GARBO

Garbo

ROBERT GOTTLIEB

FARRAR, STRAUS AND GIROUX

NEW YORK

Farrar, Straus and Giroux
120 Broadway, New York 10271

Library of Congress Cataloging-in-Publication Data
Names: Gottlieb, Robert, 1931– author.
Title: Garbo / Robert Gottlieb.
Description: First edition. | New York : Farrar, Straus and Giroux, 2021. | Includes
     bibliographical references, filmography, and index.
Identifiers: LCCN 2021032233 | ISBN 9780374298357 (hardcover)
Subjects: LCSH: Garbo, Greta, 1905–1990. | Garbo, Greta, 1905–1990—Influence. |
     Motion picture actors and actresses—Sweden—Biography. | Motion picture actors
     and actresses—United States—Biography. | Motion pictures—History—20th century.
Classification: LCC PN2778.G3 G68 2021 | DDC 791.4302/8092 [B]—dc23
LC record available at https://lccn.loc.gov/2021032233

Designed by Abby Kagan

www.fsgbooks.com
www.twitter.com/fsgbooks • www.facebook.com/fsgbooks

1   3   5   7   9   10   8   6   4   2

Frontispiece photograph by Clarence Bull.

for Irene Mayer Selznick

CONTENTS

><del><<</del>

A GARBO READER

GARBO

WHY GARBO?

※

S HE WAS NOT AS POPULAR AS CHAPLIN and Pickford had been, and she was only in Hollywood for sixteen years (and twenty-four movies), yet the impact she had on the world was as great as theirs. Yes, her beauty was incomparable, but that wasn't it. The mystery of her self-imposed seclusion was irresistible to the industry and to the world, but that was almost a distraction. Certainly it wasn't her vehicles, so many of them clichéd or worse, or the opulent productions in which M-G-M swathed her (though in her first sound film, *Anna Christie*, the highest-grossing film of 1930, she's a bedraggled whore on the dilapidated New York waterfront). Was she even an *actress*, or was she merely a glorious presence? (After *Camille*, with her universally acclaimed performance as "The Lady of the Camellias"—Bernhardt and Duse territory—that ceased to be an issue.)

M-G-M presented her first as a vamp, luring men on with her vampish ways, but she hated that.

Then she suffered, and redeemed herself through true love. Then she became an icon and an Event. But none of that goes to explain why more than any other star she invaded the subconscious of the audience: Wherever you look in the period between 1925 and 1941 Garbo is in people's minds, hearts, and dreams. You realize it as you come upon countless references to her in novels and memoirs of the period—from *For Whom the Bell Tolls* to the letters of Marianne Moore. Other Hollywood stars venerated her, accepting that she was Above and Beyond, and were as eager to meet her or just get a glimpse of her as your ordinary fan. After a while she even lost her first name—no more Greta, just Garbo: Garbo Talks! Garbo Laughs!

Who else has had this effect? No other actor until Marilyn Monroe (whom she admired and with whom she would have liked to work), and perhaps Elvis—but he was for kids, and he lost his last name, not his first. Garbo wasn't for kids; she liked them, but she had never really been one and she never had one. (She never had a husband either.) She loved her work, but she couldn't bear the surround, and she never really understood what had happened to her. She was a phenomenon, a sphinx, a myth, but also a Swedish peasant girl, uneducated, naïve, and always on her guard. She withdrew from the world when she was thirty-six, but the world wouldn't withdraw from her, even though she spent half a century or so hiding from it. She's still hiding—no one will ever know what was taking place behind those amazing eyes. Only the camera knew.

⇶1⇷

GARBO BEFORE STILLER

GRETA LOVISA GUSTAFSSON was born on September 18, 1905. She and her slightly older sister, Alva, to whom she was very close, and their somewhat older brother, Sven, lived with their parents in an unprepossessing building in Södermalm, one of the poorest neighborhoods of Stockholm, where they occupied a cold-water flat variously described as one-room, two-room, three-room, and four-room, but since 32 Blekingegaten was torn down more than fifty years ago, we'll never be sure. (John Bainbridge, whose pioneering biography of Garbo appeared in 1955, seems to have gone to the building and met the tenants, also named Gustafsson though not related. He reports four rooms, although apparently when Greta was born, Sven's bed had to be moved into the kitchen. Bainbridge also tells us that these Gustafssons had only recently learned of the Garbo connection and "were not overwhelmed by the intelligence.")

There were no indoor toilets at 32 Blekingegaten—when nature called, it was down four flights of stairs to the outdoor privies and then back up. (No elevators, needless to say.) So the Gustafssons were poor. But they were not impoverished: Karl Gustafsson, the father, was a hardworking though unskilled laborer who, even if he drank, was a responsible provider. He came from a long line of farmers in southern Sweden, but he and his wife-to-be, Anna Lovisa Karlsson, who came from a similar background, decided in their mid-twenties that their increasingly hardscrabble agrarian

32 Blekingegaten, where Greta spent her childhood

life, in a bleak economy, was just too punishing. One account puts it this way: In 1898 "they moved to Stockholm in April, they married in May, and Anna delivered their first child, Sven, ten weeks later in July." Perhaps embarrassment over Anna's premarital pregnancy had something to do with the move, but perhaps not—illegitimate birth was not severely stigmatized in Sweden, then or now.

Another account suggests that they may have met in Stockholm as early as 1896 and had settled down there together before Anna's pregnancy. In any case, well before Greta was born they—Karl and Anna, eight-year-old Sven, and toddler Alva—were already in the Södermalm apartment where Greta lived until she left Sweden and where her widowed mother went on living for many more years, refusing her movie-star daughter's efforts to move her into more comfortable surroundings. Anna, a practical, sensible, undemonstrative woman, was also a stubborn one—not unlike her famous daughter. At the time Greta was born, the family finances were so low that Karl's employer seems to have offered to adopt the new baby. Anna to Karl: "If God gives you a child, he also gives you bread." And that was that.

When Greta was a little girl, Stockholm was a bustling city but hardly a vast metropolis—the population was under four hundred thousand, and many of its inhabitants, recently transplanted like the Gustafssons from the country, remained very much in touch with nature. The Gustafssons, for instance, raised vegetables and grew flowers in a garden plot just outside the city—a long trolley ride and mile-long walk away. The whole family loved being there on weekends, and everyone pitched in—Greta, we're told, raised strawberries and, when the local kids hadn't stolen them, sold them herself in the city streets. Every extra krona helped, especially when Karl's earning power decreased severely in light of his unrelentingly worsening health.

It was Karl whom Greta adored. Tall, handsome, with a refinement remarked on as out of the ordinary in an ordinary workingman, he was fun-loving and highly musical—a singer. And also a reader. Tragically, he developed a grave kidney disease, and he died of it at the age of forty-eight, when Greta was fourteen. In the time leading up to his death, while Anna and the older children went out to work, it had been Greta's job to look after her father—to tend to him at home, and to accompany him to charity hospitals and clinics for medical help and in hopes of a cure. She never forgot the humiliations they endured as poor people in search of live-or-die attention. Years later, she would tell her friend Lars Saxon how her family's endless weeping after Karl's death angered her. "To my mind a great tragedy should be borne silently. It seemed disgraceful to me to show it in front of all the neighbors by constant crying. My own sorrow was as deep as theirs,

TOP AND BOTTOM (center): Karl Gustafsson

(*left*) Greta's mother and sister, Alva; (*right*) her brother, Sven, in later years

and for more than a year I cried myself to sleep every night. For a time after his death I was fighting an absurd urge to get up in the night and run to his grave to see that he had not been buried alive."

Karl's death not only devastated Greta but ended her education. Not that she minded that at all: She had disliked school, although she did passably well in her studies (we have her report cards), except in math—"I could never understand how anyone could be interested in trying to solve such ridiculous problems as how many liters of water could pass through a tap of such and such width in one hour and fifteen minutes . . . The only subject I really liked was history." Most of all, she was to say, she had never felt like a child, and "I don't think anyone ever regarded me as a child . . . Though I am the youngest of three, my brother and sister always looked on me as the oldest. In fact, I can hardly remember ever having felt young." Moreover, she was always big for her age—at twelve she had already reached her full height of five feet, seven inches, and was taller than all her classmates; she sticks out in every group picture from her early years.

So she was eager, almost wild, to get out into the big world: Childhood things (like school) were both boring and a waste of time. And she always knew where she wanted to go. From the first, she was obsessed with the theater, with acting. When she was still a little girl she told her Uncle David, "I'm going to become a prima donna or a princess." And her Aunt Maria "one day found her five-year-old niece deep in thought and asked what was on her mind. 'I am thinking of being grown up and becoming a great actress.'"

Even as a really young child she was putting on little shows—organizing Alva and Sven and neighborhood kids into supporting her plans. She informed her classmate and friend Elisabet Mal-

Greta (back row center) and playmates

colm that they were going to be actresses, even though Elisabet had no real interest in acting. Greta, Elisabet recalled, always took the lead roles and directed the other kids in the plays they put on. "You must come in like this and pretend you are very much surprised to see me and look like this," she instructed Elisabet, and then, "This will never do . . . Now take that chair and sit down. You can be the audience and I'll show you how one really *acts*." What's more, said Elisabet, "When we weren't actually imitating actors and actresses we would dress up as boys, making good use of her brother Sven's belongings. 'I'm Gustafsson's youngest boy, you know,' Greta told a local shoemaker, 'and this is a pal of mine.'" Sven would report that "we all had to dress up in old costumes and do as we were told. Usually she liked to play the part of a boy. Sometimes she would say terrible things. She would point to me and say, 'You be the father,' and then to my sister: 'You be the mother.' Then I would ask what part she was playing, and she would say, 'I am your child who is drowned.'" She was *always* the leader, and things always had to be done exactly her way.

Her imagination was unflagging, even when she wasn't "performing." Elisabet tells us that on warm days the two girls would climb onto the roofs of the row of outside lavatories behind their apartment house and, ignoring the smells, pretend they were somewhere else: "We are on a sandy beach. Can't you see the waves breaking on the shore? How clear the sky is! And do you hear how sweetly the orchestra at the casino is playing? Look at that girl in the funny green bathing suit! It's fun to be here and look at the bathers, isn't it?" The girls remained friends and in touch long after Greta went to America, but she ended the friendship abruptly—and typically—when in 1932 Elisabet "betrayed" her by offering these reminiscences to *Motion Picture* magazine.

She spent a lot of time at the local soup kitchens—she was a regular at the Salvation Army—not only filling up on food but entertaining the people standing in line, at the age of nine putting on skits to amuse them, and even stretching to a musical revue "in which Greta portrayed everything from the Goddess of Peace to a three-year-old in red rompers." Not that she had been exposed as a child to the theater—the Gustafssons were far too poor to waste money on entertainment. But when Greta would earn a few pennies, she would spend them on the movies and on movie magazines. (Earn them or beg them: One neighbor reported that Greta "was a real cadger in those days. On paydays when the men came home from work she would stand in the street smiling at them with an outstretched hand.") And she would acquire postcards of stage stars from the nearby newspaper kiosk in exchange for running errands for the proprietress—her favorite was the charming leading man of Swedish variety shows Carl Brisson, who went on to appear on the London stage as Count Danilo in *The Merry Widow* and as the star of Hitchcock's *The Manxman* (1929).

Many kids, of course, have dreams of becoming actors, and many kids put on shows for their families and the neighbors. And then there have been those like Mary Pickford and the Gish sisters who were themselves performing at a very early age to keep their families afloat—Mary was trouping at the age of seven, Lillian at nine. But it's hard to believe that apart from Greta, there was ever a girl of eight or nine who would walk some distance to theaters in the evening and stand at the stage door, alone, for hours, just to watch the actors and actresses come in and go out. It would get so late that her father or brother or Uncle David, a taxi driver, would go look for her and convey her home, these late hours no doubt contributing to her routine exhaustion at school. Meanwhile, though, she was beginning to be recognized by some of the actors and actresses, and the stage doorman of the Southside Theater took a shine to her and one night let her go backstage. "At last, I caught wonderful glimpses of the players at their entrances, and first smelled that most wonderful of all odors to a devotee of the theater—that backstage smell, compounded of grease-paint powder and musty scenery. No odor in the world will ever mean as much to me—none!" Slowly she became a known quantity—and, given her charm, a welcome one—at these theaters.

She was consumed by her determination to become not only an actress but a great star. But how to get there? She was dirt poor, essentially uneducated, and had no connections. Yet it happened. Nothing could or would stop her, although along with her determination she suffered from an almost crippling shyness, especially with strangers. Indeed, her strongest impulse, she would say, was to be alone with her thoughts and dreams. "I was always sad as a child, for as long as I can think back. I hated crowds of people, and used to sit in a corner by myself, just thinking. I did not want to play very much. I did some skating and played with snowballs, but most of all I wanted to be alone with myself." And she would spend much of her long life being exactly that.

As a result of this emotional independence, she could take her friends or leave them. And if she took them, it had to be on her terms. A girl named Eva Blomgren was one of her closest friends, and they corresponded when Eva went away to the country one summer—this was soon after Karl had died and Greta had just been confirmed (the Gustafssons, like everyone else, were Lutherans). "One thing I have to say," wrote Greta. "If you and I are to remain friends, you must keep away from my girl friends, as I did from yours. I'm sure you wouldn't like it if you met me with your most intimate friends and I completely ignored you. I did not mind your going out with Alva, but I realized that you intended to do the same with all my acquaintances. Eva, I am arrogant and impatient by nature, and I don't like girls who do what you have done . . . If this letter offends you, then you don't need to write to me again, but if it doesn't and you will promise to behave as a friend, then I shall be glad to hear from you again soon." And her next letter to Eva begins, "Well, so you promise to mend your ways. Then all can be as before, provided I have no cause to complain again." This need to control her relationships with others—family, friends, lovers—would manifest itself for the rest of her life, with the unique exception of her bond with the director who "discovered" her, Mauritz Stiller.

Yet despite all this prickliness, we're constantly hearing what a nice and pleasant girl she was—how full of fun! And how funny! Mimi Pollack, her closest friend from their days at Sweden's Royal Dramatic Theater Academy and for many years thereafter, said that "she was always gay and good-humored, always full of fun and ready for mischief." She was also full of energy when she wasn't lethargic and mopey. She swam, she sledded. "I was awful as a child!" she said. "We used to do all the tricks of ringing door-bells and running away . . . and I was the ringleader. I wasn't at all like a girl. I used to play leapfrog, and have a bag of marbles of my own—a tomboy."

Her first regular employment after her father died was as a "tvålflicka," a face-latherer: Her job was to dab shaving soap onto the faces of the (male) customers. She was a big success at Arthur Ekengren's barbershop, the largest in the neighborhood. Her pay was seven kronor a week (something like $1.50), and that money went straight to her mother, but she kept her tips for herself, often spending them on chocolate treats. (This and the fol-lowing information about her life as a tvålflicka comes from Karen Swen-son's biography, the most thorough account we have in English of Garbo's Swedish years.) According to Mrs. Ekengren, Greta was an immediate fa-vorite at the shop: "Some clients would phone and make special appoint-ments and then, if Greta was not there, find some excuse for postponing them." Joking with the customers, she "filled the place with her laughter and vitality."

"A good soap girl did more than simply put lather on the faces of stu-dents, sailors, and businessmen," explains Swenson. "She gently rubbed the soap into the skin, massaging each man's face and preparing him for the barber. It could be an enjoyable, even sensual experience for the patron and certainly put a teenage girl in the position of dealing with unwelcome ad-vances." Even so, one of her co-workers at Ekengren's reported that Greta "always kept her dignity and never allowed men to get fresh with her."

Spending her life lathering men, however, was not her ambition. Deciding to move on to a grander (and better-paying) job, she applied to one of Stockholm's premier department stores, known as the PUB—it was owned by Paul U. Bergström. She was accepted, and on July 26, 1920, she began work at the store and was soon promoted to the millinery department. She was still fourteen but claimed to be fifteen and looked considerably older. Her emerging beauty cannot have hurt her chances. Writing to Eva, she said, "Can you imagine me as a shop girl? But don't worry, I haven't given up my ideas about the theater . . . I'm just as faithful to them as before."

Modeling hats at PUB

The supervisor of the women's clothing department was a sympathetic lady named Magda Hellberg who remembered "employee #195" as "very conscientious, quiet," and as one who "always took great care about her appearance." When the store manager asked Miss Hellberg to suggest someone to model hats for the upcoming spring catalogue, she immediately replied, "Miss Gustafsson should be perfect for that. She always looks clean and well-groomed and has such a good face." (This may be the last time anyone referred to Garbo's face as merely "good.") Greta grabbed at the opportunity. "Aunt Hellberg can arrange anything for me," she exclaimed. "Oh, how happy I am!" Hellberg remarked that this was "probably the longest sentence I ever heard her say at one time."

The shots of Greta modeling five different hats were a success, and she was asked to repeat the experience for the next catalogue. As a result, she began modeling clothes at PUB fashion shows, and then in other stores as well. When a Captain Ragnar Ring, known as Lasse, turned up—he was making short films and commercials to be shown in movie houses—the advertising manager pointed out "a girl here who has done very well modeling hats for us; perhaps we could use her." Ring had already chosen a girl to model hats, but he hired Greta (for ten kronor a day) to play a small part. Then came another advertising film in which she played a girl who looked goofy in a deliberately outlandish costume that didn't fit or suit her. They were thinking of dropping this comic scene from the picture (and eliminating Greta entirely) when they recalled how hard she had worked and how effective she was. And then the film's producer arrived on the set and, when he saw Greta under the lights, grabbed hold of the doorpost. "She is so beautiful that it really pains my heart just to see her."

Another man who noticed her on that set was a youngish, good-looking, rich contractor—an Olympic medalist for swimming and water polo; a well-known "man-about-Stockholm"—named Max Gumpel. He had come to the store because his nephew was playing Greta's younger brother and "of course, I went to PUB to see the film being made," as he wrote in an unpublished memoir.

> She was lovely. I invited her home to dinner. She came and I remember that we had crown artichokes, which were new to her. After that we met quite often, and I willingly admit that I was very keen on her, so much so, indeed, that I gave her a tiny gold ring with a tiny diamond in it . . . and she flattered me by thinking that it gleamed like one of the British crown jewels. After a few years we parted, good friends as we had always been . . . Ten years went by; I had been married and was divorced. The star came to Sweden [this was in 1932]. One day I received a phone call at the office. A woman's voice asked if I would dine with an old friend. She was mystifying, but eventually told me who she was. At that I became very cautious, for it could easily have been someone trying to make a fool of me. Anyway, I asked the voice to put on an evening frock and come and dine in my home. When she said she did not possess such a thing, I told her just to make herself as beautiful as she could. She came—and it was she. The only jewelry she had on was my little diamond ring.

Their friendship flourished, lasting until Gumpel's death, in 1965. Along the way he did many things for her—loaned her his villa, escorted her around town, advised her on real-estate investments, even apparently worked with her during the war, passing on information about Nazi-leaning Swedish industrialists to the Allies. And she became friendly with his family. It's almost certain that he was her first lover. She was only fifteen when they met—he was thirty—but she looked older and claimed to be older, and he probably had no idea of her real age. Besides, the age of consent in Sweden was fifteen then—and still is. Her close friend Vera Schmiterlöw confirmed that Max "was Greta's first great love," and even that later on there had been talk of an engagement, given the appearance of a diamond engagement ring. Nothing, of course, came of it. One thing is definite: Whenever Garbo was in Stockholm, she and Max played a great deal of tennis together.

As a girl she was definitely aware of the other sex—she was popular with the boys in her neighborhood and, as we have seen, knew how to charm the older men whom she was lathering as a tvålflicka. And, Eva Blomgren informs us, when she was walking home every night from PUB, she deliberately walked past the royal palace. "One of the princes might catch sight of me," she explained.

In late 1920 PUB granted her a week's unpaid leave to appear as an extra in a real movie called *The Gay Cavalier*. Alva was in it, too—the sisters had been pursuing work like this for some time, and now they were cast as maids in a bawdy tavern scene. A young actor who appeared in a dance sequence claims that he chose Greta for a partner because "I was attracted by her soft, rounded curves," but then, as they danced, "I became fascinated with the thick, long curling lashes fringing the most unusual eyes I have ever seen. Smoldering gray-blue eyes that glowed like moonlight on a blue lake when she looked up at me and said, 'It must be wonderful to be a star.'" This young actor with the good memory is not credited in the cast list, but neither were Greta and Alva. Then Lasse Ring used Greta in another advertising film—she's a young girl stuffing herself with cream puffs in a rooftop restaurant.

When Ring offered her a role in a feature-length movie he was direct-

16

In a PUB promotional film

ing ("a Nordic love story"), PUB refused to give her time off from work. But when another opportunity arose—for a comedy to be directed by and starring the well-known Erik Petschler—Greta balked when the store again turned down her request for an unpaid leave. "Miss Gustafsson, in spite of her youth, is one of the best saleswomen in my entire company," said Mr. Bergström himself. As Swenson puts it, "He wanted her behind the counter where she belonged." With the full agreement of her mother, Greta walked away from the last job she would ever have outside the movies. Her official reason for quitting? "To work in film."

Peter the Tramp is a Swedish attempt at a Mack Sennett slapstick farce, all pratfalls and chase scenes and frisky bathing beauties, of whom Greta, more than a touch plump, was the dominant one. (Petschler couldn't have known that she was a big fan of Sennett stars Mabel Normand and Fatty Arbuckle.) The movie was made on a shoestring, but to Petschler's surprise, Greta turned out to be a natural comic—something Hollywood wouldn't notice until *Ninotchka*, seventeen years later. The reception of this workmanlike, uninspired film was less than rhapsodic, but Greta was noticed by a couple of reviewers: "Miss Gustafson* had the doubtful pleasure of playing a bathing beauty for Mr. Erik A. Petschler, so we have no idea of her capabilities. We hope that we shall have occasion to mention her again."

She was now without an income, and although she was making the usual casting rounds, nothing happened. What next? Back to a conventional day job? Petschler wanted to help and later claimed that it was he, one day over lunch, who encouraged her to apply for a scholarship to Stock-

---

* The spelling of her last name kept being changed. For consistency, we will stick with one "f" and two "s"s.

holm's great Royal Dramatic Theater Academy—it was the stage and not the movies that called to her. She was also encouraged by some of the actors (including her idol, Carl Brisson) whom she had met and charmed during the days when she was haunting stage doors.

As it happened, Petschler had an old friend, Frans Enwall, who was a former director of the Academy, and he brokered an introduction. According to Garbo, she told Enwall that she *"must* become an actress and asked how to go about it." Impressed, Enwall agreed to coach her for the highly competitive auditions, but he fell ill and his actress/daughter, Signe, took over. "She was extraordinarily inhibited," Signe Enwall remembered, but "she was so anxious to succeed that she was completely receptive to assistance. The fact that her knowledge of drama was not wide did not matter. What really counts in an actress is an ability to feel and understand [everyday life]. In that sense, Greta Gustafsson was extremely well-equipped."

There were to be three auditions spread out over three days, for which seventy or so applicants had to prepare scenes from three different plays. The Enwalls and she settled on a scene from Selma Lagerlöf's *The Fledgling*, a scene from Sardou's *Madame Sans-Gêne*, and Ellida's famous speech in Ibsen's *The Lady from the Sea*: "I'm haunted by this irresistible longing for the sea . . ." Late in the afternoon of each audition day, a list of those who had made the cut was posted outside the theater. Only seven of the applicants would succeed. (As with so many aspects of Garbo's life, there are contradictory versions, one of which reported that the three auditions all took place in a single day.)

As she would recall, she was so

In *Peter the Tramp*

nervous about the first audition that she persuaded Sven, her brother, to take the day off from his bakery job and accompany her. "There were about twenty people in the jury—newspapermen, critics, people from the theater, and dramatic teachers. They sat before us, in orchestra seats. [But] all I could see was that black pit—that black open space . . . I felt doomed to failure . . . I was so shy! I had never tried to act . . . I thought I was going to faint . . . At last my moment came. I stepped to the stage and recited my piece like one in a trance . . . Afterward, I collapsed in the wings, and then I just ran off. I forgot to say goodbye."

She passed this first test. And she passed the second. And she passed the third. "Oh, God, I was happy!" she recalled. "I thought I should die of joy! Oh, now, even now [1931], I can hardly breathe when I remember." Three weeks later, classes began. The date was September 18, 1922—her seventeenth birthday. And she was wearing the little diamond ring Max Gumpel had given her.

Tuition at the Royal Academy was free. But the students were not permitted to work. For most of them, coming from more or less affluent backgrounds, that was not a problem. Greta, however, had nothing other than the stipend of fifty kronor (about ten dollars) a month that the school allotted the first-year students. She scraped by, helped financially by both Alva and Sven, and by her rigor: She would walk back and forth from home to the school—almost two miles—to save on carfare, and for lunch she and Mimi Pollack would often split a twenty-cent dish.

The course was highly demanding: voice training, deportment, elocution, fencing, makeup, eurythmics, literature. The Academy taught the Delsarte/Dalcroze system, which "scientifically" broke down all movements. We have a few pages from her lecture notes: "The head bent forward equals a mild concession [or] condescending attitude. The head kept straight [signifies] calmness in the self. The throwing back of the head—a violent feeling such as love." As Barry Paris comments in his excellent biography of her, "Garbo in silent films would employ the system of gestural meaning to a high degree." The students were kept busy working together on little scenes—"Everyone agreed that [Greta's] face was beautiful and that she was particularly charming as Hermione in *A Winter's Tale*," her first and last professional exposure to Shakespeare. And they would have walk-ons or tiny roles in Royal Theater productions, earning an extra three kronor. They were also expected to attend as many of the theater's performances as possible, no hardship for stage-obsessed Greta.

Also, for the first time, she was part of a group of like-minded, ardent young people who, after their full day of study (nine to five), would stay up till all hours talking, laughing. Her closest friends were Mimi Pollack, a year older, small, cultured, a live wire; Vera Schmiterlöw, also from humble beginnings, who would become a major German film star; and the charismatic Alf Sjöberg, who would go on to be Sweden's most prominent direc-

Greta, Mimi Pollack, and Vera Schmiterlöw

tor—running the Royal Theater for decades, making prize-winning movies like *Torment* and *Miss Julie*. He would recall the great times he and Mimi and the others had together—"arguing, smoking, fighting." But Greta would sometimes sit there "alone, locked inside her androgynous silence . . . I thought, there she is sitting, only partly present above all the fighting, who was she really?" Nils Asther, who would later co-star with her in two M-G-M films (and with Barbara Stanwyck in *The Bitter Tea of General Yen*), remembered that she was *always* shy.

Her shyness was partly due to her gnawing shame at her lack of education—she was the only one of her friends who hadn't been to high school. The Swedish actor Fritiof Billquist, who wrote an early biography of her, tells us (and all later biographers) that one of her teachers remarked on how repressed she was in front of others. Once when she asked Greta to read a passage from Schiller's *Maria Stuart*, Greta whispered in horror to Mimi, "Who was Maria Stuart? Did she ever live?" When a literature professor asked when Strindberg was born, Greta answered, "In the winter." "In the winter?" he exclaimed. "Yes, I think it actually was in the winter"—possibly an attempt at dry humor as well as a cover for ignorance. Even so, "actually in the winter" became a stock gag line at the school.

In these early months at the Academy Greta attracted attention: for her beauty, her determination, her nice nature, her sense of fun ("She could be both high-spirited and maliciously funny. And she was always the first to appreciate a joke and laugh her characteristic guttural little pent-up laugh"). And her lethargy. She was perpetually late to school. In the fullest interview she ever gave in Hollywood, she talked about her tardiness. Referring to herself by her school nickname of "Gurra," she said, "The other pupils were charming, lovely girls who were always on time. Then in would come Gurra, late as usual. I'd come in the door and say, 'There's a rumor about that this school is still here. But I'm so tired; Gurra's so tired.' And nobody would say a word to me."

In December 1922 came the Stockholm premiere of *Peter the Tramp*, which she attended with Mimi and Alf. "The film surpassed every expectation," Alf would later say. "I have never seen anything so ghastly. We pulled her out of the auditorium before the lights went on. As we walked up and down the streets, we demanded she take a vow never to get involved in movies again. She obviously did not even have the most basic talent for it."

Sweden's greatest film director, Mauritz Stiller, disagreed. He had been observing her at the Academy and on the stage of the theater, and she had earlier been recommended to him by Petschler. He remembered her well. In the spring of 1923 he asked the director of the theater to recommend two young, inexperienced girls for significant parts in the major movie he was about to start filming. The movie would be a four-hour epic, *The Saga of Gösta Berling*, based on the Nobel Prize–winning Selma Lagerlöf's famous novel, whose popularity in Scandinavia can bear comparison with that of *Gone with the Wind* in the United States. This would be the most ambitious, most expensive movie ever made in Sweden.

The girls recommended to Stiller were the beautiful Mona Mårtenson and Greta Gustafsson.

Students at the Royal Dramatic Theater Academy, 1922. Standing, third from left: Alf Sjöberg;
far right: Mimi and Greta; middle row left: Mona Mårtenson, Vera. Everyone is looking at
the camera except Greta, who is looking at Mimi.

$\rightleftharpoons 2 \rightleftharpoons$

GARBO AND STILLER IN EUROPE

HERE WERE TWO DIRECTORIAL GIANTS in the booming Swedish film industry in the early decades of the twentieth century. One was Victor Sjöström, who in 1925 was already working at M-G-M in Hollywood under the Americanized version of his name, Seastrom, and who had had a tremendous success—the Lon Chaney/John Gilbert/Norma Shearer *He Who Gets Slapped*—and would go on to direct Lillian Gish in *The Scarlet Letter* and *The Wind*. He was also a formidable actor, and decades later, long back in Sweden, he would become world-famous for his performance as the old Professor in Ingmar Bergman's *Wild*

Strawberries. He and Mauritz Stiller had the greatest respect and fondness for each other—in fact, Sjöström had started out in films under Stiller's wing—and he would be instrumental in bringing Stiller (and therefore Garbo) to America.

The Jewish Stiller (his first name, Moses, or Movscha, would morph into Moje, which is what everyone, including Garbo, called him; he was only "Mauritz" officially) had been born in 1883 in Helsinki, when Finland was still a grand duchy of tsarist Russia. His mother committed suicide when he was three, his father died shortly afterwards, and he was raised by a family friend, a hatter. But from the start he was more interested in theater than in hats, and as a young stage actor he fled to Sweden (his Swedish was perfect) to avoid exile in Siberia for having fled conscription into the Russian army. At first he could barely keep himself alive—sleeping on park benches, etc.—as he scrambled for a place in the theater world, but he was soon drawn to the new entertainment form of the movies, and he appeared in a lot of them. He didn't like himself on the screen, though, and, more important, he didn't like taking direction from anyone, including directors. Soon he was directing his own films—dozens of short ones, the few of which that survive revealing an impressive pictorial style and a way with actors. Stiller always knew what he was doing, and what he wanted others to be doing. In other words, he was a born director.

His range stretched from short farces to large-scale tragic dramas to the 1920 social comedy *Erotikon*, a sophisticated story of a rich, spoiled, and fabulously costumed wife whose attention . . . strays. (Her husband is an earnest entomologist, absorbed in the study of the sex life of beetles.) *Erotikon*, which made him famous throughout Europe, covers the same territory and is from exactly the same era as DeMille's Gloria Swanson marital comedy-dramas and Lubitsch's early Pola Negri masterpieces, and Stiller's eye, his mastery of the camera, his sense of timing, and his jaundiced appreciation of human nature were as fine-tuned as those of these distinguished coevals. By then he was generally considered the leading artist of the Swedish film industry, and it was no wonder that his projected film of *The Saga of Gösta Berling*, Sweden's most beloved novel, was anticipated as a major event.

OPPOSITE: Garbo as the Countess Dohna in *The Saga of Gösta Berling*

Mauritz Stiller

Stiller was also a large personal presence in the relatively small world of Stockholm. In appearance, he was tall and striking, if rough-hewn. Irene Mayer Selznick would later describe him as he appeared to her, in Berlin, in 1924: "Stiller frightened the life out of me. He was an awesome physical sight. I likened him to the giant in 'Jack and the Beanstalk'—enormously tall, with a very craggy face; a head, hands, and feet huge by comparison even with his height; his voice had the rumble of something from deep under a mountain. When he took my hand, it disappeared. The most striking feature of his face was his eyes—blue they were, and one was disfigured and teared."

Stiller dressed exquisitely (diamond studs, platinum rings, fur coats to his ankles), ate exquisitely, and tore around town in his famous canary-colored sports car (known locally as "The Yellow Peril") with his adored French bulldog, Charlie, in the seat beside him. He had risen from abject poverty to a life of luxury, and luxury was now essential to his sense of himself. At work he was a dictator even more than he was a director—his word was law. And he was unencumbered by wives or mistresses. As Vera Schmiterlöw put it,

Greta "adored Stiller, but as far as I know there was never anything between them. Everyone knew that Stiller had a different kind of interest."

Among the many who had interested him was the beautiful Nils Asther, who decades later let it be known that when, at eighteen, he was "discovered" by Stiller, "One evening he came up to me and I was initiated into the art of loving someone of your own sex." Another interest had been Lars Hanson, Sweden's biggest young male star, who in America would twice play opposite Garbo and twice opposite Lillian Gish, and would star many times for Stiller in Sweden, not only in *Erotikon* but as Gösta Berling himself. (A major stage actor in Sweden, he would appear as the father, James Tyrone, in the 1956 world premiere of O'Neill's *Long Day's Journey into Night*.)

To keep things cozy, Asther and Hanson had also had their fling. And to make them still cozier, Hanson married another Stiller actress, Karin Molander, who had been the wife of the Gustaf Molander who, as the director of the stage academy, was the man who had recommended Greta to Stiller. (This so-called "lavender" marriage lasted until Hanson's death.) When in 1925 Stiller and Garbo were sitting around Los Angeles forlornly waiting to be put to work by M-G-M,* it was Karin Molander who, observing them "staring out at the sea and looking gloomy," remarked that "we called them Grandma and Grandpa." Molander, the biographer David Bret embroiders, "did not know the half of it—that 'Grandpa' had slept with her husband back in Sweden, and that 'Grandma' was doing so there in Hollywood." Oh, those Swedes! (And oh, that David Bret, whose pronouncements should be approached with considerable caution.)

Greta had been one of the last to be cast for *Gösta Berling*. She was terrified when she was summoned to Stiller's apartment to be interviewed, and even more terrified when she arrived. To begin with, he wasn't there, and she was kept waiting for more than an hour until he appeared, accompanied by a Russian wolfhound. At first, "without so much as a greeting, he stared at me for a long time—a very long time." Then, still staring, he made some small talk. Then, abruptly, he said, "Well, can't you take off your coat and

---

* The acronym of Metro-Goldwyn-Mayer was hyphenated until 1956, when the hyphens were officially dropped.

Filming *The Saga of Gösta Berling*. Seated: Lars Hanson and Garbo;
standing next to cameraman: Stiller

hat?" And "Then he just looked at me some more and said, 'What's your telephone number?' I knew it was all over. 'He isn't interested,' I thought. 'When they're not interested they always ask for your telephone number.'"

But in a few days he *did* call, and she was instructed to appear at the film studio for a screen test. Stiller had said to Axel Nilsson, his assistant and lover, "There is something quite extraordinary about that girl. I must discover what it is." She and her schoolmate Mona Mårtenson, the other girl recommended to Stiller, made their way by streetcar to the studio, and again she was kept waiting. "I was very shaky," Greta said in the long interview with Ruth Biery that appeared in *Photoplay* in 1928. "I come off the street, go in and they make me up and then they take me in and tell me to lie in a bed and be sick. Very sick. I didn't know what it was all about. It seemed to me like a big joke, to come off the street and be right away sick. And I was ashamed. I was ashamed to try and put myself over, as you say it. I had never done anything to put myself over before, and it made me very ashamed to do it." Mr. Stiller waited a few moments, and then said, "My God, don't you know what it is to be sick?" Then I knew it wasn't a play and it wasn't funny. I knew it was necessary in the movies and I became a very sick lady."

Stiller's screenwriter and other studio executives didn't get it, but he told them, "She has no technique, so she can't show what she is feeling, but she will be all right. I'll see to that." The crucial thing she had to do was lose weight. When she agreed to shed twenty pounds, the part of the Italian Countess Elisabeth Dohna was hers. Vera Schmiterlöw wrote to Mimi Pollack reporting that she and Greta were taking Turkish baths in order to slim down. "I'm not getting anywhere . . . but Greta just gets thinner and thinner. You can't see her breasts anymore. They're just two buttons."

There were still doubts about her performance after filming began. One fine elderly character actress remarked, "None of us could understand why Stiller was so interested in this little nobody, because he had never paid any particular attention to anyone before. To us she appeared to be just an awkward, mediocre novice." But it soon became evident what it was that

Lars Hanson as Gösta Berling

With Gerda Lundequist

interested Stiller so. For a long time he had been looking for a beautiful girl whom he could completely mold. And Greta Gustafsson was utterly malleable. "I have to break her down," he said, "but when she is broken down, what a performance she gives—such calm, such concentration, such effortless knowledge. And besides all this, her face when she is acting becomes a face to make the gods happy." Karen Swenson tells us that as the days went by—and *Gösta Berling* took many months to film—"his attitude toward Greta intensified . . . later scenes were even shot differently, with more of an emphasis on close-ups." And these close-ups are ravishing. As for her acting, it's uneven—occasionally powerful feelings emerge through her superb eyes; at other times she's tentative. But always she is beautiful.

The movie itself is so elaborate, so stuffed with characters and dramatic scenes, that although her role is central, it isn't determining—not with Lars Hanson and Sweden's most illustrious older actress, Gerda Lundequist, on hand, and not with the superb pictorial set-pieces Stiller came up with, most spectacularly the blazing fire that destroys Ekeby Hall, a template for filmed fire scenes for years to come. Poor Hanson, ordered to scramble

With Lars Hanson

across the burning rooftops on a rescue mission, was frightened for his life. "Don't be cautious," Stiller shouted—"Keep going! If the flames come closer, that's all right." "I'm burning!" Hanson shouted back. "I'm very sorry," answered Stiller. "You'll just have to burn a little longer." Greta isn't in that scene, but in the film's climax, an extraordinary pictorial tour de force, she and Larson are the couple in an ice sled fleeing a pack of wolves across a frozen lake. Audiences didn't know that it had been filmed in the park across the street from Stockholm's Strand Hotel, and that the wolves were friendly Alsatian dogs whose tails had been weighted to keep them from wagging.

Stiller not only badgered Greta mercilessly throughout the filming— "You move your legs as though they were gateposts!" and to anyone within hearing distance, "And this is supposed to be an actress!"—but he also isolated her, preferring that she listen only to *him*. One colleague reported, "We tried to make Greta one of our little family but we didn't get very far because Stiller scarcely permitted anyone else even to speak to her—he hardly let her out of his sight for a moment." (Since she was rooming with Mona Mårtenson, Stiller could hardly keep *them* apart.) "We nicknamed them 'Beauty and the Beast' . . . I can still see Stiller and that young girl— forever walking up and down, up and down, in the shade of the little grove just outside the studio. Stiller was always teaching and preaching, Greta solemnly listening and learning. I never saw anyone more earnest and eager to learn. With that hypnotic power he seemed to have over her, he could make her do extraordinary things. But we had little idea then that he was making over her very soul."

His criticism was so harsh and hurtful that she eventually dared to complain—"Stiller, I hate you!"—but although he was relentless, he would also soothe and cajole her, explaining that it was all necessary, that he only wanted what was best for her. And the results he got from her, in the face of others' persistent lack of faith, proved that he was right: It was his tyranny in conjunction with her combination of determination and malleability that created "Greta Garbo." Indeed, the most plausible of the various stories about how she *became* "Garbo" is that he chose the name and bestowed it on her. When she made the change legal, she was still so young that her mother had to sign the official application.

During layoffs in the filming, and before and after its premiere, Greta was studying and performing back at school: She had been promoted to the second year and was appearing in small roles, but she knew she needed further training. After the two parts of the almost four-hour-long *Gösta Berling* had opened—in successive weeks in March 1924—and she had been received with respect if not hosannas by the critics, her old friend Eva showed her a clipping that said, "Greta Garbo's way to stardom seems clear." "I don't think I was quite that good," she said to Eva. "I hope I'll be better in my next part." Further training, though, was not to be—except the training Stiller provided. He prevailed upon her to quit the school and put herself completely in his hands. He had long since been grooming her in non-movie matters, squiring her to restaurants to learn good food and elegant behavior; teaching her about clothes; exposing her to museums, serious music, plays—the kind of culture that had been unavailable to a girl from the slums who hadn't even gone to high school.

This conditioning would pay off when in August he took Greta and Gerda Lundequist with him to Berlin, having sold the German rights to *Gösta Berling* for a staggering 100,000 marks. "I had never been away from Sweden," Greta was to say. "I was nervous." She needn't have been: The film was received with far greater enthusiasm than it had been in Sweden, where much of what was said about it revolved around the issue of its fidelity, or lack of same, to the sacred Selma Lagerlöf text. Quickly it earned 750,000 marks in Berlin alone, and Stiller was in demand. Sending Greta back to Stockholm, he negotiated a rich contract for himself and a generous one for her with the company, Trianon, that had distributed *Gösta* and was ready to send them and several colleagues to Constantinople to film an adventure-melodrama he had written called *The Odalisque from Smolna*. Greta, of course, would be the Odalisque, who among other things is sold

Scouting locations in Constantinople, 1924

into a Turkish harem. Perhaps we need not regret that this film was never made.

The Swedish contingent, including the male lead—Einar Hanson (no relation to Lars)—preceded Stiller to Constantinople to scout locations and film backgrounds, and to spend a lot of money. Stiller, of course, had to stay in the best hotel, acquire the most luxurious appurtenances, and buy Greta her first fur coat as a Christmas present. And then, before filming could begin, Trianon's financial situation was compromised. Leaving the others behind, Stiller rushed to Berlin, only to learn that Trianon was close to bankruptcy. So much for the Odalisque. Stiller sent enough money to Greta for her to ship his things home to Stockholm, but there wasn't enough to pay for her and the others to follow, and they had to beg and/or borrow the wherewithal from the Swedish consulate to pay for their train tickets. "Don't worry," Greta told the nervous others. "Everything will be all right when we get to Berlin. Stiller will take care of everything." Years later, with the Trianon disaster still in litigation, Garbo was required to make a court deposition. "All I know is that the whole thing busted, and naturally I did not understand anything about those things."

Given the success in Germany of *Gösta Berling*, Stiller had expected pressing offers to direct there, but nothing transpired except an elaborate scheme—to be financed by the Swedish tycoon Ivar Kreuger, "the Match King"—to create an international consortium that would dominate film production in Europe. Meanwhile, he was out of funds, and with Greta and Einar Hanson on his hands, he came to an agreement with the director G. W. Pabst to lend him his two stars for a new film. This was only Pabst's second outing as a movie director, but he was highly experienced in the theater, and his talent had been immediately acknowledged.

The movie was to be called *Joyless Street*, and Pabst had already signed up two of Europe's most prestigious actors. They were Werner Krauss (Dr. Caligari in *The Cabinet of* . . .) and the Danish Asta Nielsen, the leading European tragedienne of her day and the only member of the cast who understood Pabst's choice of this pale, nervous, and inexperienced girl to portray the other leading female role—a gentle yet strong innocent young woman who struggles against becoming a prostitute in her desperation to save her family from the dire poverty that dominates the "Joyless Street" of post-war Vienna. (Nielsen, in pre-Pickford days, had been the highest-paid movie star in the world at $80,000 a year. During World War II, she refused Goebbels's pressure to stay on in Germany and ornament the Nazi film industry, returning to Denmark, where she reportedly did what she could to help save Denmark's Jews. The Austrian Krauss, on the other hand, was a virulent anti-Semite and, although acclaimed by many as the world's greatest actor, never fully rehabilitated himself after the war.)

Stiller used all his tactical genius to wangle an extraordinary contract

Viennese housewives lining up outside the butcher shop in *Joyless Street*

for Greta and Hanson—each received a fee of $4,000, to be paid in American dollars, plus many concessions to his notions of how stars should be treated. (It was too late, however, to impose the cinematographer of his choice.) At first, he tried to intervene on the set while Greta's scenes were being filmed, but Pabst chased him away, and after her sixteen-hour days, he would rehearse her privately at night. There were difficulties with the lighting and the film stock, but they were solved—for instance, a slight tic she displayed in close-ups was eliminated by slowing down the camera—and Pabst won her confidence with his sympathy and support, a far cry from Stiller's incessant bullying. She was so appreciative of his talent and his regard for her concerns that she seriously considered his offer of a five-year contract—considered it behind Stiller's back, her first gesture toward independence.

Joyless Street was made in thirty-four days and was released almost immediately, to considerable success in both Berlin and Paris. Next: the inevitable step. Stiller's dance with Louis B. Mayer and M-G-M had (quietly) begun well before the Pabst adventure and would be concluded in Berlin in late 1924, when Mayer and his family arrived there after a stay in Rome, where he was cleaning up the out-of-control mess that was the filming of *Ben-Hur.*

We have the usual different versions of what actually happened. Was Mayer determined to bring Stiller to Hollywood and took Greta only because Stiller wouldn't come without her? Or had Mayer previously determined that Greta was the real prize? M-G-M already had Victor Seastrom on board, and not only had he come through with *He Who Gets Slapped*, but Mayer liked and admired him personally. "My father was mad about

With Valeska Gert in *Joyless Street*

Seastrom," said Irene Selznick. "Simplicity, dignity, charming European gentleman, big reputation and unspoiled, no show biz about him. He had talent and poise and my father believed every word he said." And Seastrom had urgently recommended that M-G-M import Stiller.

A Berlin screening of *Gösta Berling* was set up for the Mayers to see, and a meeting was arranged. Selznick gave two accounts of what transpired, one in her trenchant autobiography, *A Private View,* and one in an interview with Barry Paris that took place not long before her death. In her book, she writes, "The only advance reservation my father had about [Stiller] was the stipulation that he wouldn't come to Hollywood without his new leading lady, an obstacle my father thought he could overcome. Instead, Miss Garbo overcame him in the first reel." Selznick was less circumspect when talking to Paris: "The first look my father got, he spoke up—'Look at that girl! There's no physical resemblance, but she reminds me of Norma Talmadge—her eyes. The thing that makes Talmadge a star is the look in her eyes.' He didn't stop talking . . . He said, 'Stiller's fine, but the girl, look at the girl!' Then he said he'd have to be careful, that tact was required—and my father was not too tactful. He kept saying if he had to choose, the director could stay, he was taking the girl. He said, 'I'll take her without him, or I'll take them both. Number one is the girl.'"

With Gregori Chmara in *Joyless Street*

What Barry Paris would discover was that sly, secretive Mayer had *already* seen *Gösta Berling*, back in Hollywood. Lillian Gish, his most important female star at the time, persuaded him to screen it because she wanted (and got) Lars Hanson as her co-star in her upcoming version of *The Scarlet Letter*, which Seastrom would be directing. The Swedish eagles were gathering.

After the Berlin screening, they all went to dinner at the Hotel Adlon, Berlin's finest, where the Mayers were staying. But before dinner, in the el-

With Jaro Fürth as her father in *Joyless Street*

evator going up to the Mayer suite, Irene, her sister, Edie, and Mrs. Mayer were joined by a girl whose "black taffeta hat was not flattering, nor chic nor youthful. Everything she wore was dark—her clothes didn't enhance her. She had on no make-up. She certainly didn't look like an actress. You wouldn't turn your head." Yet in the hotel dining room, Selznick found Greta "shy but not bashful at the table. She was contained—charming, reasonably poised. You didn't think, 'Oh, the poor thing.' She didn't try to do a rise-and-shine number. No performing, perfectly normal." Mayer didn't pay much attention to the girl at dinner, except that when they stood up to leave, he said to her, "You see, Miss Garbo, American men don't like fat women." Luckily, she didn't understand a word of English.

However it came about, the deal was agreed on. Stiller and Garbo

Werner Krauss in *Joyless Street*

would leave for America as soon as possible. He would receive $1,000 a week; there are the usual contradictions about what she would be earning, ranging upward from $100 a week for the first year of a three-year contract and inching higher from there if she worked out. As in all such matters, she simply signed what Stiller told her to sign. Yes, she wanted to go to America and become a big star, but America frightened her; she had enjoyed being in Berlin; she would not see her family for three years; her beloved Alva had been diagnosed with tuberculosis and she would not be there to help.

Stiller and she were not on very happy terms at this point—he was furious with her for having even considered staying on with Pabst. In front of Einar Hanson, as Barry Paris tells it, "he accused her of monumental ingratitude and deceit. Tearfully she promised to take no more initiatives without his approval, whereupon . . . taking her hands in his, he said, 'Stay with me, Greta. Moje knows what is best for you.'"

Stiller preceded her back to Stockholm. She had to finish her work on *Joyless Street*, and she was appreciating the wide-open life of Weimar

Berlin—among other things, according to century-old gossip, participating in a dalliance with the well-known cabaret singer Marianne Oswald, about whom Marlene Dietrich, always venomous about Garbo, said, "She looked like something out of a nightmare. She had orange hair, and she couldn't sing—and Garbo slept with her!"

When she arrived home after *Joyless Street*, Stiller more or less froze her out. But they made up. They had to—the die was cast. Stiller had tried to wriggle out of his arrangement with Mayer, thinking he might do better staying on in Europe, but for once he was dealing with someone far tougher than he was. On May 25, 1925, Mayer cabled him, saying "We have contract with you and expect you to live up to it." A month later, her family bid her a teary farewell at the Stockholm train station, and later that day she and Stiller boarded the *Drottningholm* in the port city of Göteborg, on their way to America. Greta was nineteen.

⇌3⇌

GARBO AND STILLER IN AMERICA

O N JULY 5, 1925, Stiller and Garbo sailed past the Statue of Liberty into New York Harbor. She had loved the sea voyage—she would always love the sea. Based on the excited reception they had received in Berlin, they assumed that M-G-M would pull out all the stops to welcome them. It was not to be. There had been one or two brief mentions in the papers, but who noticed them? Someone at M-G-M had assigned a young studio publicist named Hubert Voight to greet the ship, he had brought along an interpreter and had hired (for twenty-five dollars) a freelance photographer, and that was it. The photographer, having shot three or four poses, ran out of film but went on snapping away so as not to embarrass the newcomers, and Voight escorted the new star and renowned director to the not-so-prestigious Commodore Hotel (now the Hyatt) next to Grand Central Station and deposited them there. New York was in the midst of a sweltering heat wave. Garbo had never experienced anything like it and plunged into an ice-cold bath, the first of many she would take refuge in to survive the long, hot weeks during which she and Stiller were filed away and forgotten by anyone who mattered at M-G-M.

Only Voight—instantly besotted by Garbo, who after all was a stunning young woman, despite her hopeless hair and undistinguished wardrobe—was attentive. Morning, noon, and night he was at their (her) call, taking them everywhere, showing them the town (often on his own dime, although, like her a new kid in town, he didn't have many dimes to his name). Her number-one priority was seeing Coney Island, and she went nuts over the roller coaster, spending an hour going up and down and up and down. They went to some hit shows—the *Follies* (with Will Rogers and W. C. Fields) for one—and to endless movies. And Stiller had business meetings at the M-G-M offices, meanwhile bombarding the West Coast with telegrams demanding to know when they were to leave New York for California, and what the studio's plans for them were.

The studio *had* no plans for them, or maybe they had them but weren't revealing them: One conspiracy theory (Stiller's?) suggests that Louis B. was already trying to tame Stiller's independent spirit.

The break they needed came about by accident. A Swedish friend of theirs took them to meet the famous photographer Arnold Genthe. Here is how he described their meeting in his autobiography, *As I Remember*:

My friend Martha Hedman, the beautiful Swedish actress who was for several years a Belasco star and of whom I had made many studies, brought Greta Garbo and Mauritz Stiller to my studio. Stiller had known Miss Hedman in Sweden where they had worked together under August Strindberg. The newcomers were very much interested in the photographs they saw in my studio. That kind of photography was something entirely new to them. "I would love to have you make pictures of me sometime," Miss

Garbo said. (We spoke in German, as she knew hardly a word of English at the time.) "Why sometime?" I inquired. "Why not now? You're here and I'm here and I must make some photographs of you to have visible proof that you are real." She smiled, but protested earnestly, "No, not now. Look at my dress, and I don't like my hair." "Never mind that," I said. "I am more interested in your eyes and in what is behind that extraor-

A photo by Arnold Genthe that appeared in *Vanity Fair* not long after Garbo arrived in Hollywood

dinary forehead." And without making any further preparations, Greta Garbo let me make a number of pictures of her. Her face had an unusual mobility of expression and in the course of an hour my camera had captured a number of distinctive poses and expressions, all so different it was hard to believe they were of the same girl. Both she and Stiller were delighted with the result. Later on I took the pictures to Frank Crowninshield, the editor of *Vanity Fair*. I wanted to give him, I said, the opportunity to discover a great cinema star. "The pictures are very interesting, but who is the girl?" he asked. "Greta Garbo," I said. "Never heard of her," he said, "but perhaps I might use one of the pictures." "You can have it only," I insisted, "if you give it a full page." Reluctantly he agreed.

The chosen picture appeared on page eighty of the November 1925 issue of *Vanity Fair*, on the stands in October, with the caption "A New Star from the North—Greta Garbo." Before then, however, prodded by Genthe, Stiller had special-deliveried a complete set of the photos to Mayer in California, and Victor Seastrom, as always a friend and ally, had also made sure that Mayer and the rest of the M-G-M brass saw them. One story has it that an eager young Metro executive who had spotted the one in *Vanity Fair* excitedly tried to interest the studio in this new "star," only to discover that Mayer himself had already signed her up—a story one would like to take as gospel.

Meanwhile, Stiller had been negotiating the formal contracts he and his protégée were to sign. The basic deal had been made in Berlin, but M-G-M now realized that Garbo's Berlin signature had no legal standing, since she was still a minor, and they needed her mother's approval. Other details remained to be ironed out, and Stiller, as demanding as ever, succeeded in upping Garbo's weekly salary to $400. She didn't realize that this was an unheard-of starting level for an unproven young actress: Most starlets began in the $100 range. Even so, she grew upset when she heard him—brusque and imperious—crossing swords with the M-G-M lawyers. She clearly didn't want to lose this chance at stardom.

And then, after what Garbo would later refer to as the most boring and unhappy (and hot) months of her life, they were rushed onto the Twentieth-Century Limited to begin their cross-country trip. With them was a handsome young Swede named Rolf Laven whom David Bret—as always, ready with the lubricious (and questionable) detail—tells us Stiller had picked up in a gay bar, and whom M-G-M was now required to hire as his translator. Laven proved to be more than that, moving in with his boss as assistant and lover, an echo of Stiller's previous Swedish arrangements. (They were still together when Stiller returned to Sweden three years later.) What had not been ironed out, despite Stiller's importunings, were the actual plans M-G-M had for him and Garbo once they arrived—plans that couldn't be ironed out because M-G-M still hadn't made any. Stiller may have been Sweden's greatest director, and Garbo a New Star from the North, but Hollywood had seen countless great directors and new stars come—and go.

The train ride across the country didn't amuse Garbo. (Stiller, at least, had Rolf Laven to amuse him.) But at least when they finally arrived at the downtown Los Angeles station, there was a more cheerful welcome than there had been on the New York docks. M-G-M had organized a group of old friends and colleagues who were now part of the burgeoning Swedish colony in Hollywood, so that the new arrivals were greeted by, among others, the Sjöström/Seastroms and the stars Anna Q. Nilsson, Jean Hersholt, and Warner Oland, plus the American star Gertrude Olmstead—who had recently appeared opposite Valentino in *The Cobra* and would soon appear with Garbo in *Torrent*—and a brother of Stiller's whom he hadn't seen in thirty-five years. There were also two little simpering girls with bonnets, who, Karen Swenson tells us, were "six-year-old thespian Muriel Frances Dana, representing Little Miss California, and seven-year-old Evelyn Erikssen, representing Little Miss Sweden." Garbo's hair was in its riotous

frizzy mode, and apparently when a reporter asked her where she would be living, she replied, "I would like to find a room with a nice private family." The M-G-M publicity man in attendance was not pleased. Garbo was installed in the Miramar Hotel and Apartments in Santa Monica, Stiller (and Laven) in a nearby bungalow.

But Garbo was also out in the world, and often on her own—and without English. (Stiller's wasn't much better.) Obviously she needed help, and the studio came up with the perfect person. He was Sven-Hugo Borg, an extremely handsome Swede in his late twenties, who had wound up in Los Angeles with the vague idea of becoming an actor, and whose English was excellent. Registering his interest in finding employment, he left his name and credentials with the Swedish consulate, who suggested him to M-G-M when they came looking for someone to act as interpreter for the new Swedish import.

They met in late 1925, just as *Torrent* was beginning production— Garbo terrified, approaching "the making of her first Hollywood film with all the excitement of a condemned person walking to the electric chair." "Borg, Borg, do something!" she cried. "Make them let me have Mauritz! Why won't they let me have Mauritz?" That was something that was not in Borg's power to achieve, but in everything else he was hers to command for the next four years. In a series of articles he would write about her and about their relationship for the British magazine *Film Pictorial*, he said,

> Not only did I act as her interpreter from 1925 to 1929. It was I who taught her her first words of English [not literally], and I who guided her through those first hectic months . . . For more than a year after her arrival in Hollywood she did not have a personal maid, except of course, to dress her. Garbo's demands on me for personal service were so exacting that it was really embarrassing to me, especially when a motion-picture magazine carried the following: "The first personal maid Garbo had in this country was a man, and I'm not kidding." Interpreters are O.K., reasoned Garbo, but why let her countryman waste his time? So Sven was commissioned to carry Garbo's shoes from her dressing room to the set (she wore carpet slippers between scenes), and to lug her wraps and make-up box. There

was poor Sven, trailing after her, complaining, "I was hired to be an interpreter, not a lady's maid," and Garbo, impervious as ever, saying, "Sven, bring me my make-up mirror."

He also drove her all over the place, and indeed taught her to drive—and took the rap when several times, with her at the wheel, they were stopped by the cops. The L.A. police, as always, did everything they could to protect the studios' interest.

With Sven-Hugo Borg

It seems plausible that he also spent a good deal of time in her bed. (Like everyone else, he assumed that her relationship with Stiller, however close, was non-sexual.) They were both young, they were both beautiful, they were both Swedish, and neither of them had anyone else, until—temporarily—she had John Gilbert. At various times they spent weeks together out of town and in seclusion. The relationship was interrupted when he published his articles about her in England—a far greater act of treachery as far as she was concerned than his taking another lover—but eventually their complicated friendship resumed.

(Starting in 1933, Borg would play scores of bit parts in the movies—a sailor, a logger, a German sniper, a masseur, "a Swede"—until his final, mysterious credit, in *The Prize*, in 1963, as "Dead make-up artist." Garbo was dismayed when, in 1981, she received word of his death. She would survive him by nine years.)

While Garbo, with Borg's help, was slowly adjusting to her new life, Stiller was very low. He exhausted himself besieging M-G-M with requests for an assignment and with projects of his own—an English-language version of the *Odalisque from Smolna* script, for instance. (Oddly enough, the studio said no.) Nor was he a well man—although he was only in his early

ABOVE AND OPPOSITE: Typical starlet poses of the day

forties and looked so imposing, his health had always been unsound. Had he made a terrible mistake coming to America, where it became clearer and clearer to him that he was a nobody? Which only made him behave more aggressively and therefore offensively to Mayer and his "boy genius" Irving Thalberg, who was in charge of production at M-G-M, both of whom were obviously remembering their recent difficulties with Erich von Stroheim (the "von" was of his own devising). Just a year earlier, in 1924, "Von" had completed his version of Frank Norris's *Greed*—eight hours long. Today, based on the two-and-a-half-hour version that the studio hacked it down to, it's considered (by some) a masterpiece. Back then, there was unanimity, among the only twelve people who ever watched it all, that it was unbearably long and boring. (Fifty years after seeing it, Irene Mayer Selznick was still outraged by it.) Stroheim's megalomania had enraged M-G-M, and they obviously feared that in Stiller they had another such monster on their hands.

When he wasn't raging, he was brooding—friends remember the two newcomers as "a melancholy pair." Garbo, at least, had things to do: English to learn, horseback riding to learn; her hair to tame, her teeth to be seen to, although stories of major work on them were highly exaggerated—they didn't need to be capped and at most required only some minor re-alignment of two in the front. In fact, Swenson tells us, the studio dentist reported that she had the only perfect teeth of all their stars. M-G-M had begun insisting on her doing the kind of ridiculous publicity stunts starlets were subjected to—the most notorious, and the one she hated most, had her sitting in a cage, terrified, next to the very docile lion whom the world would come to know as the studio's mascot, Leo. (It is also far from impossible that the published picture was a montage of separate shots of the Lady and the Lion.)

There was a rotten screen test, then Stiller insisted that he direct a second one, and this one Thalberg paid attention to. Suddenly, she was assigned her first role at M-G-M. As usual, we have conflicting stories about how it happened, the most appealing (and unlikely?) one being that the well-known director Monta Bell was looking for an actress for his current film and was going through newsreel flood footage for the movie when up popped the new Garbo test, which had been photographed, at Lillian Gish's suggestion, by the superb cinematographer Hendrik Sartov. Eureka! Garbo

Torrent: as a devout girl who becomes the great diva La Brunna

was to report to the studio immediately for costume fittings, et cetera. If you're cynical, you can choose to believe that the bosses at M-G-M had suddenly realized what they had in her and imposed her on Bell. In fact, the Boss of Bosses, Mr. Mayer, was quoted as saying, "Maybe I'll never win a fortune at the race track but that won't keep me from betting. I'll take a chance on Garbo."

By late November she was at work, playing the female lead in a major film—this was only a few months after her arrival in Hollywood, however long it may have seemed to her at the time. Stiller, naturally, was disheartened at not directing her first American film, but he was realistic and urged her to comply. He would, of course, be coaching her unofficially.

The movie was at first called *Ibanez' Torrent*, Blasco Ibáñez being the internationally bestselling author of two novels already turned into sensationally successful movies: Valentino's breakthrough hit, *The Four Horsemen of the Apocalypse*, and his equally successful *Blood and Sand*. (Ibáñez's *Mare Nostrum* was already in the works, a gorgeous epic directed by Rex

Ingram and starring Antonio Moreno . . . who would soon be appearing opposite Garbo in her second outing.) In *Torrent*, she would be playing opposite another sexy "Hispanic" star, Ricardo Cortez, who was born Jacob Krantz on New York's Lower East Side. (When sound came in he quickly ceased being Hispanic.) As for his sexiness, one seeks it on the screen but fails to find it. Times change. He was rude and unwelcoming toward Garbo, but she just dismissed him as "a pumpkin." No doubt he was angered by all the attention she was receiving. Word had gotten around the studio about how exciting the daily rushes were, and what Garbo was like on the set. "I've been watching that new girl work," one M-G-M writer told a journalist. "I don't know what it is that she has but I do know that everyone on the lot who can get away from whatever he is supposed to be doing goes to watch her. There is a stillness about her, a power . . ."

Torrent follows the life of a naïve young Spanish peasant girl who is dumped by the rich boy whose mother forbids their marriage and who seamlessly goes on (off-camera) to become the world's most famous opera singer—La Brunna! In her wake straggle millionaires, grand dukes, tsars, all flinging furs and tiaras at her, but her heart remains true to Cortez until he lets her down once too often and she bravely faces life alone with her tiaras and tsars (and personal record company). The big excitement of the film is the fabulous flood—the Torrent—that is its climax, and it is Garbo's transformation from sweet ingénue

With Ricardo Cortez

to sophisticated glamour that fixed her early image as a vamp, the character established by Theda Bara (anagram, Arab Death), and which Garbo hated and resented. But for us today what impresses is how completely natural and enchanting she is as the young lovestruck girl in the early scenes.

Garbo, Stiller, the entire Swedish colony thought the movie, and she in it, were a disaster and a disgrace—typical Hollywood melodramatics with typically elaborate M-G-M trimmings. Only the critics and the audience loved it, helped along, no doubt, by ads like this one:

Ibanez' *Torrent*! Rising flood of mighty emotions!

Sweeping us on—ever on—breathless!

Greta Garbo—Perfection!

Discovered by Metro-Goldwyn-Mayer in stark Sweden!

She is setting the heart of America aflame!

Torrent: bystanders envy her glorious life, but we know how she suffers

Garbo was on her way.

She, however, had been unhappy making *Torrent*, and not just because she had been denied Stiller as her director. Writing to Mimi Pollack, she said, "You have no idea how my head spins sometimes just from unhappiness." She describes her daily routine: up at 6:00 in the morning, back to her hotel residence twelve hours later, and right to bed. "And lonely, lonely.

God, it is horrible. This ugly, ugly America, all machine, it is excruciating." She rarely went out, she said, except for having dinner with Stiller. She had no energy left to meet and converse with other film people, and no desire to make small talk. The only thing that gave her pleasure was to go to the bank and send money home to her family. But eventually she settled in, and the correspondence with Pollack tails off. (Her less agitated letters to Salka Viertel circa 1935 echo the same feelings and complaints. She's settled in, but she hasn't changed her tune.)

M-G-M, having blundered into an image for her that galvanized the public, rushed her into *The Temptress*, another vamp role from another Ibáñez novel. She is the impossibly elegant Elena, married to a marquis who has bankrupted himself to slather her in jewels and regal residences. His old friend Manuelo Robledo (Moreno) turns up in Paris, he and Elena take one look at each other, and soon she and the ruined marquis are following Robledo to "the Argentine," where he's building a great dam—yes, he's a genius engineer. There she vamps every male in sight, including Lionel Barrymore in a relatively restrained performance and a ferocious bandit who serenades her, conveniently murders the marquis, and in a fit of pique, dynamites the dam.

The high points of this farrago of melodrama and exoticism are the flood that follows the destruction of the dam, the fight with bullwhips between the bandit and Robledo that leaves the bare-chested engineer blinded (but only temporarily) and scarred, and the final scene in Paris, years later, when Robledo, now a hero and newly married, comes across bedraggled, unrecognizable, alcohol- and drug-ridden Elena outside a café, buys her a drink, and goes off, leaving her to bestow her last valuable possession, a ruby ring, on a deadbeat artist at the next table, believing that he's Jesus Christ.

Garbo hated this movie, too, but its success secured her position as the most promising young actress in the world. And the most beautiful. During the making of *The Temptress*, however, she suffered the greatest blow of her life, apart from the death of her father. Her cherished sister, Alva, only twenty-three, died in Sweden—another Gustafsson beauty, who was just beginning her own career as an actress.

It was Stiller who, on the set, handed her the cablegram with the terrible news. She had never been told how ill Alva had become. After nearly collapsing, she said to Stiller, "Come, Mauritz, let us go on," but she did not turn up for work the next day. One person tried to comfort her. Lillian Gish, working on a nearby set, remembered that "I couldn't speak to her [because of the language barrier] and tell her I was sorry. So I sent her some flowers with a note." When Garbo awkwardly tried to thank her, Gish put her arms around her and they both burst out weeping. (Lillian, of course—so close to her own beloved sister, Dorothy—understood sister-love.) Garbo never forgot her kindness.

With Lillian Gish

Whereas the on-screen story of *The Temptress* was ludicrous, the story off-screen was tragic. M-G-M had acceded to Stiller's insistence that he direct Garbo's second outing, and he filmed her for five weeks and then was summarily fired. The parts of the film he did direct and that were retained are highly elaborate, brilliantly textured, fascinating—and hopelessly unsuited to M-G-M: His *Temptress* was a highly artistic European movie, imbued with the very qualities that had impressed the studio to begin with. Stiller had also seriously offended Antonio Moreno, an important star, insisting, among other things, that he do away with his trademark elegant mustache. Moreno helped Stiller dig his own grave, but it was already more or less dug. Stiller's highly personal and dictatorial way of filming was also wildly expensive, and he was falling further and further behind in the shooting schedule. Post-*Greed*, that was Stiller's death knell at M-G-M. Lars Hanson reported Thalberg saying to him, "Is the man mad? Has he ever been behind a camera before?"

Garbo was in despair. "When this thing happened to Moje, I thought the sun would never rise again," she wrote to a friend. And "How I was

The Temptress: (*above*) Stiller directing Garbo and Antonio Moreno before being fired; (*left*) Moreno whipped and nearly blinded as the result of her vampish ways; (*opposite top*) the dam bursts; (*opposite bottom*) years later, down-and-out in Paris and destroyed by absinthe and other excesses, she fantasizes that the drunken bum at the next table is Jesus, and gives him her last possession— her ruby ring.

broken to pieces, nobody knows." She was frightened of going on without him, and aware of how this would affect him, both personally and professionally. But, again, he counseled her to keep going with the highly experienced Fred Niblo, who had directed the triumphant *Ben-Hur* and who treated her tactfully and gently, even though he was told to reshoot much of what Stiller had already shot. What might have been a masterpiece is lost to us, but a worldwide hit was born—one that cemented Garbo's dizzying rise to fame.

By now, M-G-M knew what it had, and knew what to do about it. Their biggest male romantic star—and with the recent sudden death of Rudolph Valentino, the entire industry's—was John Gilbert, who in ten years had gone from earning two dollars a day to ten thousand dollars a week. Quickly the studio paired him with Garbo in *Flesh and the Devil*, yet another vamp role for her, to her chagrin. She pleaded with the studio to let her rest. And she was distressed by this new role she had been assigned. As she would later say, "I cannot see any sense in dressing up and doing nothing but tempting men in pictures," but she had no choice other than to obey. (She would make sure that that would never happen again.)

The third star in the love triangle that constituted the plot of *Flesh and the Devil* was her old colleague from *Gösta Berling*, Lars Hanson. And a very peculiar triangle it was, since the many scenes between Leo (Gilbert) and Ulrich (Hanson), beginning in their boyhood and continuing through their army camaraderie and their involvement with the fatal Felicitas, are so ardent in their depiction of male friendship that whenever they meet after an absence, their eager embrace leaves their lips barely apart, an inch or so away from a kiss. Didn't anyone notice this? What did Gilbert, who was as straight as a guy can be, make of it? What did Clarence Brown, the director, make of it? And he was straight, too. Inevitably, the rivalry between the two young men over Felicitas—who is married to one of them but in love with the other—jeopardizes their sacred bond of friendship. But fortunately their duel-to-the-death over her is interrupted when at the last possible moment, in the only honorable act of her life and in gorgeous furs, she falls through the ice to her death while hurrying to prevent her husband and

Lars Hanson and
John Gilbert as
best friends in
Flesh and the Devil

Flesh and the Devil: (*above and opposite*) Garbo and Gilbert in the most sexually explicit
scenes ever seen in a commercial movie—and the ones that made her
the world's greatest female star

(*above*) Her black veil tells us that her husband has been killed in a duel; (*below*) Barbara Kent, Gilbert, Garbo, and Hanson at the altar rail, where she has committed blasphemy by sipping from the communion cup where her lover's lips have just been

her lover from slaughtering each other. (My friend Jeanine Basinger, ushering in a South Dakota movie house where *Flesh and the Devil* was being revived, reports that a woman in the audience shouted out, "Save the fur!")

What astonished the world were the highly charged sex scenes between Garbo and Gilbert. They kissed with their mouths open! They made love horizontally! She was lying on top of him! Nothing this erotic had ever been seen on the screen. *And* the photography by the young William Daniels was so exquisite! (He would go on to film almost all her movies.)

Flesh and the Devil ended with the duel interruptus and the two friends reunited and in each other's arms, but M-G-M covered its bets by filming an alternate scene for exhibitors who wanted a different kind of happy ending. This time round we have a pastoral scene in which Leo is holding a hank of wool for his mother as she winds it into a ball while Ulrich lies at their feet,

reading. And then, in a twinkling, Leo succumbs to the schoolgirl pash Ulrich's little sister (Barbara Kent) has always had for him, and joy reigns unconfined. Both endings are available to be seen. But the plot was never the thing, although there's certainly a lot of it. It's the two stars who are everything, plus some clever business devised by the writers and director. We learn who died in the first duel—Leo or her cuckolded husband—by watching the new widow, Felicitas, with a smirk of satisfaction, trying on a chic hat with a black veil. We see Felicitas kneeling at the communion rail in church, turning the wine goblet around so that her lips will touch it where Leo's just have been. (Blasphemy on top of adultery!) This is a well-made movie—Mayer and Thalberg, having realized what they had in Garbo, gave it their all.

As for Garbo herself, she has a new, assured beauty and command. Brown and Daniels and Gilbert helped her in every possible way, but they

Clarence Brown directs; William Daniels is behind the camera.

didn't invent her. Not even Stiller invented her. And she herself didn't understand what she was all about. The world simply grasped that she was unique and to be treasured, and it flocked to see her. With the tremendous worldwide success of *Flesh and the Devil*, Garbo was canonized as the leading actress of the cinema, a position she never relinquished. She was now central to M-G-M's sense of itself, and she realized the power that gave her. She and Hanson had been billed under the title, which didn't bother her, but she was earning "only" $750 a week, which did. That would soon change.

Fortunately for Stiller, an old friend from Germany, Erich Pommer, was now in charge of production at Paramount. M-G-M, all too relieved to be rid of the impossible Moje, released him from his three-year contract so that he could move to Paramount and direct the major star Pola Negri in *Hotel Imperial*, a considerable success when it was released. He finished two more films with Negri, including the effective anti-war *Barbed Wire*, in 1927, and then—his career petering out and his health having seriously deteriorated—he left for Sweden. Garbo saw him off at the station, both of them trying not to cry. But although she would miss him, he was right: She really didn't need him any longer. And they would never see each other again.

Back in Stockholm, although no new film presented itself, Stiller directed an acclaimed and successful production of the American hit play *Broadway*, George Abbott's first success, that had run in New York for a year and a half. He had plans—grandiose ones, naturally—for new films, but he was soon so ill that he could barely function. There had been letters between him and Greta, confused, sad, guilt-ridden on both sides. He was out of money, almost bankrupt, and protracted stays in the hospital and major operations could not restore his health. Sjöström, arriving back in Sweden for a vacation, rushed to the hospital, and over the next days he and Stiller had intense, at times delirious, conversations. And then Moritz Stiller was dead—at forty-five. Tuberculosis? Pleurisy? No one knows for certain. It is said that he died clutching one of Genthe's portraits of Greta to his chest.

Sjöström wired Garbo the terrible news. Again, as with Alva's death, the cablegram was delivered to her while she was at work, this time on *Wild Orchids*. Immediately at the end of filming, she left for Sweden, defying telegrams from Thalberg to return to Hollywood for retakes. (She was suspended, but what did she care?) Once she was back in Stockholm, nothing took precedence over coming to terms with Stiller's death. Accompanied by his lawyer, Hugo Lindberg, she visited the storehouse where his effects were gathered. Lindberg: "I remember vividly how she walked about the room, touching this item and that. She seemed very moved and talked about Moje in a hushed voice, almost a whisper. 'This was the suitcase he took to America,' she said, picking up the bag. 'And these rugs—I remember when he bought them in Turkey.'" (This event was clearly the trigger for the famous scene in *Queen Christina* when Garbo wanders around the room in which she and Gilbert have spent the night, touching the bed, the chairs . . .) She was allowed to take away with her a portrait of Stiller and the heavy oak chair she had sat in while waiting for him to interview her the first time they met. She was also allowed to buy a chest of drawers that had stood in his study.

A few days later she went to Stiller's grave in Stockholm's Jewish cemetery, leaving behind a large floral cross. Returning the following day, she found the cross gone, its flowers scattered. A passing stranger explained "what I in my ignorance had not understood—that the cross is a Christian

symbol that has no place in Jewish life." (There are cynical commentators who dismiss this story as sentimental hooey.) On her subsequent visits home, she would always visit Stiller's grave, always alone. And back in Hollywood, on the set, she would frequently murmur, "He says this . . . he does so and so." Jacques Feyder, who directed her twice, referred to him as "the green shadow."

Without question, Stiller was the person with whom Garbo had the strongest bond, a bond that did not end with his death. There were others who influenced her, guided her, took care of her, but no one who so dominated her psyche. The relationship between them may have frayed toward the end, but her devotion to him and to his memory never faltered. (Nor his to her. He never seems to have resented her dazzling ascent to fame, only wanting her to be happy and fulfilled.) We know their story well, because Hollywood has told it again and again—art unwittingly imitating life. They call it *A Star Is Born*.

GARBO AND GILBERT

E MET AT A DINNER PARTY," wrote Ben Hecht, the screen-writer, playwright, novelist, and much more,

and Jack came home with me and talked all night. In the time of Hollywood's most glittering days, he glittered the most. He received ten thousand dollars a week and could keep most of it. He lived in a castle on top of a hill. Thousands of letters poured in daily telling him how wonderful he was. The caliphs for whom he worked bowed before him as before a reigning prince. They built him a dressing room such as no actor ever had. It was a small Italian palace. There were no enemies in his life. He was as unsnobbish as a happy child. He went wherever he was invited. He needed no greatness around him to make him feel distinguished. He drank with carpenters, danced with waitresses and made love to whores and movie queens alike. He swaggered and posed but it was never to impress anyone. He was being Jack Gilbert, prince, butterfly, Japanese lantern and the spirit of romance.

That was not the way he started out. His father ran a third-rate touring company, his mother playing the leads, until they divorced when he was a toddler. Clearly he was unwanted, and his mother was a mother in name only—she never even registered his birth (in 1897) and let him believe he

John Gilbert

was illegitimate; he didn't meet his father, whose name he had never been told, until he was twenty-six. She left little Cecil—Jack's birth name—here, there, and everywhere throughout his childhood, palming him off on uninterested relatives and near-strangers. He often went hungry. When she had men in her bed she would stuff him away in the closet. He spent most of his time backstage, where he managed to teach himself to read. His spotty education ended—like Garbo's—when he was fourteen. His bitter and angry mother died in her late thirties, and after the funeral his stepfather handed him a ten-dollar bill and put him on a train for San Francisco. He was on his own.

But he was charming, smart, and ambitious, and slowly he made his way. He was a show-business child and quickly turned to show business to earn a living—it was all he knew. He tried the stage, but it was the movies with which he fell in love, though he was hardly movie-star material—tall, gangly, painfully thin, with a big nose (though perfect teeth). Finding himself employed by the pioneer producer Thomas Ince, he worked as an extra at two dollars a day, then started writing scenarios, and finally found a mentor in the superb French director Maurice Tourneur. (Important mentors who happened to be first-rate directors were another thing that he and Garbo had in common.) There were lots of girls, one of whom (he hardly knew her) he married, then divorced—on his pal Charlie Chaplin's advice—when he fell madly in love with a young actress named Leatrice Joy, whom Cecil B. DeMille was turning into a star.

Meanwhile, he was filling out and growing more handsome, and his indefatigable spirit, ravening curiosity, and compulsive work ethic were drawing attention. Through the midteens of the century he was working his way up from extra to bit player to studio contract player to second and first leads, punctuated in 1919 by playing opposite the movies' greatest star, Mary Pickford, in *Heart o' the Hills* and climaxing in a terrific performance in 1923 as a riverboat gambler in a Fox film called *Cameo Kirby*, directed by John Ford and featuring Jean Arthur in her film debut.

Garbo and Gilbert as photographed by Edward Steichen for *Vanity Fair* in 1928

Alexander Walker, in his insightful book *Stardom*, identifies Gilbert's quality:

It was [his] temperamental boyishness, [his] emotional un-formedness, [his] absolute ability to yield to his feelings . . . which gave John Gilbert his romantic dash and self-charging energy. It matched his screen looks to perfection: His smile, his broad forehead with its crown of curly hair, his eyes whose mascara make-up provided a hypnotic darkness against which the whites flashed like phosphorus, and especially his wide-wide grin and cocky chin. It is the romantic look American-style as opposed to the romantic look Valentino-style. Gallantry is the word rather than seduction. It is that of the pirate of romantic fiction, not the gigolo of the ballroom floor.

Gilbert's greatest successes: (*clockwise from opposite top*) with Lillian Gish in *La Bohème*; in *The Big Parade*, the most successful silent film after *Birth of a Nation*; with Norma Shearer in *He Who Gets Slapped*; with Mae Murray in *The Merry Widow*

LEFT AND OPPOSITE:
Enjoying
themselves
off-camera

In 1924 Gilbert was introduced by his friend Howard Hawks to Irving Thalberg, and he signed a five-year contract with the recently organized Metro-Goldwyn-Mayer. Thalberg, who became one of his closest friends, had recognized his star potential and quickly shepherded him through the series of excellent performances and tremendous hits—among them *He Who Gets Slapped*, *The Merry Widow*, *The Big Parade*, *La Bohème*—that made him the highest-paid leading man in pictures. And brought him the tag "The Great Lover," which he loathed. It also made it inevitable that he would be paired with the studio's latest sensation, Greta Garbo.

Some months before the two stars met, Garbo and Stiller were at a dinner party at which the director Rowland Lee, one of Jack's closest friends, was seated next to her. He didn't find talking to her easy, he remembered: "She spoke very little English. Sometimes she pretended to know even less. But when Jack Gilbert's name came up . . . her eyes lit up. Then when I told her I knew Jack Gilbert, that I practically brought him up, she roused herself to a pitch of excitement . . . She asked me question after question about him. Jack Gilbert was all she wanted to talk about, how marvelous, how wonderful, how charming he was . . ."

Their first encounter was on the M-G-M lot. "The Swede isn't a bad looker," Gilbert reported to his gang at lunch in the commissary, as recorded by Frances Marion, the famous screenwriter. "Bones are too large but she has amazing eyes. I ran into her the other day and said 'Hello, Greta,' and I'll be damned if she didn't freeze. '*Miss* Garbo,' she said, then turned on her big flat feet and walked off. Imagine upstaging *me*." Their first formal meeting took place on the first day of their working together on *Flesh and the Devil*. In *Dark Star*, the excellent book about Gilbert by his daughter Leatrice Gilbert Fountain, we're told that when the director Clarence Brown (who would work with Garbo seven times) brought the timid Swedish girl over to meet the great star of *The Big Parade*, "She was so nervous . . . that Jack warmed to her immediately. She started to relax from the moment he smiled at her and he soon had her laughing. If it wasn't love at first sight, it was something very close to it. Garbo had clearly developed a crush on Jack before their meeting. Jack, for his part, was certainly flattered by it and charmed by her vulnerability. There were also those eyes. However it started, by the time their first love scene was filmed they were madly, exuberantly in love."

Brown remembered it this way: "It was the damnedest thing you ever saw . . . When they got into that first love scene . . . well, nobody else was even there. Those two were alone in a world of their own. It seemed like an intrusion to yell 'cut!' I used to just motion the crew over to another part of

All is bliss . . .

the set and let them finish what they were doing. It was embarrassing."
Brown knew what he had: "I am working with raw material. They are in
that blissful state of love that is so like a rosy cloud that they imagine themselves hidden behind it, as well as lost in it."

Almost at once Jack swept Greta up to his mountain aerie, although she
maintained her official residence at the Miramar Hotel in Santa Monica. He
pampered her, indulged her, worshipped her. She didn't like the bathroom?
His decorator recalled, "When Mr. Gilbert started seeing Garbo in 1926, I
installed black marble walls and a sunken black marble tub with gold fix-
tures in the master bathroom. But Garbo complained that the marble glis-
tened too much. So workmen fluted the walls to remove the shine." It all
cost fifteen thousand dollars. Jack built a cabin on his property for her, and
put in a pine grove, because, Barry Paris says, "She missed the sight and
sound of Swedish trees." He opened an account for her in a leading Stockholm bookstore. But most important was what he did for her on the set,
making sure that she had the best camera angles and calling for retakes if he
didn't think she had been shot to her best advantage. Clarence Brown said,

. . . until it isn't.

"He watched everything she did and corrected it. Garbo was so grateful. She recognized his long experience in the movies and she hung on his every word," later telling a journalist, in one of her rare interviews, "I don't know how I should have managed if I had not been cast opposite John Gilbert . . . through him I seemed to establish my first real contact with the strange American world. If he had not come into my life at this time, I should probably have come home to Sweden at once, my American career over." Meanwhile, both in private and in public he never stopped begging her to marry him. She, having a lot more common sense than he had ever displayed, wouldn't do it.

What would a marriage between two such incongruous people have been like? To begin with, as he reported to his great pal the columnist-reporter-novelist Adela Rogers St. Johns—and as *she* reported in both her autobiographies—they had mutually exclusive views of marriage. "I didn't know Garbo well, and that is an understatement," St. Johns wrote, "but I knew Jack Gilbert very well. What I know of their romance is told here exactly as Jack told it to me.

"You are in love with *Garbo*," Greta once said gloomily to him. "Damn right," the dashing Gilbert . . . said to her. When he told me about it he said, "I told her yes, I am in love with *Garbo*. I want to marry *Garbo*. She wants to leave the screen and buy a wheat ranch and have seventeen children and don't think she can't. I love people and cities and *conversation*—so I say I will not marry her unless she goes on being Garbo. She says she will not marry me unless she can leave the screen forever. So there we are."

"But," Jack told St. Johns, "the glorious woman I loved was the Garbo of the screen. I knew what would happen if we bought a wheat ranch. She'd wear flat-heeled shoes the rest of her life. No, no, it wouldn't work."

Even so, it almost happened, and more than once, if you believe the stories that later went the rounds (and are still going the rounds). The most elaborate event/nonevent was a purportedly scheduled double wedding between Greta and Jack and director King Vidor and actress Eleanor Boardman, with much of Hollywood royalty in attendance at the home of Marion Davies. According to this account, Garbo just didn't turn up, and finally the Vidor-Boardman wedding had to proceed without her and Jack. It featured a report that Jack and Louis B. Mayer came to blows when Mayer said to him, "Why do you have to marry her? Sleep with her and forget about it." No one who was present at the Vidor wedding has confirmed this story, which was put about only many years later by Boardman, who seems to have had a deep animus toward Garbo—"the most fascinating woman I ever met, but . . . also the most selfish. She had no real love for Jack. She promised at least three times to marry him and then backed off . . . I wish I knew why Garbo treated him so badly but I don't. She took everything he had to offer and gave nothing." The most telling evidence about the supposed aborted wedding is that it went unmentioned in all the gossip columns and feature stories of the time and the countless memoirs to come. And let's not forget that on the fatal day, September 8, 1926, Jack and Greta had known each other for only three weeks.

Other stories of elopements, most or all of them fabricated, would come and go, grist for the columns and fan magazines. The most inventive had them on their way to a justice of the peace somewhere out of town, and when they stopped at a gas station, Garbo locked herself in the bathroom, climbed out of the window, and escaped back to L.A.

Eventually, Gilbert had to acknowledge that Garbo did not want to marry him, or anyone else. But there's no doubt that in the first flush of their romance, she blossomed in ways no one had ever witnessed before—or would again. Many people remember what she was like while she was living up there in Gilbert's "castle." She tried hard to be a "hostess" for him. "Every Sunday there would be an open house on Tower Road," said writer/director Carey Wilson, one of Jack's closest friends, who was often living at the castle during this time. "Entertaining was second nature to Jack, but agony for Garbo. But when she realized that these people wanted only to exchange sociability and friendship, she did gradually relax and lose most of her shyness . . . She entered heartily and effectively into all the games, from tennis to murder mysteries." (Coached by Jack, she quickly became a fiercely competitive tennis player. According to Wilson, she "played the most unorthodox tennis you can possibly imagine. Grasping the racket up toward the throat, she would smack the ball so heartily that there wasn't much to be done about it in the event it happened to land in the court.")

Salka Viertel, the closest and most trusted friend Garbo would ever have in Hollywood, said, "Garbo was at her best with Jack. She came out in society, she laughed and went to parties. People will never forget how she was then, warm and vibrant and wildly beautiful." A young actress who had once worked with Jack said, "I remember the days when Garbo was in love with Jack Gilbert. She looked as if she had a light shining from within." Jack got the ultra-reclusive Greta to go with him to the premiere of one of his films, even to spend a weekend with him at Hearst's San Simeon. And when she wasn't with him, he thought and talked of nothing else. Joan Crawford, paired with him in *Twelve Miles Out* in 1927, would write, "He was still madly in love with Garbo, and the romance was not going well. He was like a caged lion. He resented every moment he was not with Garbo." One morning, Crawford says, he turned up near-hysterical and told her, "She wouldn't sleep with me last night! . . . She hates Hollywood and everything in it."

Hollywood was not really the problem, though. She was a bewildered, unsophisticated twenty-two-year-old suddenly transported to Oz, lacking a language in common with the Oz-ites, her mentor and protector taken from her, dealing with a studio with its own interests at heart. One moment she was an uneducated Swedish peasant girl, the next she was world-famous. She didn't know enough about Hollywood to hate it. And Jack Gilbert was the best thing that had happened to her since her arrival—not only a tremendous star but supportive, generous, rich, deliriously in love with her. Of course she fell in love. And of course, given her cautious, self-absorbed, practical nature, she drew back in the face of his impetuous, driven, boyish (childish?)—and alcoholic—behavior. And she was conflicted not only about him but about herself. Yes, she wanted to raise wheat and seventeen children in Montana, but she also was determined to be both a great actress and a great star. No wonder he too was bewildered. Finally, this collision of passions and egos was taking place in a frenzy of public attention. The Garbo-Gilbert relationship had quickly become the biggest Hollywood story since the Pickford-Fairbanks marriage, and millions around the world were caught up in it. That she survived—and flourished—is testimony to her unyielding strength and determination.

Given the huge promise of *Flesh and the Devil*, it was inevitable that M-G-M would want to pair them again, as soon as possible. But how? Gilbert was making other films with other leading ladies (Crawford, Boardman, Renée Adorée, Jeanne Eagels), but Garbo—the new jewel in the crown—was assigned to something called *Women Love Diamonds*, another vamp role. She simply refused to appear in it. Threats and suspensions did not budge her from her refuge in Gilbert's castle. From November 1926 to May 1927 she did not work, and finally M-G-M folded. It was agreed that her next vehicle would be a modernized *Anna Karenina*—at last something serious! Her old nemesis, Ricardo Cortez, would be Vronsky, and a pretentious Russian, Dmitri Buchowetski, whom Garbo did not like, was directing. They started filming, she became ill, and everything was put on hold. What's more, Irving Thalberg didn't like the Buchowetski rushes. Suddenly, Cortez was making a movie with Lon Chaney and Buchowetski was gone—from *Anna Karenina* and from Hollywood. And guess who the new Vronsky would be?

Post-Tolstoy, Gilbert and Garbo were to appear together in only two more films. The first one, *A Woman of Affairs* (1929), was another big hit—but no thanks to Gilbert. It was the role, though, not his performance, that sank him. This neutered version of Michael Arlen's scandalous international sensation, *The Green Hat*, pulled every punch—even the title and the heroine's name had to change: The famous "Iris March" became "Diana Merrick," and her young husband (John Mack Brown), who in the novel

Together again in *A Woman of Affairs*

commits suicide for the sake of "purity," is here revealed as an embezzler, not a syphilitic. Poor Gilbert, as the man who has loved her through thick and thin but keeps abandoning her for reasons of plot, is completely passive. Clarence Brown, directing again, spoke of his extraordinary generosity and professionalism:

> Gilbert's part was a weak man, dominated by his father. I quite naturally thought that Gilbert might object to the short footage he had in the picture . . . Before even waiting for any objection from him, I proposed that I add something to his part, making it a bigger and more manly role. [But he] said, "I'd rather you didn't touch my part a bit, Clarence. If you do we might weaken our story. My character is weak and he's got to be handled

that way. Footage doesn't matter. I'd rather play the part of a butler in a good picture than have every foot in a film that's a flop." That's what I call idealism in an actor, and God knows it's rare enough in Hollywood.

Iris March/Diana Merrick was an extreme embodiment of the twenties—restless, sophisticated, gallant, full of pluck. She lives the life, and then she dies the death, driving her Hispano-Suiza into a tree to protect Gilbert's dull marriage and approaching fatherhood. This is Garbo's first "modern" movie, and she looks wonderful: The costume designer, Adrian, gives her a sporty, casual look that's ravishing; the art director, Cedric Gibbons, gives her Art Deco settings with an M-G-M gloss; the cinematographer, Daniels, gives her a diffused glow.

And she plays one of her greatest scenes when, lying in a French hospital bed near death from—from what? nervous breakdown? abortion?—she scoops up the big bouquet of roses Gilbert has sent her and rhapsodically buries her face in them. "With only a melodramatic situation, a jug of flowers, and herself," wrote Richard Corliss, "Garbo convinces us that she is incarnating the spirit of Greek tragedy instead of Michael Arlen. It's a minute of screen acting that by itself makes *A Woman of Affairs* one of her most imposing achievements. Something beautiful has been created out of almost nothing—which is less a case of skating on thin ice than of walking on water." It was another immensely profitable venture for M-G-M.

But soon it was 1929, and with sound overtaking silence at breakneck speed, they managed to squeeze three more Gilbert-less silents out of Garbo before she and the studio took the plunge into sound with *Anna Christie*, which was a triumph. But Gilbert's career was tanking. The tangled story of his supposedly ultra-high voice, of Louis B. Mayer's vendetta against him, of bad luck and foolish choices while he was raking in a fortune from his unbreakable long-run contract, has never been properly untangled. Mostly, it seems to me, the times were against him. He was a figure of romance, and as the thirties and the Depression deepened, Hollywood was caught up in gangsters, snappy dialogue, musicals. Garbo survived by virtue of her unassailable position (particularly abroad) and her beauty and glamour. Gilbert didn't. None of his sound films prospered—except one.

By 1933, Garbo was in full command of her situation at M-G-M—greatly thanks to Harry Edington, who had been Gilbert's agent and whom he had convinced her to take on as her business manager. Always in search of prestige, encouraged by Salka Viertel (who was one of the officially credited screenwriters) and others, she chose to make *Queen Christina*, a fanciful account of the life of Sweden's famous seventeenth-century queen who abdicated (something Garbo herself was always threatening to do). A hokey and completely invented romance was cooked up between Christina (in real life notoriously unattractive and sexually ambivalent) and "Don Antonio," a Spanish ambassador come to Stockholm to see if Christina might like to marry the king of Spain. They meet in an inn, in a snowstorm, and since she's dressed as a man, it makes sense that they share the only available bedroom. Guess what happens in that bedroom? Antonio, however, doesn't realize that she's the queen as well as a woman. What follows, follows— and at the very last, he is killed in a preposterous duel.

M-G-M had signed the young Laurence Olivier to play Don Antonio, but when he arrived in California, things did not go well between him and Garbo. He was frightened. She was beyond cold. And then she exploded her bomb. I will only proceed, she announced to Mayer, if I can have Jack Gilbert. Mayer's fury was incandescent, since he and Gilbert despised each other, but there was nothing he could do. Olivier was paid off and scampered back to England, and, to Jack's astonishment, he was summoned to the studio and signed for the role. (His old contract had run out.) He was in bad shape. His marriage to the celebrated Broadway actress Ina Claire had quickly petered out, and although he was now happily married to Virginia Bruce, he was certain that he was finished and was stunned when the call came from M-G-M. He did an obligatory screen test with Garbo that Olivier watched, reporting, "Garbo's face softened. Into her eyes came a strange, beautiful light. Something seemed to be happening deep down inside her."

When reporters demanded to know how it felt to be working with Garbo again, Gilbert said, "She was exactly the same today as six years ago, and she will always be the same—just as bewildering. Three years ago I would have sworn that she would never look at me again, and now she has fought to get me this part, when I am down and most need encouragement.

Incredible." His friend Colleen Moore remarked that "she remembered all the times he'd helped her career." Gilbert put it differently to Adela Rogers St. Johns: "There's never been a day since [she] and I parted that I haven't been lonely for her. I think she has always been lonely for me."

He was, uncharacteristically, afraid of failing—*Queen Christina* might well be the road back to his former preeminence. Once shooting began, he would later say, "I was nervous and gun-shy. The executives were looking at me with the old-time, too-familiar suspicion and hostility. I felt that only Garbo wanted me there." He was not sleeping and was drinking too much, and it all showed in his demeanor on the set—and everyone was watching. How would their first love scene go? When he grew too ardent, Garbo made things clear: "Mr. Gilbert is a married man now, with a wife and baby." "I was sick over the way I was playing my part," he said. "I was afraid of giving a bad performance. I was working under terrific pressure. The whole thing kept twisting around in me like a knife." Virginia Bruce, his loving and supportive wife, recalled, "Sometimes he'd be awake drinking all night. Then in the morning he'd get me to throw him in the pool so he could clear his head . . . He had bleeding ulcers. He used to throw up blood in the morning until he fainted." At one point he had to be hospitalized.

Garbo behaved wonderfully. One of their co-workers would comment, "Often we saw her watching him, when he didn't realize her eyes were upon him. There was pain and pity in her eyes, as though a bitter-sweet memory was taunting her. Gilbert never reacted to her efforts. He was like a man who had been floored by life, and was too tired to make the effort to get up from the canvas and continue the fight."

They made it to the end, and although Gilbert's reviews were mixed, today he looks right in the part—working hard, the voice masculine enough, and with touches of his earlier gleefully romantic self. He had, after all, played versions of Don Antonio, the impassioned lover, for years, and there was a lot reminiscent of silent film about the entire production. But he would make only one more film—*The Captain Hates the Sea*, as an alcoholic journalist—before dying in 1936 at the age of thirty-eight. Another pre-echo of *A Star Is Born*.

I haven't come across a single negative remark ever made about Garbo by Gilbert after their run-in before they officially met. At different times in her life, Garbo said various things about *him*, notoriously "There never was a romance, and now I wonder what I ever saw in him." Replying to the playwright S. N. Behrman, who had asked her, "How could you ever have got mixed up with a fellow like that," she said, "I was lonely—and I couldn't speak English." To a companion as they passed Gilbert in a car: "*Gott*, I wonder what I ever saw in him. Oh, well, I guess he *was* pretty."

Yet I keep returning to words from an early draft of Behrman's script, in which Christina says as she kneels over Antonio's lifeless body after the fatal duel: "Antonio, is this you? This is not you, Antonio. To you I cannot speak. But to that Antonio who was, to whom I did speak endlessly of love, I say again, I love you—I love you now and will always love you." Yes, it's fanciful, but I can't help feeling a sense of premonition and elegy—and truth.

At the end—of *Queen Christina* and of Gilbert and Garbo

$\rightleftharpoons 5 \rightleftharpoons$

GARBO AND M-G-M: THE SILENT YEARS

E VEN BEFORE *Torrent* was finished, Louis B. Mayer had tried to get Garbo to extend her three-year contract to five years. Summoning her to his office, she would recall, "He just said he couldn't afford to advertise my pictures and put money into me if I would not sign for five years with them." She said no. "I tried to explain—in my bad English—that I was satisfied, that I wanted no changes until I had at least played a part for him." "We're spending all this money on you," said Mayer. "Don't you think you should cooperate?" She didn't. He sweet-talked, he threatened, she demurred and went on doing so. Stiller was no longer in charge of her professional life, but she knew her own mind. It just made no sense to her—why would they want to extend their commitment to her before the public had ever laid eyes on her?

With the traumatic four-month filming of *The Temptress* finally behind her, she was exhausted, depleted, and in mourning for her sister. "I'm so sick and tired of everything," she wrote to her friend Lars Saxon, "all I want is to run away. I've had trouble with Metro-Goldwyn, been forced to turn to the manager [Mayer], and tried to talk to him although I don't know anything about how to run his business. I've become so nervous that one day I will make a scandal and leave everything."

Mayer saw her as ungrateful; she saw him as heartless. Ordered to the studio for costume fittings for *Flesh and the Devil*, she said to him, "Mister

Louis B. Mayer, Garbo, Lars Hanson, and Sven-Hugo Borg

Mayer, I am dead tired. I am sick. I cannot do another picture right away. And I am unhappy about the pictures." "That's just too bad," Mayer replied. "Go on and try on your clothes and get ready." She stopped going for fittings and rehearsals, didn't answer her phone, and on August 4, 1926, a messenger delivered to her, at the Miramar, a memo ordering her to turn up at the studio that day or, at the latest, the following morning. "Failure by you to comply with this demand, particularly in view of the attitude heretofore displayed by you, and your general insubordination, will be treated by us as a breach of your contract of employment . . ." Et cetera, et cetera. She stayed home. On August 13, M-G-M dismissed her from *Flesh and the Devil*. She didn't reply, although she did hire a lawyer. At last, on the seventeenth, she gave in, returned to the studio, and met John Gilbert. And as we have seen, she hated the script, she hated her role, but she didn't hate him.

Even before the hated movie was released—although everyone knew it was going to be a sensation—M-G-M had assigned Garbo to *Women Love Diamonds*, in which her character battles the disgrace of her illegitimacy by raising the children of a chauffeur of whom she is enamored. "I could not do that story," Garbo said. "Four or five bad pictures and there would be no more of me for the American people." She stayed home.

And, again, she ignored orders to appear. Mayer suspended her salary; Thalberg sent the director, Dmitri Buchowetski, to the Miramar, and after listening to him praise himself, she said to him, "But I do not wish to work for you." He was replaced, she was replaced, and the film went on to total eclipse. It was in late 1926 that Garbo took on Harry Edington, who "said

With Lionel Barrymore in the aborted version of *Anna Karenina*

he would handle . . . my contracts. My money, my work—everything." Strangely enough, Edington worked for M-G-M, and it was they who paid him whenever an arrangement was made. Garbo never liked paying people.

It was Edington who would negotiate her new contract, since obviously a star of this magnitude could not be kept on the old terms. Garbo's demands? Five thousand dollars a week! The press excoriated her for her "greed." She didn't yield, yet Mayer—who had already okayed *Anna Karenina* as her next project—took her off suspension and went on paying her at her old salary. She stayed home; she stayed out of sight; she became invisible.

So began one of the strangest episodes in Garbo's life. As we have seen, for six months she not only didn't appear for work, she disappeared from public view. There is no photo of her during this period; there is no confirmed spotting of her. Eventually, she turned up at the studio to begin work on *Anna*, with Cortez as Vronsky, but after a few days she became ill and disappeared for another two months. By now, the studio, the industry, and the public were getting used to her unyielding demand for privacy. But how—and why?—does so famous and conspicuous a woman vanish away, at the height of the world's consuming fascination with the saga of her and

With her hairdresser and maid

Gilbert? Mark A. Vieira sums it up this way in his invaluable (and beautiful) book on Garbo:

> Did Gilbert get Garbo pregnant in August 1926? Did she have a child prematurely and give it up to be raised by Swedish friends? Did she have an abortion? Did Gilbert abuse her, causing a miscarriage and complications? Did he shoot her? Did she shoot him, causing him to be hospitalized "for observation"? Was her April illness and her subsequent female trouble a result of this stress? Was her fear of strangers indicative of a more serious psychological disorder? Did she have a nervous breakdown as a result of the combined trauma of her sister's death, her separation from Stiller, her too-sudden romance with Gilbert, a possible pregnancy, a possible abortion, and the strike?

(*above*) As Anna Karenina, with Gilbert, in *Love*; (*opposite top*) with Philippe de Lacey as Seryosha; (*opposite bottom*) with director Edmund Goulding and Gilbert

Meanwhile, however, Edington and M-G-M were tortuously working out the new contract, and finally it was signed. It gave her $2,000 a week for the first year; $4,000 the second; $5,000 the third; $6,000 the fourth. When on May 18, 1927, it was announced that *Anna Karenina* was back in production, the new director would be the suave and experienced Edmund Goulding, the script would be by Frances Marion, and William Daniels (hero for his work on *Flesh and the Devil*) would be the cinematographer. Gilbert, of course, was inevitable: After *Flesh and the Devil*, and the worldwide hoopla surrounding the stars' relationship, how could M-G-M not reunite them?

And now the movie's title could be changed to *Love*, so that the campaign could proclaim "Gilbert and Garbo in *Love*!" Although the shutdown and new start cost the studio over $100,000—$2,000,000 or so today—it was worth it.

Filming went smoothly, but the results were mixed. (Gilbert would later call it "a cheap interpretation of Tolstoi's story, which, though containing

some memorable moments, is at best a sob sister's love tale. A Russian *East Lynne*.") Garbo looked wonderful, of course; Gilbert did not, though no one seemed to notice. Nor did their love scenes have the impact of those in *Flesh and the Devil*. The lack of sympathy between them was hardly surprising—by this point their romance was more or less over, Gilbert acting out with drunken driving, pistol-waving, and confrontations with the police. Far more convincing were her love scenes with Philippe de Lacey, the highly experienced ten-year-old—he had been in more movies than she had—who was playing her little boy. Here Garbo's feeling for children, her tenderness, break through, so that their scenes together give us a happy Garbo, and she is always entrancing when happy. There were no Kitty and Levin, no Dolly and Stiva. Gilbert was right—*Love* was hardly Tolstoyan. But it went on to great popular success. (After *Ben-Hur*, *The Big Parade*, and *The Merry Widow*, it would be the company's most profitable silent film.) *Variety* predicted, "They are in a fair way of becoming the biggest box office team this country has yet known." It seemed plausible at the time, but it was not to be.

This turbulent period in Garbo's career was beginning to reveal certain realities about her physical condition. As usual, she was a contradiction: seemingly robust and athletic, yet languorous, exhausted. Going out at night was impossible if she were to function well at the studio the next morning—she came home, studied her part, collapsed into bed. When she fell ill filming the scrapped *Anna Karenina*, the doctor diagnosed her as suffering from "an intestinal affliction, probably ptomaine poisoning." Thalberg told Cortez that she was suffering from anemia. She had serious difficulties with her monthly periods—the company tried shooting around them, but they were irregular and painful. (Finally, she acknowledged that she had a recurring ovarian infection.) It was also thought that she might be suffering from *pernicious* anemia, a compromised ability to take in vitamin B12—a far more serious condition than simple anemia and potentially life-threatening. (Many years later, however, Dr. Donald Reisfield, the gynecologist husband of her niece, Gray, reported that her problem had *not* been pernicious anemia.) Whatever it was, it clearly combined with her other dissatisfactions to put her out of commission.

Many of those dissatisfactions would soon be a thing of the past, however. Under her new contract, she now had what she had always wanted: not only a huge salary, but freedom from submitting to interviews or cooperating with foolish feature stories or appearing in ads for commercial products. And—crucial to her—she had the right of veto over her roles, co-stars, and directors. Lillian Gish had these prerogatives at M-G-M, but Gish over the years had risen through the ranks as a D. W. Griffith discovery after a childhood trouping around the country in corny melodramas. Pickford, Chaplin, Fairbanks, Valentino, Swanson—the biggest stars who preceded her—all had served lengthy apprenticeships. Garbo's only serious apprenticeship, if you can even call it that, consisted of two films of substance in Europe, followed by three Hollywood melodramas in which she was compelled to play vamps.

What do you do with a unique star like Garbo after a role like Anna Karenina? You cast her as another unique actress who happens to have been the greatest star the theater has ever known. "The Divine Sarah"— Sarah Bernhardt!—had died only a few years earlier, in 1923, having given the film industry immense prestige in 1912 when she appeared on the screen as Queen Elizabeth. As it happened, M-G-M owned a mediocre play about Bernhardt, but well before it could be turned into a satisfactory screenplay, it had disappeared, Bernhardt having already disappeared from it. Now Garbo would be an artless young peasant girl during World War I who joins her demimondaine mother in Paris and falls in love with a nice young fellow. The war happens, the fellow becomes a deserter from the army, and the girl becomes a great star (so we get to see Garbo in furs and jewels and swanky outfits and glamorous venues). Being good at heart, though, she gives it all up for love of "Lucien." She suffers, he suffers, she sinks into degradation, but true love prevails and eventually Lucien takes her away from all that swank and suffering and they begin over again on a small ranch he conveniently owns in South America.

All this we know only from the reviews and the stills, because this is the one Garbo film that has disappeared—a disaster, because it's the one Garbo film directed by the superb Victor Seastrom. In 1993, however, a single early reel of *The Divine Woman* was miraculously discovered in a

The Divine Woman: (*above and opposite*) with Lars Hanson

Moscow archive, and it's a revelation. Here is a Garbo we've never seen before—natural, joyous, darting around in her little housedress, cooking, raining kisses on her guy (her old co-star Lars Hanson). Goodbye to vamp-hood and melodrama, and a preview of what might have been if she had turned away from prestige and importance and become one of the great romantic comediennes of the thirties—an Irene Dunne, a Jean Arthur—instead of Queen Christina and Napoleon's Countess Walewska. As it was, she had to wait a dozen years until *Ninotchka* to show what she could have accomplished in that genre. (Of course, we got *Camille* in recompense.)

It's fortunate that Bernhardt was erased from the film—can you imag-

ine Sarah in a little housedress and ending up on a ranch in South America? All that's left of her in *The Divine Woman* are a few moments in which Garbo is wearing her hair frizzed. It's clear that the movie—a substantial hit—had grown more and more conventional as it proceeded. But then everything Garbo did in this period was a hit. And the Swedes—Seastrom, Hanson, Garbo—had a happy time making it. A major opportunity had been missed, however: With the exception of Ernst Lubitsch, she would never again have a director of Seastrom's quality. (Think of *The Wind*, of

The Scarlet Letter, of *He Who Gets Slapped*, and of his major Swedish films.) Seastrom recalled that after the first preview of *The Divine Woman*, "Management came up and paid me quite a few compliments. But on our way home, my wife sat quite silent. 'Why don't you say something,' I finally asked, rather irritated. 'Since you want to know,' she replied, 'I'll tell you. You shouldn't make films like that, Victor.'"

With Lars Hanson and director Victor Seastrom (Sjöström)

And then came something called *The Mysterious Lady* (an M-G-M employee got fifty dollars for coming up with that title). And guess what! The mysterious lady is a SPY!

In 1931, in *Dishonored*, Marlene Dietrich, spy, faces the firing squad, famously refusing a blindfold.

In 1933, in *After Tonight*, Constance Bennett, spy, is caught but gets away with it, to be reunited with Gilbert Roland.

But in 1928 Garbo, spy, got in there ahead of them with *The Mysterious Lady*, and she too gets away with it. (She'll be back four years later as spy Mata Hari, and we know what happened to *her*.)

The Mysterious Lady is one of her most entertaining silents, despite a script whose logic is, to put it tactfully, porous. But who cares? Watch her play with young Austrian officer Conrad Nagel (born in Keokuk, Iowa), luring him into her spyish trap. Watch her falling in love. Watch her (of

The Mysterious Lady

course you can't hear her) entertaining everybody with her glorious singing. Watch her struggle with her vile spy-boss (Gustav von Seyffertitz;
he'll be Dietrich's spy-boss, too) and then—shoot him (Garbo murders!),
although she only does it to save Nagel. (There's a lot of *Tosca* behind this
story, and in fact it's *Tosca* that's being performed on the stage when Garbo
and Nagel first meet—"by accident"—at the opera. He, if you care, is then
convicted as a traitor for allowing the crucial secret papers he's carrying to
Berlin to fall into the hands of "Tania Fedorova." But he escapes from

In *The Mysterious Lady* she enjoys an idyll with Conrad Nagel (*above*), fends off spymaster Gustav von Seyffertitz (*below*), is the toast of Warsaw (*opposite top*), and flees to safety with Nagel (*opposite bottom*).

prison and rushes to Warsaw to find and punish her. Fortunately, he's not only a brilliant soldier, he's a brilliant pianist, so that in Warsaw he can masquerade as a Serbian musician-for-hire in fancy restaurants until he finds her. And plot, plot, plot . . . until love conquers all, and they make their getaway together.

It's not a surprise that Garbo is wonderfully, subtly seductive in the opening scenes, and beautiful, if tired, throughout, but the movie does have a surprise. After their ecstatic first night together, the lovers spend the day in the park and she's running, skipping, clambering over the rocks, laughing, kissing, picnicking. Yes, over the years Garbo talks, Garbo laughs, Garbo murders, but here Garbo *romps*. And is enchanting. When she lures, when she suffers, when she sacrifices she's as old as time, but here in the woods she's a happy young woman in her early twenties, like Garbo herself, who was twenty-two when it was being shot.

Reliable Fred Niblo is her director again (*The Temptress*), and he does an excellent job: He can do glamour and he can do tension and he can do sex. It's true that the early setup scenes are over-extended and the dramatic finale is over-rushed, but despite some risible dialogue ("I came to you as the woman who loved you—I leave as your enemy"), you go along with it all. This movie is fun.

Well, not everyone did go along with it at the time, but *Life*'s besotted critic said, "She is the dream princess of the ages . . . Miss Garbo does it all and does it gorgeously, and for once in her none-too-even career she is supported by an excellent cast, and directed with imagination and sense by Fred Niblo. I recommend *The Mysterious Lady* highly, even to those who don't feel about Greta Garbo quite as I do." And everyone commented on the "scores" of passionate kisses.

Next came the castrated, bowdlerized version of *The Green Hat* that paired Garbo with Gilbert in their last silent film together. We've seen how *A Woman of Affairs* was not a happy venture for Gilbert, but it revealed a new Garbo—modern, game, British (sort of). She takes loving care of everybody but herself, although not even she could make anything less than ludicrous of Douglas Fairbanks, Jr.'s frenzied performance as her young brother. Nor could she help Gilbert seem anything more than passive in the

A Woman of Affairs: with
Gilbert; with roses and
Lewis Stone; with the fatal
Hispano-Suiza

Nils Asther is annoyed with his servant in *Wild Orchids*.

weak role he was stuck with. No sparks flew, the sensationalism of the novel was muted out of recognition, but Garbo is splendid, and, as we've noted, in her famous scene with the bouquet of roses Gilbert has sent to her in the French sanitarium where she's recovering from something or other, she's an excellent actress—perhaps for the first time. She also looks swell out of historical drag and as a figure from her own era. (She looks particularly great behind the steering wheel of her Hispano-Suiza.) Since everyone knew that *A Woman of Affairs* was a pseudonym for the proscribed title *The Green Hat*, it hardly mattered that names and plot points had been altered. M-G-M had scored another big moneymaker.

And then Garbo's off to Java (where else?) as the sexy young wife of the much older Lewis Stone (he would work with her seven times before finding his greatest fame as Judge Hardy, Mickey Rooney's wise old dad, in fifteen Andy Hardy movies). He loves "Lillie," but his libido, if he ever had one, is a thing of the past. She tosses and turns in her bed while he sleeps the sleep of the just, his attention reserved for the cablegrams he keeps receiving on the ritzy ship that's bearing them to the tea plantations he's on his

way to inspect in Java. He treats his gorgeous wife like an adored daughter, spoiling her, cuddling her, patting and petting her. No wonder, then, that she's both fascinated and repelled by the Javanese Prince De Gace—handsome, exotic, seductive, and a touch brutal—whom she first encounters whipping his cringing servant in a corridor of the ship.

It's *Wild Orchids*, directed by the experienced and successful if unthrilling Sidney Franklin ("What I know about Java you could put in your hat"), and it's got something going for it—one of the few sexually compelling leading men Garbo ever was granted: There were Gilbert, Gable (once), and now? It was

Garbo got up in Javanese drag

Nils Asther, her fellow Swede, whom she knew well and liked, and he was a beauty, sporting that spellbinding pencil-thin mustache. What matter that he was predominantly gay? All Hollywood knew, but the public didn't, and Garbo certainly didn't care. And what a happy coincidence that, as we've already recorded, when he was very young he had been initiated into homosexual practices by Mauritz Stiller. It sort of kept things in the family.

The pairing worked so well that Asther and Garbo would make a second film together, but his career didn't really develop—there was only one other peak when, in 1933, Frank Capra cast him opposite Barbara Stanwyck in *The Bitter Tea of General Yen*, this time Chinese rather than Javanese, but who's counting?

As for *Wild Orchids*, it gives us good jungle, plus Garbo doing a

Will she succumb to the ardent Asther?

demented "Javanese" dance in a demented "Javanese" outfit (until her husband tells her that she just looks silly and to take off all that junk), plus a climactic tiger hunt with the predatory prince lured to his near-death by a suddenly jealous Stone. But all ends happily when Lillie opts to stay with her husband: "John, you blind, foolish darling, will you never remember that you are the only man I love?"

Although *Wild Orchids* is a "silent," it incorporated many sound effects into its pre-recorded musical score: the tiger's growl, the palace gongs, the roaring crowd of well-wishers who have come to wave goodbye to the passengers as the ship carrying the Sinclairs to Java pulls away from the San

Francisco dock. (At the orders of the ship owner, the sailing has been delayed because the Sinclairs are going to be just a little late—they arrive with a flourish and a motorcade escort, Garbo radiant.)

The whole movie is solidly made, and although Garbo had no interest in making it (she just wanted to get out of town), she's excellent—natural in all the emotions the plot puts her through, believable at every point, even when she runs her fingers through her hair in anguish once too many times. Despite its Javanese hokum—or perhaps because of it?—*Wild Orchids* turned out to be one of 1929's top-grossing films. (Legend has it that it was originally to have been titled *Heat*, until someone noted that announcing "Greta Garbo in *Heat*" was perhaps not such a good idea.)

It was during the shooting of *Wild Orchids* that Garbo received the news—in Seastrom's cablegram, delivered to the set—of Mauritz Stiller's death. This was almost an exact replay of the way she had learned of Alva's death. As Asther would remember, "Greta turned deathly white after reading the wire, and for a moment I thought she was going to faint." She tried to go on with the scene, but Franklin stopped work for the day and sent her home. Asther also reports that as he was on his way out, he passed her dressing room and heard laughter. "Just then the door flew open and she asked me to come in. 'I have something to show you, Nils,' she said. She was still trembling, but suddenly she laughed again, holding a small perfume bottle in one hand. The tiny bottle was half filled with brandy. Attached to it was a note from Louis B. Mayer, saying, 'Dear Greta, My sympathy in your sorrow. But the show must go on.'"

She finished the movie on November 23 and within a few days was on the train to New York, on her way to Stockholm for her first trip home in more than three years, just in time for Christmas. When she didn't show up for retakes on December 3, M-G-M wired the Santa Fe Chief, demanding that she return. She didn't bother to answer, and yet again the studio put her on suspension. So? A day or two in New York, and she was on board the SS *Kungsholm*, enjoying herself with a new friend, Prince Sigvard of Sweden.

They were together at the captain's table and took to each other. (Greta, you may remember, had always been on the lookout for a prince.) But this was not a romance—she was now twenty-three, and he was a mere twenty-one. ("I don't play around with kids," she was to say.) Even so, their friendship, which carried over once they were back in Stockholm, caused some consternation to the royal family—Sigvard, after all, was third in line to the throne.

Also at the captain's table was someone who would play a much more important role in her life. A large segment of the Swedish aristocracy was returning home from attending the wedding of Count Folke Bernadotte to an American: not only Sigvard and one of his brothers but also royal cousins, a flock of other Bernadottes, and the Count and Countess Wachtmeister, Nils and Märta. They were friends of Mimi Pollack, who had written to Greta about them—he was a royal equerry and owner of one of the oldest and grandest estates in Sweden; she was a kind and generous woman, known as Hörke, who was ten years older than Greta. The Wachtmeisters were as close to being royalty as you can get without being royal, and with a magnificent home—a castle! with seventy-five rooms!—outside Stockholm, which Greta and Mimi went to visit. Greta had never seen anything like its luxury and comfort, and soon she had her own special room, and an intimate friendship with Hörke that extended to the entire family. And its dogs and horses. Over the years to come, she and Hörke would ski together,

Reunited with her mother in Sweden, 1928

travel together, and correspond faithfully, sharing each other's secrets, travails, and thoughts until the relationship, interrupted by the war, slowly petered out, although it never fully died. Apart from Mimi, Hörke was the closest friend Greta had in Sweden during this period of her life.

Early in her stay in Stockholm, she met, through Sigvard, one of his most intimate friends, Wilhelm Sörenson, the twenty-four-year-old son of a wealthy industrialist, who was at present

The Wachtmeisters' manor, Tisdat. The far-left room on the third floor was traditionally Garbo's.

a law student. Soon he was escorting her everywhere. They danced; they laughed; they had a good time—the kind of frivolous good time she had never before had. Sören, as she called him, was (naturally) yet another handsome young Swede. The couple, if that's what they were, had a tearful, public farewell as she boarded the ship to carry her back to work in March.

Half in seriousness she had told him to get in touch if he turned up in California. He, who was as fascinated by Hollywood and movie-making as he was by her, took it *completely* seriously and wrote to her saying that he would soon be on his way. "If you really want to come you are heartily welcome," she replied, "but I must warn you that you may never understand me completely—*how* I really am, and *what* makes me so. If I am working on a movie when you are here, we would not see much of each other, because then I must be alone."

Of course she spent some of

Hörke, Nils, and Gunnila Wachtmeister

her vacation time with her mother and brother, Sven, and some of it mourning Stiller. But most of the time she was going around with her old theater friends—she even agreed to act in a stage version of Tolstoy's *Resurrection* but backed out before the dress rehearsal. She loved Stockholm, she loved Christmas there, she loved being with her old pals, but she was horrified to discover that lunatic interest in her was just as intense in Sweden as it was in America: She was beset by crowds of people, journalists, photographers. And when in early March 1929 the time came for her to return to Hollywood, she was not unwilling to go.

And M-G-M was relieved to have her back—Mayer and Thalberg had had no assurance that she would ever return. Yet the greatest crisis of her career was approaching: Could she succeed in the new world of sound? Although there had been sound in film before *The Jazz Singer*, in October 1927, it was Al Jolson's talking and singing in that gigantic hit that made universal sound inevitable. Though not everyone agreed—Thalberg, for one, couldn't believe that the glory of silent film could be superseded, and Metro was the last major studio to make a silent film: Garbo's *The Kiss*. Only Chaplin, with his own studio, stayed silent.

It took about two years to iron out all the problems the switch to sound would lead to, problems that Garbo was well aware of. But she was also aware that she had no choice if her career were not to vanish—it was speak or shut down. Even so, her fans still turned up for the two more silents M-G-M crammed her into before they took the big leap. The first was *The Single Standard*, her second outing with Nils Asther, and she's a daring young modern girl, determined to lead her life with all the rights and privileges a man can enjoy under the *double* standard. It helps, of course, that she's rich and looks great in the sporty outfits Adrian concocted for her (he would be with her until the end), and that she's surrounded by stunning Deco sets—"Arden's mansion," as Mark Vieira puts it, "was not the gingerbread edifice that a San Francisco setting would imply, but a 'Moderne' marvel of soaring sandstone setbacks and geometric black-and-gold interiors." She's Arden Stuart, an all-American San Francisco deb, who's stifled by the rules and restrictions of her society world, so that when she wanders into an art gallery and encounters Asther as a fascinating—and rich—artist-cum-boxer-cum-yachtsman (he's known as "Packy"), she hops on his yacht and off they go around the world. We see her—she's stunning—sunbathing and diving and splashing around in bathing suits. We see their passion and perfect contentment until his need to be alone (his yacht is called the *All Alone*) makes him send her away, although he'll always love her.

To ease her heartbreak (and escape society's censure) she now marries good-looking John Mack Brown, who's been carrying the torch for her

OPPOSITE AND RIGHT:
The Single Standard

With John Mack Brown, husband

since forever. And a little boy is born. When Packy shows up, following a ridiculous episode "in fever-haunted China," it's a toss-up whether she'll go off with him again, abandoning spouse and tot. But after everyone behaves with consummate nobility and self-sacrifice, she chooses to stay with her child, thus placating conservative Midwest audiences who welcomed the notion that sublime mother-love can erase the sins of a young woman who has tried to live by the Single Standard.

With Nils Asther, lover

The Kiss: Monsieur (Anders Randolf) and Madame Guarry at home

Yes, the story (by Adela Rogers St. Johns) is ridiculous, but Garbo's modern affect and modern acting are startling. The sultry vamp is gone; the tragedy queen is a thing of the past. Here she's natural, happy (when not being noble), fun to watch—likable! You see once more what she might have been in talkies if she and M-G-M hadn't conspired to keep her in lugubrious romances and high-flown "classics" and historicals. (She didn't help by letting it be known that she hoped to play Joan of Arc.) Box-office returns for *The Single Standard* were strong, but they were slightly less solid than they had been for *Wild Orchids*, so that was the end of her being paired with Nils Asther. Not, however, the end of their relationship. They had known each other in the old days in Stockholm, and now they became close friends—he was even allowed to come to her house! They traveled together, holed up in a cabin in the woods together; according to Asther, he even proposed to her. So what that he was gay *and* married?

As for her final silent film, the important thing about it was the director, the highly esteemed Jacques Feyder, who had come to Hollywood with his equally esteemed wife, the actress Françoise Rosay (their most famous film

Madame struggles with Monsieur to save Lew Ayres

together, made in 1935, was *Carnival in Flanders*), and it was he who pro-posed *The Kiss* to her. M-G-M had hired him to direct Garbo in a Ger-man version of *Anna Christie*, to be made on completion of the American version—which was to be Garbo's first venture into sound.

The Kiss has certain real virtues, apart from its star. It's not only set in France, it *feels* like France: Feyder was known for the naturalism of his mises-en-scènes and character actors. And it's a snazzy Deco France, since everyone is rich and chic. Also exemplary is the movie's brisk pace. Given

Garbo shoots!

In the dock, defended by her lawyer/lover, Conrad Nagel

that "Irene" has *three* men in love with her—it's a quadrangle—and that the plot involves a shooting and a murder trial, it's a miracle that it comes in at just over an hour. Apparently, at least ten scenes that were shot died on the cutting-room floor.

It's just as well. This old-fashioned vehicle couldn't survive longueurs. Garbo is beautiful, of course, and is revealing a newly expanded spectrum of feeling, from her genuine affection for her elderly, bossy mogul husband to her passionate commitment to her conventional lawyer/lover to her amused kindness toward the young boy (he's still at school) who thinks he's in love with her. She looks splendid in her first outfit—cloche, furs around the neck; in her tennis whites (good legs); in her Deco-like evening dresses and negligees; in her uncompromising in-the-dock black. She's excellent in the most violent scene she ever played, struggling fiercely to prevent her enraged husband from beating her young admirer to death. Yes, she shoots her husband, but only to save an innocent lad's life—she's outgrown vamp-hood once and for all and ascended to noble self-sacrifice. But let's face it: For all its felicities, *The Kiss* is glorified junk—derivative, predictable, and clichéd. "Your husband can't refuse you a divorce." "I have always been a faithful wife and have nothing to reproach myself for." And Conrad Nagel as her supposed great love looks terrible, acts worse, and is an awful lover—their kisses are unbelievably tepid. Come on, Conrad, you're kissing Greta Garbo! (Nagel had been more ardent—and more enjoyable—in *The Mysterious Lady*.)

Fortunately, the young, importunate "Pierre" is played by the twenty-year-old Lew Ayres in his first role and only a year before he starred in *All Quiet on the Western Front*. He's completely charming in his ridiculous boyishness, though handsome as all get-out when tuxed up. Ayres credited Garbo with extraordinary generosity and consideration toward him—imagine being a callow, totally inexperienced young actor suddenly playing opposite the star of stars! Forty years later he told Barry Paris, "I was a little greenhorn of twenty, bouncing my way around, and she was the most sophisticated performer on the screen. I worked with her for six weeks, that's all, I was a nobody." Yet not only was she generous professionally but they also had fun together, on location playing tennis and going out for lunch. It reminds us that she was only four years older than he was. *Screenland* got it right, as fan magazines so often did: "Next to Greta, the most interesting thing about *The Kiss* is the film debut of young Lew Ayres, a smouldering boy who is a real find." Who could have predicted that one day he would star in nine Dr. Kildare movies! Or that he would marry Ginger Rogers . . .

Even in M-G-M's, and the industry's, last silent film apart from Chaplin, Garbo-power pulled it off. Efficiently made, with no extravagant salaries other than hers, *The Kiss* would prove to be one of her most profitable movies. But the moment for the plunge into talkies could no longer be delayed. And Garbo was ready, now that the early technical problems of sound had been ironed out. "If they want me to talk," she said, "I'll talk."

⇒6⇐

GARBO TALKS

B
ETTE DAVIS was speaking for the world when she described how in 1930, the year she moved to Hollywood and before she had ever made a movie, she was filled with anxiety waiting to hear how Garbo, her idol, would sound in *Anna Christie*. And how relieved she was when she first heard the sound of Garbo's voice on the day the movie was released, and the voice was so exactly right. "The voice that shook the world!" said *Picture Play*, and this was no hyperbole. Garbo was at the peak of her extraordinary fame, her hold on the imagination of the world's audiences as powerful as ever.

Bette Davis—and M-G-M, and Hollywood, and Garbo—were not the only ones holding their breath. Naturally, the first reviews focused on the voice itself. What was it like? Did it fit the Garbo image? Richard Watts, Jr., in the *Herald Tribune*: "Her voice is revealed as a deep, husky, throaty contralto that possesses every bit of that fabulous poetic glamour that has made this distant Swedish lady the outstanding actress of the motion picture world." Her accent? "Anna" has been raised by Swedish relatives on a Minnesota farm, so it's no surprise that she *has* an accent. In fact, the Swedish accent is underplayed—Garbo had been working on it both in California and back in Sweden, and some reports say she had to exaggerate her normal Swedish intonations to find the right balance. She herself reported in one of her rare interviews, "I do not know how my voice will record since I have

LEFT: Anna Christie: "Gimme a whiskey . . ."

OPPOSITE: With Marie Dressler

made no tests, and do not intend making any until I have my part to play. I am not taking voice culture or staying up nights practicing Shakespeare. I will speak naturally and as I feel the lines should be spoken, just as I play any character now. If I cannot play a role naturally and without artificial devices, I cannot give a sincere performance."

Even so, she was nervous. Her young Swedish friend Wilhelm Sörenson had indeed followed her to Hollywood. She had written to him, "They are making sound movies here now and nobody knows what is to happen to me. Perhaps I will not stay here much longer." After he arrived, she had him run lines with her at home. Her first day filming in sound was to be October 14, 1929. She telephoned Sörenson the evening before and said, "This is it, Sören. Tomorrow's the day when silent Greta gets a voice!" And then called him again—at 2:30 a.m.—demanding, "Come over here immediately and drink coffee with me. Step on it!" They talked until after 6:00, and then while they were on their way to the studio it occurred to him that she was suffering from stage fright. Silence. "Then I heard a voice from underneath the rug beside me in the car. Instead of a deep, rich timbre, I heard the moving plaint of a little girl. 'Oh, Sören, I feel like an unborn child just now.'"

When she joined him for lunch in her dressing room after the first scene had been shot, she said, "Well, it wasn't really so bad, though I became a

little scared when I heard my own voice." She had said to the sound engineer, "My God! Is that my voice? Does that sound like me—honestly?"
Everything went as well as could be expected, except that two weeks later,
on October 29, there came news from New York of an event even more
cataclysmic than the talkie revolution. It was Black Tuesday. Despite the
catastrophe, filming went ahead and was completed on November 18. A
rough cut was rushed to a sneak preview in San Bernardino, and the audience, which had paid to see *The Kiss*, was thrilled to be seeing *Anna Christie*
instead, and the preview was a sensational success—"It's in the bag!" Louis B.
Mayer declared—and Thalberg decided to release it just as it was, no retakes needed. Garbo, as usual, had refused to attend, nor did she attend the
premiere in January, but the following day she went with Sörenson and
Jacques Feyder to see it in a theater. While it was playing, she seemed positive about it, but afterwards she said to them, "Isn't it terrible? Who ever
saw Swedes act like that?"

   Anna Christie is very far from terrible. And Garbo is extraordinary, as
usual. When she slouches into the film, sixteen minutes after it begins, she's

With Charles Bickford

so low-keyed she's a little hard to understand, but even so her first words are electrifying: "Gimme a whiskey—ginger ale on the side. And don't be stingy, baby." The bartender: "Shall I serve it in a pail?" Anna: "That suits me down to the ground." What's really startling is not the voice or the accent but the character. Garbo—the prima donna, the vamp, the spy, the flaunter of furs and jewels, the doomed driver of an Hispano-Suiza, the murderess, the mistress of Deco—as a bedraggled, world-weary, sickly prostitute from St. Paul swigging whiskey in a waterfront bar? The big challenge wasn't vocal, it was artistic.

Eugene O'Neill's Pulitzer Prize–winning play—filmed as a silent with the excellent Blanche Sweet in 1923—is awkward and strained, and Frances Marion's script doesn't solve the problems. The first scenes are dominated by that old vaudevillian and character actress Marie Dressler, co-star with Chaplin and Mabel Normand in the wonderful 1914 *Tillie's Punctured Romance*, often identified as the first full-length film comedy ever made. ("Of all the scene-stealers I've ever watched," wrote Hedda Hopper, "Marie Dressler was tops.") Having mugged and carried on outrageously as a

At the amusement park

drunk old wharf rat—you either love her or can't stand her, or both—she just disappears from *Anna Christie* except for one brief scene in the middle of the movie. Everyone back then loved her, including Garbo, and her career skyrocketed, but the focus on her, followed by her disappearance, distorts the movie. And then there's that endlessly repeated and endlessly irritating O'Neill line "That old Devil sea!" And all that fog!

So what? Garbo underplays, does nothing to mitigate the cynical, angry wreck Anna has become, revealing her anguish at her past life, her abandonment of hope for something better, and then her gradual transformation by love (and sea air) through exquisite modulations of her eyes, her expression, and—yes—her voice. She can't help being beautiful, but she doesn't *play* being beautiful in her cheap skirt and sweater, her small, low-slung breasts clearly prominent. And at the crisis of the plot, her explosions of rage at life, at fate, at *men* are deeply felt and powerful. "Oh, how I hate them—every mother's son of them!" and "Nobody owns me . . . I am my own boss." Yet when she and Matt, the sailor with whom she falls in love, spend the day on shore at Coney Island, she's charming in a frilly feminine dress, laughing, adoring,

"Nobody owns me . . . I am my own boss."

so overjoyed when she realizes that he wants to marry her. (She's even been knitting him a sweater—"Garbo Knits!") This is the Garbo we've had only glimpses of before—in *The Divine Woman*, *The Mysterious Lady*, *The Single Standard*: the *happy* Garbo. Love transforms her—and here propels her into the 1930s and romantic comedy.

Can it last? Not until that old Devil sea has its way and forces her to reveal her horrible past to her father and lover—her abuse at the hands of her farm family, her time in a "house." She can't, in honor, marry Matt without his knowing the truth, and Matt, with all his Irish pride, can't live with it. Until he can, because he loves her so deeply. But he can't marry her until he exhorts her to swear on his dead mother's rosary that despite what she's done, he's the only man she's ever loved. She swears it—we believe her—and then it emerges that she's Lutheran. So much for the rosary! As Richard Corliss puts it in his indispensable book on Garbo's films, this creaky business makes *Abie's Irish Rose* look like *Romeo and Juliet*. (Matt, by the way, despite the awful stage Irishisms he's stuck with, is vigorously and appealingly played by the young Charles Bickford, giving Garbo one of her few virile leading men.)

The crucial thing is that in her first talking film, Garbo successfully plays a real woman, however stagy much of the dialogue and action may be. *Anna Christie* is the announcement to the world that, like her or not, she's an *actress*, not simply a spectacular look. And the public certainly *did* like her—the movie broke box-office records everywhere, made M-G-M over a million dollars in profit, and became the top-grossing film of 1930. Its success was helped immensely by the advertising campaign, perhaps the most famous ever launched in Hollywood. Thalberg didn't like anything he was being shown—silent-era portraits weren't going to sell a talking film about a prostitute. Then Frank Whitbeck, a longtime publicity/exploitation executive at the studio, picked up an envelope, drew an immense blank billboard, and added two words: "Garbo Talks!" History was made. Some time later, Whitbeck walked into an M-G-M office where Garbo was in conference. "Miss Garbo," someone said, "I think it is high time you met the man who first said "Garbo Talks!" Looking up at him, she said, "Aren't you ashamed?"

Garbo is said to have preferred her German Anna (shot by Feyder) to the American version, but although she's a somewhat more tarnished and despairing whore in German, and has been given many more close-ups by Feyder, her two performances are not very unalike. (Her German is perhaps a little more comfortable than her English.) The two *movies*, however, *feel* unalike. Just as Feyder's France in *The Kiss* seems highly French, the ambiance here seems very German. The sets are the same—we're still in waterfront New York, in the same waterfront dive; Garbo still enters through the door labeled "Ladies Entrance"—but we feel we're in Germany. And Feyder's imported German actors are very, very German. He's done what he was supposed to do—made a German film for a German audience—but to me the result is somewhat schizophrenic.

Marie Dressler's role has been recast with Garbo's greatest friend, Salka

The German *Anna Christie*

With Salka Steuermann (Viertel)

Viertel, using her actress name, Steuermann—she's not only younger than Dressler, she's more Lotte Lenya than vaudevillian. The new Matt is tamer than Bickford; the new father is a younger and less eccentric father than George F. Marion. They've had to omit the Irish-Catholic/Lutheran business with the rosary, since it would make no sense in Germany. (No loss!)

The whole thing was made in twenty days, but that doesn't mean Garbo wasn't paying attention. Barry Paris illustrates her attention to detail: "In the Brown film, she slices some bread, downward, on a galley table; in the Feyder, she holds the loaf and cuts it upwards, toward herself, European style." Actress and director liked and admired each other—Feyder speaks of her warmly in his memoirs—but of his feelings about following in the footsteps of Clarence Brown he says not a word. While in the same book of memoirs—never translated into English—Madame Feyder (Rosay) is conspicuously less warm about Garbo than her husband was. Perhaps actress and director "liked and admired" each other a little too much.

WHILE WAITING FOR FEYDER to complete another project before starting on his *Anna Christie*, M-G-M had hustled Garbo into the first of two really crummy movies—*Romance* and *Inspiration*. "Of all Garbo's films, *Romance* is the one without a single redeeming little minute of dramatic or cinematic charm. The only spark of spontaneity comes when her pet monkey bites a respectable old woman on the ear." So wrote Richard Corliss, thereby making it redundant for me to say the exact same thing here, except to add that Garbo, portraying an Italian diva, has named her monkey Adelina. For Adelina Patti, of course—the greatest diva of them all.

Why not let Corliss carry on? "Gavin Gordon is better-looking as the eighty-year-old man who narrates the film-long flashback than as the twenty-eight-year-old curate who falls in love with a coquettish diva. With her Marguerite Gautier curls and her 'be gay or die' insouciance, Garbo's Madame Cavillini is a very rough sketch—more like a finger painting—for *Camille*. And her suicidal self-sacrifice gives off faint emanations of the doomed ballerina of *Grand Hotel*. But these are only promises, and the rest of *Romance* leaves them unfulfilled."

Romance

And yes, Mr. Corliss, "It was a bad idea to cast Garbo, in only her second talkie, as an Italian opera singer. She does her best to get the speech patterns down right—with musical vowels, blurred consonants, *r*'s that roll like the Tuscan hills—but at times the Italian accents elide carelessly into her natural Swedish, and once in a while it's difficult to tell whether she's speaking Italian or English. Her idea of Latin body movements is even further afield. She smiles, frowns, winks"—yes, Garbo winks!—"inhales—all mischievously—and relies heavily on extravagant hand signals, as if translating simultaneously for the deaf."

Clarence Brown did a clumsy job on *Romance*, and for once the photography of William Daniels doesn't do justice to Garbo's beauty. Her frequent co-star Lewis Stone, cast as Cornelius Van Tuyl, a distinguished Olde New York aristocrat who is her wise and loving "protector," has snow-white hair and a face to match but keeps telling us that he's fifty-one. (Barry Paris remarks that "Lewis Stone with speech is no more interesting than Lewis Stone mute.") Gavin Gordon, in his only important role, not only lacks

With Gavin Gordon and Lewis Stone

appeal but simply can't act. What were they dreaming of! Gordon, by the way, went on to a drastically diminished career playing bits (he's a now-you-see-him, now-you-don't Lord Byron in *The Bride of Frankenstein*) and then anonymous appearances such as "Night club singer" in *I See Ice* and on to "Druggist—uncredited" in *King Creole* and "Executive on Golf Course" in *The Patsy*. On the other hand, he had a long and presumably happy relationship with comic sidekick Edward Everett Horton.

And then there's the dialogue. "Love is just a little warmth in all this cold." "Thank you for having loved me." And, from the aged Gordon, now a retired bishop, to his grandson (who wants to marry an . . . actress!), the climactic message of the film: "It's the greatest thing in the world—romance!" Not for Madame Cavillini, who, we learn, having sacrificed her career in order to become pure, dies in a convent, offstage.

Garbo, who for once had allowed herself to be talked into a script she disliked, was mortified by the result. Reported Sörenson, "[She] could have wept when she heard her supposed Italian accent . . . She thought it was terrible. At times she couldn't understand her own words. She knew she had made a mistake."

In the wake of *Anna Christie*'s great success, and in the flush of excitement over Garbo talking, *Romance* was praised by several of her idolizing critics, and it made hay at the box office. But don't be fooled. If you're still tempted to watch *Romance*, proceed with caution, and don't say you weren't warned.

DURING HER FIRST YEARS AT M-G-M, Garbo was a vamp, an actress, an opera singer, a mother, a technically faithful wife, a spy, and Anna Karenina. She sacrificed herself by crashing a car into a tree, and she killed—killed!—to save an innocent young man. She was reduced to streetwalking. These movies, of course, were all silents.

But in her first four sound films, she took on a new identity: the Woman with a Past who redeems herself through True Love. She's a prostitute in *Anna Christie* who hates all men, but then she meets Charles Bickford. She's a Kept Woman in *Romance* but redeems herself by giving up her career and entering a convent. (Did she take her pet monkey with her?) And in *Inspiration*? As Yvonne, a glamorous, Bohemian, devil-may-care, serially kept woman, now in love for the first time, she is once again redeemed—this time by her devotion to that unlicked pup Robert Montgomery, and by her noble withdrawal from his life so that he can marry the nice rich girl his relatives have chosen for him and successfully pursue his career as a diplomat. (Shades of *Camille*!) As luck will have it, an ex-lover conveniently turns up in time to marry her so that they can begin a new life together, I believe in South America. Or was that in *The Divine Woman*?

The Garbo we have in *Inspiration* is both quicksilver and . . . tired. "I'm so tired"; "Oh. I'm so tired." Not too tired, though, to keep from sidling up

The toast of Paris, in *Inspiration*

With Robert Montgomery, happy in the country

to young Montgomery, whom she's spotted at a party: "I like your eyes. Who are you?" Soon she's assuring him that "nothing that happened before I met you matters," and "I wish you didn't mean everything in my life, but you do," and "I never cared for any of those men. I swear to you," and "I love you and that makes up for all the misery." Followed by glorious renunciation. Along the way: furs, Russian specialty dancers (they fling swords from their mouths!), and Deco, Deco everywhere.

Yes, it's Clarence Brown back at the helm, and doing a marginally better job than he did with *Romance*. And we're in modern Paris instead of old New York, with Garbo sexier, better dressed, and better photographed, so that this movie is a definite improvement on its predecessor. But it's also the *same* movie, and, yes, Lewis Stone is back too, with no plot responsibilities and still full of avuncular wisdom, barely ruffled when his mistress (Karen Morley), whom he's casually dismissed with a generous payoff, jumps from a window to her death. That gets Yvonne thinking.

Garbo is beautiful, charming, relaxed (when not anguished). In her very first shot she's laughing. Except for one envious bitch, all her pals (and ex-lovers) adore her, and she's in great demand as a model. She's believable in love, she's believable in despair, and she's more comfortable talking than she was in her first two outings. This movie, though too long and totally derivative, would be enjoyable enough if not for M-G-M's perpetual problem: finding appropriate male leads for her.

Poor Robert Montgomery, barely into his long and triumphant career, here defines the word "callow." He's so naïve, so out of his depth, so . . . American! It wasn't until the movie was almost over that, despite his being called André, I realized he was meant to be French. Gleaming with health and boyish good will, madly in love, he's on his way to becoming the sexy master of sophisticated comedy and romance he would become in his years of playing opposite Shearer, Crawford, Myrna Loy, Tallulah Bankhead, Rosalind Russell, Marion Davies; the years of *Private Lives*, *Letty Linton*, *Haunted Honeymoon* (he's Dorothy Sayers's Lord Peter Wimsey); the turn to serious dramas and war films (*They Were Expendable*) and becoming a director; the years of his Oscar nominations for *Night Must Fall* and *Here Comes Mr. Jordan*. In *Inspiration* he tries hard and is even touching at moments, but as a successor to John Gilbert? Unsurprisingly, he was never paired with Garbo again. (They didn't get along very well off-screen either.) It's not just that they lack chemistry together, it's that they're in two different movies.

The New York Times summed up the whole thing succinctly: "Miss Garbo, no matter what may be said of the story, gives a stunning performance as the girl who is the toast of the Paris studios." Other reviews said more or less the same thing. And even at the depth of the post-Crash economy, *Inspiration* netted a highly profitable million dollars. Garbo power.

AND THEN IN 1931 came *Susan Lenox: Her Fall and Rise*, in which she will suffer, suffer, suffer until she wins Clark Gable back, redeemed from her tarnished past by her unwavering love.

It took more than twenty writers to put together (the word "write" somehow seems inappropriate here) the script for *Susan Lenox: Her Fall and Rise*, based on a notorious thousand-page novel whose author had been murdered years before. He might well have died of chagrin had he lived to see the hodgepodge of nonsense M-G-M made of it. As James Agate, the British critic, remarked, "Neither hero nor heroine at any moment behaves like a sentient human being." (Well, that's also been true of countless other movies, then and now.)

The opening scenes work. Garbo is an abused farm girl whose mother died giving birth to her "without a ring." Now she's being forced into marriage with a vile lout who tries to rape her, which is why she flees into the stormy night and finds herself cowering in the garage of a young engineer who turns out to be Clark Gable. So far, so good. "Rodney" is of course drawn to her. "Who are you anyway?" he asks. Quickly he figures it out: She's a *girl*, and a mighty pretty one. But he's more gentleman than wolf, and soon he's wringing out her rain-soaked garments while, behind a closed door, she's donning his striped pajamas.

This is pre-mustache Gable, and their charming idyll is in the vein of light romantic comedy. "Helga" cooks breakfast for him, they go fishing down at the brook (she's never fished before! she catches one!), they chase each other around the room, she's laughing, she's happy, and she helps him

Susan Lenox: Her Fall and Rise: in *noir* danger; safe with Clark Gable in his kitchen; Garbo fishes!

pack to go to the big city, where he's entered a competition to design a bridge. Into his bag goes the framed picture of his parents, which—he's somewhere in his twenties—he never goes anywhere without. He'll be back in six days, with a wedding ring.

Alas, her wicked uncle turns up to force her home, but she escapes, wielding a pretty whip as she jumps into his buggy, lashes the horses, and gets to the station just in time to find herself in a railway car conveying a troupe of carny players to their next gig. (They're playing poker, the good-natured tattooed lady exclaiming, "That's the best hand I've had since Sitting Bull sat down.") Helga joins the carnival as a specialty dancer, because what else can she do? And so the plot thickens as she goes from good to bad to worse— that's the "Fall" of the title—picking up the name Susie along the way. But she's always pining for Rodney, even when she's hostessing a swank soirée in the Manhattan Deco penthouse of her crooked-politician sugar daddy. Somehow she's maneuvered to have Rodney invited to the party so that she can humiliate him the way he humiliated her when he came upon her, compromised, in the carnival. Now he bitterly rejects her, but, realizing that she still loves him, she abandons lover and penthouse to begin her (moral) Rise.

So far we've been in an Expressionist noir farmhouse, an idealized forest cabin, a seedy carnival, a glamorous penthouse. She's been a victim, a fisher-girl, a cooch dancer, a soignée mistress dripping in gowns and jewels—the way Garbo's audience liked to see her. Next stop: Central America and a sleazy whorehouse (she's dancing, not whoring) in "Puerto Sacate," to which she's tracked Rodney down and where she's waiting for him to return from the fever-ridden swamplands where he's been slaving away, a despairing and unshaven cynic. Throughout the protracted filming, and despite (or because of) the brigade of scriptwriters, no one had figured out how to bring this thing to an end. Oh yes—rich, handsome, noble Ian Keith has popped up out of nowhere, begging Susie to let him take her away from all this on his magnificent yacht.

The ending they came up with flashes by so quickly you can't believe it's over when it's over. In a nutshell: She pleads with "Rrrrodney" to believe she's always loved him. He says no. She pleads some more—"Since I last saw you, no man has had a minute of me, not even a second." He says

From traveling carnival . . .

no. She says, "I'll make you believe in me." He says yes. Final clinch while Tchaikovsky's *Pathétique* soars on the soundtrack. She's now in purest white and he's shaved.

Garbo is once again assuring us that true love redeems a fallen woman, particularly since it's *men* who have brought about her fall. The crucial thing is to convince your man that whatever depths you've fallen to, he's the only one you've ever really loved. (Quite a message! It's okay to have sex for money, but a no-no to do it for love.)

And yes, the story is corny, and the dialogue too, but this movie is *alive*. And, for once, Garbo is encouraged to be likeable. Robert Z. Leonard, an old-timer who had directed far worse potboilers for his wife, Mae Murray, does a good job of keeping things going and making individual scenes effective. William Daniels's lighting is ravishing. Garbo is gorgeous in her many modes and outfits, and moment-to-moment she's emotionally believable. Most important: Her unlikely pairing with Gable is a success. Appar-

. . . to New York luxe

ently she found his acting wooden, and it more or less is, but he's masculine, sexy, and a real Presence. He's not just in support of her, like the Nagels and Montgomerys—he holds the screen in much the way she does. In other words, he's a star.

This was the watershed year of Gable's career. In 1930 he didn't exist. In 1931 he had already slapped Stanwyck around, co-starred (and a lot more) with Crawford, dominated Shearer, and emerged as M-G-M's biggest male attraction. *The Hollywood Reporter* summed things up: "A star in the making has been made, one that, to our reckoning, will outdraw every other star. Never have we seen audiences work themselves into such enthusiasm as when Clark Gable walks on the screen." He stayed The King for thirty years, until 1961 and *The Misfits*, by way of *It Happened One Night* and Rhett Butler. Can we imagine any other actor starring opposite both Greta Garbo and Marilyn Monroe?

Susan Lenox was a big hit, even though the reviews couldn't get past the

idiocies of the script. (Well, Andrew Sarris did: "*Susan Lenox: Her Fall and Rise* is the closest thing in Garbo's oeuvre to an out-and-out fun movie, exhilarating even in its badness.") And it's proof that Garbo really did have a sense of humor. Years later, as Barry Paris tells us, "viewing her films with Richard Griffith at the Museum of Modern Art, this was the one that most amused her." "She loved to mimic herself," Griffith reported, murmuring "'R-r-rodney, when will this painful love of ours ever die?'"

TOP AND BOTTOM: In a "Puerto Sacate" brothel (but chaste) she reclaims Clark Gable.

❥7❧

GARBO OFF-SCREEN

THE TRANSITION TO SOUND was not the only change taking place in Garbo's life during the late twenties and early thirties. She was perpetually on the move—from one house to another, always in search of more watertight privacy. What had begun as a natural inclination toward solitude had been exacerbated by the relentless, almost maniacal, assault on her that was caused by the avidity of the public for information about her, encouraged by the ruthlessness of the press—particularly photographers—in pursuing it. There were times when even M-G-M didn't know where she was living. Clarence Brown tells us that once he was summoned to her house to read lines with her only to discover that for the past year they had been living across the street from each other.

Her domestic arrangements changed as well. For about a year in the late twenties a young Swedish couple—Gustaf and Sigrid Norin—had been in charge of the household: shopping, cooking, cleaning, chauffeuring, and lying about her whereabouts to almost anyone who telephoned her. Garbo herself, of course, never answered her phone. The Norins eventually "betrayed" their employer by talking at length to the one reporter—Rilla Page Palmborg—with whom she had had a pleasant relationship, and who was now "betraying" her, writing a book called *The Private Life of Greta Garbo* (which Edington tried to stop Doubleday, Doran from publishing). Presumably Palmborg paid the Norins well for their highly detailed, very frank account of life with The Divine One, who was just about their own age—twenty-four or so. Whatever Palmborg paid them was worth it—it is in her book that we find by far the fullest account we have about how Garbo lived at that time and what she was like to live with. Which is why it's quoted extensively in just about everything written about her since its publication.

Her eating habits? For breakfast she favored juice, creamed dried chipped beef, toast, a poached egg, fried potatoes, homemade sponge cake, coffee. When she was working, lunch was "Fresh berries . . . cooked up and sweetened with powdered tapioca . . . a cheese or meat sandwich and a bit of fresh fruit. Garbo carried her lunch (salad, sandwich, milk or beer) done up in a paper bag, like some shop girl who was getting only twenty dollars a week"—anything rather than eat in the commissary with everybody else. If she was home, lunch was more or less the same. As for dinner, it would be ready for her by six-thirty or seven, but often she would decide to rush out for a long walk instead of eating, then would rummage through the icebox when she got home, hours later.

Pets? Her chow, Flimsy; her talking parrot, Polly; and her two kittens, Pinten (half-pint) and Mira.

Expenses? "She told us that we were to do all the buying for the house, but she expected us to keep the bills down. A hundred dollars a month was to be the limit on household expenses . . . By careful buying I kept food bills as low as eighty-five dollars a month for the first two months." Yet Garbo complained. "We found we couldn't please her, no matter how we schemed. She scolded on general principles. It was a comedy at the end of each month . . . A few days after we took charge of her house, Garbo handed me fifty dollars in cash and a little black book. She said the money was to make purchases for her from time to time. I was to get a receipt for everything I bought. Then I was to enter every purchase, with the date it was bought, in the little black book. Each receipt was to be pinned on the page of its entry. At the end of the month Garbo went over this book, drawing a line through each item and receipt as she checked them off. Believe me," said Gustaf, "I saw to it that they balanced to the cent . . . Don't ever let anyone tell you that Greta Garbo doesn't know how to handle money."

Her clothes? "Part of my job was to look after her wardrobe," said Sigrid. "I never saw her wear any of the evening dresses that hung in her closet . . . Several of them she had never had on, and she was sorry she had bought them. In her closet Garbo kept the old plaid suit she wore when she was on location in Turkey with Mauritz Stiller. She cautioned me to see that it was kept free from moths." All her clothes were simple, most of them tailored. "She wore men's pajamas, most of them made of silk, with collars buttoning tight around her neck. The blouses she wore with her jersey and tweed suits were men's tailored shirts. She had a big assortment of men's ties in all kinds and colors that she wore with them . . . Most of the time she wore light-weight woolen hose, such as we buy in Sweden." As for her shoes, Gustaf tells us that he used to buy most of them for her. "She wore the smallest size of men's oxfords. She didn't believe in pinching her feet or tottering around on high, pointed heels. I bet she had a dozen pairs of these tan shoes sitting in her closet. Often when I brought home a new pair she had ordered, she would say, 'Just the thing for us bachelors, eh, Gustaf?'"

Cosmetics? "Garbo was never fussing around with face lotions. I never saw her with a bit of cold cream on her face. Occasionally she would rub a piece of ice on her face 'to freshen up a bit' as she said. In fact, she had nothing on her dressing table but some face powder and a plain silver toilet set. Neither did she care for perfumes. She had one bottle of gardenia, but it had nearly the same amount in it when we left as when we came. The only scent she used was lavender in her soap." As for her hair, "After a shampoo, which she took under a shower, she would rinse her hair in camomile tea that I brewed for her from camomile seeds. This kept it light and gave it a lovely sheen. Her hair is straight as an Indian's and at home she never had a bit of curl in it, brushing it back from her forehead and tucking it behind her ears."

Her day? Up at seven. Twenty-minute swim in the pool. Breakfast in bed (always served by Gustaf). Scan the papers for items about herself in the theatrical section, which she would tear out. (Her business manager was expected to paste them in a scrapbook.) Play with the pets in bed. Sudden rush to leave for work. "Hurry, Gustaf. Drive fast. It makes them mad when I am late at the studio." When she wasn't working, she would occasionally stay in bed two or three days at a time, getting up only to have her swim and sun bath. "She was always reading. Books in Swedish, German, and English." Long walks at night—"She would put on a plain topcoat, pull a slouch hat down over her face, thrust her hands in her pockets, and start out." She loved walking in the rain. She loved riding—three or four times a week when she wasn't working. She was frightened of burglars and didn't want the Norins out of the house at night.

Guests? Sörenson, Nils Asther, the Feyders and the John Loders. (Loder was a minor movie star, at one time married to Hedy Lamarr.) "John Loder was an Englishman, his wife an Austrian," Palmborg points out. "Jacques Feyder a Belgian, and his wife a Parisian. And Garbo was Swedish. Yet, when they were together, they always spoke German—a language foreign to them all." These were her first real friends in Hollywood—"She would sit around the fireside and talk and joke with them like a schoolgirl." Other social life? "She never had any desire to go out to the nightclubs and cafes that the other motion-picture stars frequented. She didn't like to dance. 'What fun is there dining in a room crowded with a lot of strangers?' she would ask. 'In Sweden friends meet to be sociable over a bottle of champagne or a glass of wine or beer. Here people try to look as if they were having a lot of fun stealing a drink from a bottle hidden under the tablecloth. Then they have to sit there and pretend they are drinking iced tea or ginger ale. It is all so silly.'" This was under Prohibition, of course. Garbo hosted a few gatherings, including an elaborate Christmas Eve celebration—the décor, the food, the drink all traditional Swedish. Christmas dinner the next day was equally festive. After the guests were stuffed with food, Garbo moved everyone outside. "There was plenty of excitement and noise in Garbo's pool that night," said Gustaf. "You would have thought there were twenty people out there instead of only five."

After almost a year, the Norins decided they had had enough. Gustaf had been brought up in comfort and was well educated, and now his parents were close by, living near the Los Angeles Country Club in an attractive house with a walled-in garden and big swimming pool. They were not happy that their son was making his living as a servant. The adventure of housekeeping for a star was over. The young couple gave notice, trying to time their departure conveniently for Garbo, but one day, when she was "in one of her moods when nothing and no one pleased her," Gustaf reminded her that he and Sigrid were leaving in two weeks and that she would soon have to find someone who would suit her. "She changed quick as a flash. 'Can't I call attention to a little dirt if I want to? Everything is all right. Forget all about it.'" He persisted: "But Garbo didn't seem to take us seriously. She made no effort to find anyone to take our place. The last night we were there I went in to have a talk with her. She was in bed, as usual. When I told her that we were going the next morning she said, 'But you can't leave me like this. There will be no one to look after the house.'

"Early the next morning Mr. Edington, her business manager, came over to try to persuade us to stay on—was it a question of salary?—but I told him that I had a position at one of the studios. Not as an actor, but in the modeling department, where miniature sets of the pictures to be made are modeled in plaster of Paris, and where ornaments for the complete sets are made. We said our good-byes, and since then we have not seen Garbo."

But they thought about her. "Neither of us will ever forget the months we lived in the same house with this strange girl. Day after day we saw the real Garbo without pose or pretense. Yet we never felt we actually knew her. There was something distant about Garbo that neither of us could penetrate. She is different from anyone we have ever known."

Of course the Garbo whom the Norins knew was the twenty-four-year-old émigré, essentially unsophisticated and essentially on her own, with Stiller gone from her life, with no family nearby and no old friends, and living in a doubly alien world: America and Hollywood. And she was the target of crazed worldwide curiosity. She would find her way.

Yet although the Norins' observations caught her early in her development, to a remarkable degree they apply to her entire life—not only did her personal habits remain surprisingly fixed, but her attitudes did as well. She remained abrupt in her dealings even with people she was more or less close to, refusing, for instance, to say whether she was coming to dinner and turning up—or not—on the evening in question; suddenly getting to her feet and walking out of a gathering, or telling her guests that it was time for them to leave. She was both needy and imperious. Gustaf Norin reports that one day when he was serving lunch to Garbo and Edington, he "heard him call her Garbo, as he often did. She looked him over coolly and said, 'Miss Garbo, if you please.' He couldn't take her seriously. 'You always call me Harry, and I have always called you Garbo.' Without changing her expression she answered, 'Miss Garbo, if you please.' And after that I noticed that it was always Miss Garbo." Why Edington put up with such behavior—she wasn't even paying him—remains a mystery.

GARBO, SALKA, AND MERCEDES

G ARBO'S ISOLATION would soon be alleviated when in 1929, at a party in Ernst Lubitsch's house, she was introduced by Jacques Feyder to a woman she would be very close to for the rest of her life—Salka Viertel, the wife of a distinguished German writer and director, Berthold Viertel. Garbo, Salka tells us in her fascinating memoir, *The Kindness of Strangers* (recently republished), "was the only woman who

Salka Viertel

The Viertel house in Santa Monica

wore an austere black suit and not evening dress." It was a chilly night, yet
Feyder and the two women spent the rest of the party out on the terrace "in
a highly animated mood." Garbo "was intelligent, simple, completely without pose, with a great sense of humor, joking about her inadequate German
and English, although she expressed herself very well."

The next day, Salka wrote,

We had just finished lunch, when the doorbell rang and in the open window of the entrance appeared the unforgettable face . . . Gaily she announced that she had come to continue the conversation of last night, and
stayed all afternoon. We went for a short walk on the beach and then sat in
my room. She told me she was pleased I had only seen her in *Gösta Berling*,
as she did not care much for her other films. She was very funny, carica-
turing the repetitiousness of the seduction techniques. She lived not far
from us [in Santa Monica], and in the evening Berthold and I walked her
home. After he said good-night to her, we exchanged our impressions.
What had charmed us was her great politeness and attentiveness. She
seemed hypersensitive, although of a steely resilience. The observations

she made about people were very just, sharp and objective. "Probably all that fame prevents her from living her real life," I said. "It's a high price to pay," said Berthold. She came very often early in the morning when the beach was deserted, and we took long walks together.

In a recent biography of Viertel, Donna Rifkind writes that these first encounters

sparked the longest, and most important relationship either of them would ever have in Hollywood. Instinctively they must have known that each had what the other needed: as a major film star at the peak of her earning potential, Garbo had power, while Salka had stability, patience, ironclad loyalty, and a gift for advocacy. Along with advice and total discretion, Salka offered Garbo a refuge on Mabery Road, where the actress could be herself, relaxed and without airs. Garbo lived in eleven different houses during her years in California, but each of these was a fortress, not a place of comfort. They could never be home, as Mabery Road came to represent for her. And Garbo offered Salka as much as if not more in return. Salka wrote to a friend in the mid-1960s that Garbo "is a kind of deus ex machina responsible for the strange turn my life took, and kept me in America."

Salka was not only a talented (and, in Europe, successful) actress, and a woman with a rich and generous sexual history, she was an earth figure, an earth *mother*, and indeed she and Berthold had three sons on whom she doted. (The glamorous middle one, Peter, was supposedly the inspiration for the Robert Redford character in *The Way We Were*; he would become a screenwriter and a novelist, his best-known book, *White Hunter Black Heart*, modeled on his close friend John Huston.)

Garbo's relationship with her own mother was certainly not a standard one—there was affection, perhaps, but at a distance. She wrote to Anna, sent her piles of clippings and reviews, tried to get her to move to a more comfortable apartment (eventually she succeeded), managed to bring her and Sven and Sven's family to America in 1939 as war neared. But she certainly didn't encourage her mother to live with her or near her. Money yes, closeness no. When Anna died in late 1944—in Scarsdale, New York—hardly anyone was told. Cecil Beaton, in his diaries, reports: "Mercedes [de Acosta] touches on the subject of Greta's family: 'But don't ever mention it to Greta. It's a sore subject. She doesn't like it talked about, but it makes me very sad, for she doesn't see her mother & I fear when her mother dies she will have great remorse & sadness.' 'But isn't the mother dead? I thought she died 2 years ago.' 'No, she's here in Connecticut staying with her son—& they are very unhappy that they never hear from Greta.'" Another friend, even later on, asked Garbo whether Anna still missed her home. "Greta looked up to the sky. 'How would I know?' she said quietly." It doesn't take much psychological acumen to infer that in Salka, sixteen years her senior, Garbo found the warm, forceful, maternal protectress she had never felt she had.

And Salka provided something even rarer than a home and a mother. To her famous salon out there in Santa Monica, every important European refugee (and many who were unimportant) regularly came for stimulating talk, convivial atmosphere, and magnificent food. Here were the Thomas Manns and the Heinrich Manns, Stravinsky and Schoenberg, Max Reinhardt (with whose son, Gottfried, Salka had a long live-in affair), Chaplin and Eisenstein and Murnau and German-born Billy Wilder. In his memoirs, actor/director/writer Robert Parrish recalls, "I walked in the back door one day and there was a guy with short hair cooking at the stove. In the living room, Arthur Rubinstein was tinkling on the piano. Greta Garbo was lying on the sofa, and Christopher Isherwood was lounging in a chair. 'Who's the guy in the kitchen,' I asked no one in particular. 'Bertolt Brecht,' came the reply."

Garbo savored being part of this atmosphere, and she soaked it up—she never ceased aspiring to the cultural and intellectual life she had never even known existed when she was growing up. It's not surprising that Salka remained the most important influence on her tastes and attitudes throughout the thirties and forties, encouraging her in her demands for roles of historical or literary significance, and involved with a number of her scripts. In fact, she was officially employed by M-G-M as a screenwriter, though it is generally understood that her real importance was as the only channel the studio had to its mercurial and exacting star, who not only was a tremendous money-maker but also brought it unparalleled prestige both at home and around the world.

Salka and Louis B. were usually at odds, but she and Thalberg liked and respected each other, united in their wish to protect Greta. When he died in 1936 (at only thirty-seven), everything changed. We can be certain that if he had still been in charge of production five years later, Garbo's career would not have ended with *Two-Faced Woman*. The only area in which Salka failed to influence Garbo was political: Salka devoted a tremendous amount of her time and energy to assisting refugees fleeing the Nazis to get to America, and to other liberal and left-wing causes. Garbo was barely interested, though after the war the United States government was: Salka was investigated by HUAC and, if not persecuted, was harmed professionally, although she had never been a Communist.

IT WAS AT THE VIERTEL HOME that Garbo met the other woman who would become a large part of her life for many years—the ubiquitous lesbian rake Mercedes de Acosta, who numbered among her fifty-odd lovers (or so she claimed) Marlene Dietrich, Eva Le Gallienne, Isadora Duncan, Alla Nazimova, Tallulah Bankhead, Pola Negri, Katharine Cornell, and—are you ready?—Edith Wharton. (And then there was her husband.) De Acosta titled her notorious memoirs *Here Lies the Heart*, notorious not so much for its scanty revelations as for its abounding inaccuracies. Le Gallienne said it should have been called *Here Lies the Heart and Lies and Lies*—all too true—and yet de Acosta's book, written with both clear-eyed perception and the eyes of love, somehow rings true in its sense of who and what Garbo was.

One of her most elaborate stories had to do with her first sight of Garbo. She was in Constantinople:

One day in the lobby of the Pera Palace Hotel I saw one of the most hauntingly beautiful women I had ever beheld. Her features and her movements were so distinguished and aristocratic-looking that I decided she must be a refugee Russian princess. The porter said he did not know her name but he thought she was a Swedish actress who had come to Constantinople with the great Swedish director, Maurice Stiller. Several times after this I saw her in the street. I was terribly troubled by her eyes and I longed to speak to her, but I did not have the courage. Also I did not know what language to use. She gave me the impression of great loneliness which only added to my own already melancholy state of mind. I hated to leave Constantinople without speaking to her, but sometimes destiny is kinder than we think, or maybe it is just that we cannot escape our destiny. Strangely enough, as the train pulled out of Constantinople I had a strong premonition that I might again see that beautiful and haunting face on some other shore.

Mercedes de Acosta, 1934, by George Hoyningen-Huene

Karen Swenson tells us drily, "Unfortunately, Mercedes' own passport records contradict this rather romantic story. She did visit Constantinople—with her husband, Abram Poole, in August of 1922; Greta Garbo appeared as that magnificent apparition in December of 1924 through January 1925—and never the twain did meet (for at least another seven years)."

Mercedes—always dressed in black and white with pointy sporting shoes, and frequently wrapped in a black cloak—was a clever, provocative woman, born in New York in 1893 (or thereabouts) to a large family of semi-aristocratic Hispanics. Among her sisters was the internationally famous Rita Lydig, one of the most fashionable and extravagant woman of her day and friend to such luminaries as Debussy, Rodin, Tolstoy, Bernhardt, Duse, and Degas. Asked why Rita had never expressed herself artistically, her great friend (and portraitist) John Singer Sargent replied, "Why should she? She herself is art."

Author of a number of plays (most of them unproduced) and a determined but failed poet and novelist, Mercedes came to Hollywood with the intention of becoming a screenwriter, and indeed she sold a script called *East River* to RKO for Pola Negri (it was never filmed) and later worked for Paramount and M-G-M. (Thalberg himself, she tells us, telephoned her to come and help with the script for *Rasputin and the Empress*, the one occasion on which the three Barrymores worked together.) When she was introduced to Garbo, "As we shook hands and she smiled at me I felt that I had known her all my life; in fact, in many previous incarnations." "Her beautifully straight hair hung to her shoulders and she wore a white tennis visor pulled well down over her face in the effort to hide her extraordinary eyes which held in them a look of eternity." It was love at first sight—on Mercedes's part, though Garbo was certainly taken by her unorthodox look and outspoken adoration. In a matter of days they were walking on the beach together, dancing with each other in the (empty) house of a friend of Salka's. "'You're Driving Me Crazy' we sang and danced over and over again."

Garbo summons her to her house, but then

"I am not going to take you into the house and you will have to leave soon. I am very tired and I have to shoot again tomorrow very early on that ghastly *Susan Lenox*." "Aren't you happy about the film," I asked innocently. "Happy? *Who* is happy? No one making films can be happy." "I'm sorry. I hoped you were. You were happy this morning." "But now it is nearly evening. Soon it will be night, and I will not sleep, and then it will be morning, and I will have to go again to that terrible studio. Let's not talk. It is so useless talking and trying to explain things. Let's just sit and not speak at all." And so we sat silently as the shadows of the eucalyptus trees began to stretch out across the lawn and finally the sun grew fiery red and slowly sank behind the hedge. Greta sighed and broke the silence. "Now you must go home," she said. Whenever I go to see her and it becomes time to leave, she asks me to go home as she did this day, it is a joke between us. She always has to remind me to go home.

Quite a joke. This passage is not only a fair indicator of de Acosta's writing style but a presage of a relationship that endured (sort of) for three decades, until, desperate for money, Mercedes published her book and Greta slammed the door violently and permanently. In essence: Mercedes was madly in love; Greta was responsive, then fed up with her friend's stifling and dramatic jealousies and sufferings. But Mercedes was intelligent and worldly, and she was *useful* in many ways, always there when Greta needed someone to find her a suitable new house or for occasional companionship. Greta's speech? "George Cukor used to say in Hollywood that I taught Greta her beautiful English and it was generally credited to me that I did. But this was not really true. It is possible that her English was in some small way influenced by mine, but she had such innate taste that she could never speak any language other than beautifully." Greta's career? "I had for some time thought of an idea for a film for her—the role of Queen Christina of Sweden. I had many notes and had written an outline of a story. When she arrived I told her about it. But as things often go in the film world in Hollywood, the idea was taken from me. Before I knew it, two other people were working on the story." One of those two (actually, there were at least three) was Salka Viertel, Mercedes's arch-rival (in her own mind) for Greta's attention and loyalty—a rivalry in which Mercedes had no chance of prevailing.

She was, however, instrumental in getting Garbo "to exchange her sailor pants for slacks. Looking back, it seems difficult to believe that at this time people were still shocked to see women in trousers. Once we were photographed in them on Hollywood Boulevard without our knowing it. The photograph came out in the newspaper with the caption under it: 'Garbo in pants! Innocent bystanders gasped in amazement to see Mercedes de Acosta and Greta Garbo striding swiftly along Hollywood Boulevard dressed in men's clothes.' Considering what walks down Hollywood Boule-

Garbo and de Acosta shock the world in pants.

vard now, it seems strange that Greta and I could have caused a sensation such a comparatively short time ago."

Soon after the two women met, and just after the filming of *Susan Lenox*, an exhausted Garbo needed to get away and, through the ever-useful Edington, had borrowed the keys to a cabin belonging to Wallace Beery located on a small island in Silver Lake in the Sierra Nevadas. She left in her car being driven by the chauffeur who had replaced Gustaf Norin, a laid-

back, charming African-American called James. (When Greta would ac-
cuse him of being very lazy, Mercedes reports, "far from disagreeing with
her he would answer, 'Yes, ma'am' in a soft drawling voice.") Soon, however, Greta telephoned: "I am on the way back. I have been to the island but
I am returning for you . . . Can you come to the island?"

Yes, Mercedes could and *did* come to the island:

On the island, snapshot by de Acosta

How to describe the next six enchanted weeks? Even recapturing them in
memory makes me realize how lucky I am to have had them. Six perfect
weeks out of a lifetime. This is indeed much. In all this time there was not
a second of disharmony between Greta and me or in nature around us. Not
once did it rain and we had brilliant sunshine every day . . . The days and
hours flew past far too quickly. They did more than that. They evaporated. There was no sense of time at all . . . There in the Sierra Nevadas she

used to climb ahead of me, and with her hair blown back, her face turned to the wind and sun, she would leap from rock to rock on her bare Hellenic feet. I would see her above me, her face and body outlined against the sky, looking like some radiant, elemental, glorious god and goddess melted into one.

Those "six perfect weeks" turn out to have been "less than two—if that much," as Swenson points out. There was no time—Garbo was due in Hollywood for "extended retakes" and was then going straight into *Mata Hari*. Beery would tell reporters that when he gave Edington the keys, the cabin was to be Garbo's for three weeks, but "Two weeks later he returned them." David Bret gives the likely duration of this idyll as ten days, and, he adds, despite the fact that they swam naked in the lake, "There may have been nothing remotely sexual in this: Garbo had done exactly the same thing during her vacation with Nils Asther and, by her admission, they had slept in separate rooms. The only difference is that Mercedes photographed Greta topless and, it would appear from studying the expression on her face, with her full approval." But then Garbo was famous for shucking off her clothes to swim—in her pool, in the ocean, wherever. She was never embarrassed by being naked. (A Swedish characteristic?)

Six weeks? Ten days? Sex? Not? Mercedes de Acosta was a fabulist, yes, but in her book she was a discreet one: There was no hint of anything sexual. The important thing is that Garbo, so famous for wanting to be alone, wanted Mercedes with her. What in reality Garbo wanted was to be in charge, and in Mercedes she had intuited what amounted to a love-slave. It was a relationship that neither of them could permanently break away from, despite Garbo's increasing aversion to Mercedes's clinging dependency and Mercedes's eternal suffering at Greta's indifference. This dismaying dynamic, despite long separations, lasted for thirty years.

$\Rightarrow 9 \Leftarrow$

GARBO GOES ON TALKING

A NNA CHRISTIE had been an artistic and commercial triumph. *Romance*, *Inspiration*, and *Susan Lenox* were box-office successes, but no one could (or did) call them major efforts. It was time, both Garbo and M-G-M sensed, for her to cut down on the number of movies she made and to make sure that each of the ones she *did* make was presented—and received—as An Event. *Mata Hari* had all the elements. The real woman—born Margaretha Geertruida "Margreet" Zelle MacLeod— was a notorious and successful Dutch exotic dancer who claimed Indonesian blood and who was executed by the French during World War I,

having been convicted of spying for Germany. What's more, one of her lovers—"the love of her life"—had been a Russian aviator who had been blinded in combat. She became one of the legends of her time, despite the fact that she hadn't been a very good dancer and was a completely ineffectual spy. But she was a perfect template for an M-G-M–glamoured movie about an exotic dancer/martyred spy who dies the death.

In *Susan Lenox*, Garbo had been wearing a sweater and skirt and catching a dear little fish in a mountain brook. Now, in *Mata Hari*, she's wearing a pagoda on

TOP AND LEFT:
The real Mata Hari

OPPOSITE: June Knight
subbing for Garbo

her head and dancing lasciviously before a gigantic idol, while crooning, "Shiva, I dance for you tonight as the Bayadères dance in the sacred temples of Java." Or, as *Variety* put it, "She did a polite cooch to Oriental music." (As it happens, she had a dancing double, June Knight, for much of this ludicrous exhibition, which in any case was censored for the 1939 reissue.)

Everyone, of course, knew that the real Mata Hari had died before a firing squad, so everyone knew from the start that Garbo was doomed. But not everyone knew—until M-G-M told them—that she went to her execution pretending to her (temporarily) blinded lover that they're meeting for the last time in a hospital where she's about to undergo an operation rather than in a prison cell, surrounded by weeping nuns, where she's waiting for the soldiers to take her away to her death. She's in stark black, her hair pulled tightly back—a look that Mercedes claimed credit for proposing.

Before this, however, she's dressed in a series of costumes extreme even by Adrian standards, one of which "took eight Guadalajaran needlewomen nine weeks to complete." There are the obligatory lavish flowers, the obligatory furs. There's the obligatory Lewis Stone, but no longer avuncular—he's the cruel, implacable head of the German spy ring. There's the typically hammy Lionel Barrymore as a Russian general whom Mata has co-opted.

(*left*) Dealing with Lionel Barrymore; (*below*) pretending to the temporarily blinded Ramon Novarro that she's going into a hospital for an operation, but (*opposite*) really going to face the firing squad

And there's the typically tender young man who falls into worship-at-first-sight and whom she comes to care for with all her trademark sexual/maternal love. (He's the heroic Russian aviator, unwittingly caught up in her spyish lures.)

He's Ramon Novarro, one of the great male stars of the day—*The Prisoner of Zenda*, *Scaramouche*, *The Student Prince of Heidelberg*, and, of course,

Ben-Hur; he's Hollywood's leading Latin Lover in the wake of Valentino's death. And why not? As Mark Vieira put it, "Even if he was Mexican, he could pass for Russian. He had passed for Jewish in *Ben-Hur*, after all." Forget that he was six years older than Garbo, he looked six years younger with his baby face and boyish manner and charming little mustache. He was handsome and appealing, though hardly a virile presence—his voice is as soft as his looks. The two stars got along well—perhaps he was a relief after the ultra-virile Gable, and perhaps she felt secure with him, given his homosexuality, which was an open secret in Hollywood. Garbo hated rehearsing (as did the director, old-timer George Fitzmaurice, who had directed Valentino's final film, *The Son of the Sheik*), but Novarro desperately needed it, and she graciously accommodated him.

Many things happen in *Mata Hari*, all of them unbelievable, although there's the ring of truth to her proclamation "I'm Mata Hari, my own mas-ter" and her statement "That's how I am, and that's how I had to be." Mata Hari, like Garbo herself, remains her own woman, even if in this case she's a woman who's pure construct—the closest Garbo comes to Dietrich's ex-ternal approach to roles. Can she have been sulking because, not for the last time, she couldn't get M-G-M to present her as Joan of Arc?

At least one serious critic took her to task—Mary Cass Canfield, in a "Letter to Garbo" in *Theatre Arts Monthly*: "Your playing was, more often than not, a highly finished piece of somnambulism. You merely walked through it, like some superior and unperturbed mannequin." Even the commercial reviewers were dubious. But as Mark Vieira (again) put it, "No one was reading reviews in January 1932. They were either looking for work or watching *Mata Hari*." Today, it's a hard movie to watch, and cer-tainly hard to like—even as camp. (By the way, in case you're curious, "Mata Hari" was said to mean "eye of the dawn" in Malaysian.)

In the long run, however, M-G-M knew best. *Mata Hari* was probably the most financially successful film of Garbo's career, its profit well over a million dollars.

FROM NOW ON, with almost no exceptions, it's class, class, class all the way. (Garbo's own preference, always, and now she had Salka encouraging her and running interference for her with the studio.) So she graduates from being a Dutch exotic dancer to being a tragic Russian ballerina. She doesn't dance in her next movie, *Grand Hotel*, and she doesn't have much screen time in it, but it's still her movie, despite the vigorous competition.

Were the plot strands of *Grand Hotel* clichés before Vicki Baum incor-porated them into her internationally bestselling 1929 novel (*Menschen im Hotel*—People at a Hotel), or did she come up with them herself? Let's give her the credit, if that's what it is. After all, she was a dynamic woman—Austrian-Jewish, well educated, who among other things was for years a successful concert harpist, went in seriously for boxing (not a normal avo-cation for the Viennese young women of her day), wrote more than fifty books, and ended up as a Hollywood scriptwriter.

It was Thalberg who saw the potential. For $13,000 he bought the screen rights to the book, then commissioned a play based on it—a hit first in Berlin, then running on Broadway for more than a year with the enchanting Eugenie Leontovich as Grusinskaya. Thalberg had come up with the revolutionary idea of making movies with a whole bunch of stars rather than as vehicles for a single star—a Valentino, a Pickford, a Garbo. (*Dinner at Eight* would follow.) And M-G-M had the stars to do it with, more than there are in Heaven, as the studio liked to boast. For *Grand Hotel* they had Joan Crawford, in her way as big a star as Garbo; they had not one but two Barrymores; they had Wallace Beery, big at the box office (*Min and Bill*, the Oscar for *The Champ*); and they had the inevitable Lewis Stone, here an embittered doctor with a face disfigured by a war wound, whose sole function is to keep pronouncing the ironic message "Grand Hotel—always the same. People come, people go. Nothing ever happens." What makes this doubly ridiculous is that so very *much* happens to our stars.

Garbo in her limited number of scenes, with only Barrymore (John) playing opposite her, dominates the movie. She's a fading ballerina, and she's tired, tired, tired. ("I've never been so tired in my life.") Alone in her room, she decides to end it all with veronal, but, fortuitously, Barrymore—a baron down on his uppers, who's there to steal her pearls—reveals

(*above*) Tragic ballerina; (*opposite*) with John Barrymore

The other major players: Joan Crawford, Wallace Beery, and Lionel Barrymore

himself to her and not only convinces her to live, but talks his way into her bed. It's true love, for both of them, and they plan to go off together. Alas, before that can happen, the baron is murdered by the desperate industrialist Preysing (Beery, the only one in the cast of supposed Germans who speaks with a German accent—apparently, he made it a condition of his accepting the role; Garbo's accent is Russian by way of Sweden).

Then there's Flaemmchen, the stenographer-cum-whatever with a heart of gold, who is Joan Crawford, thrilled to be in a movie with Garbo. (Unfortunately, they have no scenes together, and in any case Garbo did all her rehearsing at home.) Crawford is modestly accoutered—she was to have only a single dress but bludgeoned Thalberg into granting her not only a second one but a negligée as well—yet she looks like a million bucks and gives a terrific performance, clearly aware of what's at stake for her appearing in such a prestigious event and in such company. Flaemmchen is her best M-G-M role except for the vicious Crystal of *The Women*, and she's believable both as the hard-boiled girl on the make in a tough world and as the tender-hearted young woman who lovingly takes charge of the dying bookkeeper, Kringelein—Lionel Barrymore, whose overacting is unbearable, even by Lionel standards. (Lonely, dying old men don't have to be hams. Consider Takashi Shimura in Kurosawa's great *Ikiru*.)

The various plot lines interweave cleverly and fluently; Cedric Gibbons's astounding circular set holds everything together; director Edmund Goulding keeps control of his band of prima donnas. (Thalberg had chosen him on the theory that a sympathetic bisexual man would get better work out of temperamental actresses than your average Hollywood Joe.) But what finally matters in *Grand Hotel* is Grusinskaya and von Gaigern, her baron.

Garbo is superb. We believe in her depressed exhaustion (the famous "I want to be alone . . . I just want to be alone . . ." and "Fame always brings loneliness. Success is ice-cold and lonely as the North Pole." Well, Garbo would know). We believe she's a great ballerina, even though she doesn't look like a dancer or move like one. Most of all, we believe in her ecstatic joy when Barrymore restores her sense of being a woman who is loved and who loves, and for whom there's a future. "For the first time in my life I'm

M-G-M lined up the all-star cast for a publicity shot. Needless to say, Garbo would not cooperate, so they pasted her into the picture.

happy!" she tells us. But we don't need to be told. It's in her face, her smile, her laugh—her radiant energy. Who would have thought we'd ever see Garbo twirling gleefully through a hotel's revolving doors? As she rushes off in the morning to catch the train for Italy—the train on which von Gaigern is to meet her—everyone colludes to keep from her the news that he's dead. It's a masterstroke that we're not shown her despair, only her rapture.

As for John Barrymore, I find him disappointing. The love scenes seem a little calculated; he's a little self-conscious. The Great Profile isn't really so great anymore—he's fifty to Garbo's twenty-seven. His reputation as America's greatest actor was so overwhelming that it was assumed he was *still* America's greatest actor, and he'll be swell two years later in *Twentieth Century*, where instead of sharing tragedy with Garbo he's romping with Carole Lombard. But here he's not really much of an improvement over Garbo's other male foils of this period. Apparently, though, they got along very well, each of them in awe of the other and she covering for him on mornings when he was hung over and couldn't make it to the studio: She'd stay home, "indisposed." Noblesse obliged.

Is *Grand Hotel* a great movie? No, but it's a dazzling one, and the world was dazzled. It was one of Garbo's three biggest box-office successes to date, along with *Mata Hari* and *Anna Christie*. It was the only movie ever to win the Best Picture Oscar without being nominated in any other category. Clever (and knowledgeable) Ethan Mordden put it this way: "Sure, everyone's in a different style; that's what all-star casts are for. Garbo invents her own genre, John Barrymore is high comedy, Lionel is weepie, Beery . . . is blood-and-thunder melodrama, Stone is austere and military, and Crawford, in superb Adrian outfits, is from life. It's the best thing she did." Grusinskaya is not the best thing Garbo did, but, like her Queen Christina, like her Camille, like her Ninotchka, it's imprinted on our memories.

Pauline Kael would nail it years later:

From her first line, "I have never been so tired in my life," Greta Garbo sets the movie in vibration with her extraordinary presence . . . Intellectually you have every reason to reject *Grand Hotel* as an elaborate chunk of artifice and hocus-pocus: there are no redeeming qualities in Vicki Baum's excruciating concepts of character and fate, and anyone who comes to see this movie expecting an intelligent script or even "good acting" should have his head examined. But if you want to see what screen glamour used to be and what, originally, "stars" were, this is perhaps the best example of all time.

Actually, M-G-M had already nailed it—in the Marion Davies movie *Blondie of the Follies*, which Edmund Goulding directed right after *Grand*

Hotel. Here is Davies at her charming and funny best, as she erupts from her lower-class background into the *Follies* and the arms of Robert Montgomery. After she's crippled (don't worry, she'll recover), she throws a last fancy party before returning to her roots. Out of nowhere, into it cavorts Jimmy Durante, then a contract player at Metro, and they fling themselves into a glorious spoof of Garbo and Barrymore. The Baron: "Can I stay with you for a little while?" The Ballerina: "Well, just for the week then . . ." Davies was always a superb mimic, and here she looks like Garbo, talks like Garbo, and suffers like Garbo. She's hilarious . . . and completely sympathetic; no wonder Mr. Hearst was crazy about her. Hurrah for her and Goulding and M-G-M. History does not relate whether Garbo saw *Blondie*, and if she did, whether she was amused.

Marion Davies and Jimmy Durante doing a Garbo-Barrymore parody in *Blondie of the Follies*

WE CAN ALL AGREE that Pirandello is a classier writer than Vicki Baum, if not always as much fun. And M-G-M (and, no doubt, Salka) had no difficulty in assuring Garbo that the Nobel Prize–winning author of *Six Characters in Search of an Author* was about as classy as you could get. (By now, of course, she had veto power over everything.) Yet if you had to vote on which was Garbo's worst sound film—*Romance? The Painted Veil? Two-Faced Woman?*—you could do worse than go with *As You Desire Me*, although its reviews were generally favorable. Didn't the reviewers notice that the script was terrible, the acting was terrible, and the direction was worst of all? Garbo had been more tired than usual after *Grand Hotel* and desperate to get home to Sweden for a vacation; her M-G-M contract was running out in only a few weeks, and to add to the stress, no one knew (and the press speculated and speculated) whether she would ever come back—to M-G-M, to America, to film. One prominent columnist declared, "I'm for a law that will bar Garbo from leaving the country."

Not surprisingly, Pirandello's play featured his familiar theme of illusion versus reality. But the screenwriter assigned to the film was no Pirandello. He was Gene Markey, a good-looking, athletic charmer-around-Hollywood who would go on to marry Joan Bennett, Hedy Lamarr, and Myrna Loy, and whose skimpy film-writing credits included *Inspiration*, another contender in the worst-Garbo-movie sweepstakes. If there had been time for serious reconsiderations of the script—for bringing in collaborators and for considered rewrites—the results might have been better. But there wasn't any time. Garbo was on her way to Sweden.

The most famous thing about *As You Desire Me* is that when we first encounter Garbo—chanteusing away in a nightclub—she's in a platinum-blond wig and singing to the enraptured crowd. She's "Zara," the toast of Budapest, sounding like Marlene Dietrich, her new supposed rival, although of course her singing is dubbed; and she's hard-faced, like the early Dietrich. Some commentators have assumed that this was all meant as a parody, and maybe it was. Her best moment comes when she flips a wineglass up in the air and catches it coming down—she's getting drunk. ("Garbo Drinks!") And it's a good drunk scene, too. Unfortunately, she's wearing one of the ugliest outfits Adrian ever concocted for her—a black pantsuit with a hideously distracting collar. Who is sabotaging this movie?

Here's the question on which *As You Desire Me* pivots: Is Zara Zara? Or is she Contessa Maria Varelli, missing for ten years since her villa was savagely "invaded" during the war? Her husband, Bruno—the count—has been pining for her all this time, and when they're reunited, he's convinced she's the real thing. But is she? Even *she* doesn't know, because she's been traumatized, because she's been suffering from amnesia, and because she's been effectively hypnotized by the evil novelist Salter, played at her insistence by Erich von Stroheim, depressed and in bad health. (Mayer hated him, Thalberg hated him, but Garbo insisted on him.) He barely made it through the filming, consistently late, unable to remember his lines, stuttering, offending everyone, although Garbo, with her usual generosity toward her fellow performers, covered for him when he couldn't make it into the studio by pretending that it was she herself who was unwell. No wonder that he gave a badly clichéd performance, barely rising to the heights of sadism required of him.

When "Maria"—aka "Zara"—is restored to husband and home outside Florence, does her beloved maid recognize her? Does Bruno's faithful Alsatian recognize her? All is ambiguous, but Bruno himself has no doubts: "I've got to believe that you're Maria." And she's made it clear from the start: "I don't want to remember—all I want is to forget."

The plot fractures when wicked Salter turns up with the supposed "real" Maria in tow, a pathetic creature who's been in a mental institution since the night of the "invasion" and is seen now only behind a dark veil. And then there's Maria's sister, played by Hedda Hopper, who has ulterior motives, and there's Tony, Bruno's great friend, who's an artist and who's apparently spent the decade searching everywhere for his friend's missing wife until he spots her in Budapest . . . or was that Zara? (Or Dietrich?)

We'll never know, but luckily it doesn't matter, since—of course—Bruno and Zara/Maria fall in love all over again. (Or for the first time?) She's resisted his embraces, but now she comes to him in the night, because he's so . . . "*good*." Now she can forget her profound aversion for "men, men, *men*." The trauma of what happened the night of the "invasion" is erased, her memory may (or may not) be coming back, a preposterous explanation for the veiled Maria is wheeled out, and all ends happily, except for poor wicked Salter, who gets what he deserves.

With Erich von Stroheim in *As You Desire Me*

And what of Bruno himself? A very inexperienced Melvyn Douglas has been thrust into this role. At least he's tall, although, hidden behind an unbecoming mustache and utterly ill at ease, he's hopeless. It's not just that he hasn't yet learned to act, it's that he's completely confused about what's going on. As he wrote in his autobiography, "I never knew at any moment what I was supposed to be doing. It was beyond the understanding of any of us." By the time seven years later when he and Garbo were doing *Ninotchka*

With Melvyn Douglas in *As You Desire Me*

together, he had learned to act—*and* they had the benefit of a coherent script and accomplished director.

As for George Fitzmaurice, his direction of *Mata Hari* had been acceptable, but here he was totally amateurish. The staging is stagy—there's nothing cinematic about it, once we get past the opening nightclub scene. Nor does he help his actors: Stroheim was undirectable; Douglas, just not ready for the challenge of Garbo; even *her* performance is thin, except for the few high spots. Worst of all, through much of the film Garbo isn't really very beautiful. (I know this is heresy and am prepared to be burned at the stake.) An ambivalent review in *The New Yorker* said, "I am inclined to think that there is altogether too much discussion of Garbo these days. It is enough to say that this is not one of her most ambitious offerings." On the other hand, suddenly bitten by the Garbo bug, Stark Young, America's most respected theater critic, said of her in *As You Desire Me* that "for the first time she seemed to me to show in her playing an inner delight and happy dedication to the love and joy of it . . . The secret luminous center of such playing cannot be conveyed, of course, any more than its shining fluency can be forgotten." And a Los Angeles review, after opening with some lines of Heine (in German), went on to say: "Why speak of a fine performance by Melvyn Douglas, or say that von Stroheim was excellent as always; why mention that it is a Pirandello story, when afterward all you remember is a woman going aboard a boat with swelling sails and sailing away into a moonlit night, leaving one with a sense of ineffable beauty."

No doubt asking herself what she was supposed to be doing in this bizarre movie

AND THEN CAME THE MOVIE that was probably closest to Garbo's heart: *Queen Christina*. The idea of her playing Sweden's most famous historical

figure had been in the wind (and undoubtedly in the back of her mind) for some time, with various people—Marie Dressler one of them!—claiming it was their idea. Mercedes de Acosta, of course, claimed credit (although she received none). The movie was shepherded into completion by Salka Viertel. It was she who, working with M-G-M writers, developed the concept, and who conferred with and counseled Garbo every step of the way. She may not have written actual passages of the final script, but her influence was all-pervasive and she deserves all the credit she received. Producer Walter Wanger imported S. N. Behrman to spiff up the dialogue and write pages of new material.

Clearly, Christina resonated with Garbo—a figure of authority who must be obeyed; a queen who liked dressing up as a man, whose favorite courtier was a woman, and who refused ever to marry ("I shall die a bachelor"); a no-nonsense, highly educated and cultured monarch—Garbo's Christina reads Molière and speaks knowledgeably of Velázquez. As for Christina's abdication, hadn't Garbo tortured her studio—and the world— with threats to abdicate her own supreme position in the world of film?

What emerged from this synchronicity between subject and star is a highly peculiar creature that begins as one kind of movie and ends as another. The first half, for all its authentic historical trappings, is pure romantic comedy, though togged out with swords and capes and caparisoned horses: Female dressed as Male meets Male who likes Females. *She* doesn't know he's Don Antonio (José Miguel de la Prada, Count Pimentel, Knight of the Holy Roman Empire, Envoy Extraordinary of His Majesty Philip, King of Spain, Aragon, and Castille), Spain's emissary to Sweden, who is conveying his king's proposal of marriage to the queen; *he* doesn't know she's the queen. In other words, standard Hollywood, though robustly and charmingly presented. One can't help thinking, as she struts around as a young fellow, what a wonderful Rosalind she might have made.

The rest of the movie is High Historical. Christina's advisers as well as her subjects reject the idea of Catholic Spain—and its personification, Don Antonio. She doesn't want to marry Spain, but she does want the right to love its ambassador: "I'm tired of being a symbol—I long to be a human being." There's a great deal of pageantry—solemn and impressive and not

Garbo (in drag) and Gilbert giving a pretty girl the once-over in *Queen Christina*

very stimulating. Since everyone knew that the real Christina had abdicated, had never married, and had never been sexually or emotionally involved with a Spanish functionary, the film romance could only end tragically—with him dead of a convenient duel. At which point we are given Garbo, in what is perhaps the single most famous shot in movie history, standing alone at the prow of the ship bearing her into exile, staring blankly ahead, her face a mask, her thoughts and feelings impenetrable. Alone at last.

And who was it who portrayed Don Antonio? As we have seen, to the astonishment of all and to the fury of Louis B. Mayer, Garbo insisted on her old playmate John Gilbert, whose career had plummeted in talkies and who was on the ropes. She held all the cards, though, and Gilbert was hired, despite the supposed fatal inadequacy of his voice. Yes, there are a few moments of silent-film eye-popping, and the voice does have a slightly odd texture, but he's ardent and accomplished; M-G-M could have done—*had* done—far worse by her.

Gilbert had been generous to Garbo about billing in the early days, when he was a great star and she was a newcomer, and now he was billed beneath the title (no doubt Mayer's revenge), but he was deeply grateful to her. "She was magnificent to me while we were working together," he said. "She knew that I was nervous, raw, almost sick with excitement and the thrill of the thing. And never once did she fail in consideration of me, in tact, in saying and doing the right thing at the right moment . . . She sensed every one of my feelings and was tender toward them." It is a rare moment in Garbo's history when we can fully admire her, even love her, as a human being, not only as an artist.

Garbo threw herself into this project intensely and personally. Her Christina would be authentic: On vacation in Sweden, she spent a good deal of time exploring the real places in Christina's life which M-G-M would try to reinvent, taking notes and making sketches that, M-G-M reported, "proved invaluable." (When Salka suggested making the film abroad, she wrote back that "Metro was the best studio and Thalberg the most capable producer.") She read everything there was to read about Christina and certainly felt closer to this character than to any other in her career. And the

With Gilbert and director Rouben Mamoulian

correspondences between them were extraordinary, including the fact that she was twenty-eight when she played Christina and Christina was twenty-eight when she gave up her throne.

The studio went to extreme lengths to keep the historical details accurate, hiring an expert who produced a detailed report on the errors the film was making. "When I saw apples, oranges and grapes carried in, I pointed out the impossibility of having them served at the inn, even if it was suggested [that the ambassador] had brought them from Spain. He had been travelling for weeks, and, besides, no fruit could be kept edible in the very cold winter climate of Sweden." You can imagine how seriously the studio took all this. (Years later, however, Garbo did advise that eating grapes while lying on your back wasn't a very good idea.) The level of the studio's seriousness about *Queen Christina* is suggested by the trailer they released for it. "Garbo Returns: A Queen Whose Love Affairs Were as Modern as Tomorrow's Tabloids! A 17th Century Maiden Who Lived with 20th Century Madness!"

What accounts for *Queen Christina*'s artistic success, apart from Garbo's convincing performance and despite all the plot nonsense, is the mostly excellent direction of Rouben Mamoulian, who had made a distinguished name for himself in Hollywood—the innovative *Applause* and *Love Me To-*

Pondering her choices

night, the Fredric March *Dr. Jekyll and Mr. Hyde*, and the latest Dietrich extravaganza, *Song of Songs*—and who also enjoyed a distinguished stage career: *Porgy and Bess, Oklahoma!, Carousel*. Mamoulian was intelligent, low-key, and firm—not for him Garbo's preference for keeping her directors out of sight. They got along extremely well, and even had a brief "relationship," whatever that meant. (There may even have been an aborted

elopement.) It was he who famously conceived the indelible shot of Christina at the prow of her ship. Answering Garbo's question "What do I express in this last shot?" Mamoulian told her, "Nothing, absolutely nothing. You must make your mind and heart a complete blank. Make your face into a mask; do not even blink your eyes while the camera is on you. You see, with a tragic ending like this, no matter what feelings are portrayed by the actress, and these could range from hysterical sobs to a smile, some of the audience would disagree, find them wrong. This was one of those marvelous spots where a film could turn every spectator into a creator." It was also Mamoulian who orchestrated the movie's other most famous sequence:

Christina, now definitely seen as a woman, emerges from the bed she's shared with Antonio at the inn and slowly, lingeringly, moves around their bedchamber, stroking and fondling its artifacts—"I've been *memorizing* this room." "It was a graphic poem," Mamoulian said.

And it was Mamoulian, with the help of Behrman, who made sure that the film's solemnity was tempered with humor, and that there was some snap to the action scenes. He also extracted excellent performances from Lewis Stone, for once in a role of some real consequence (and a full close-up!) as the queen's most trusted councillor; from Ian Keith as the villain and C. Aubrey Smith as the queen's most loyal and intimate servant. What a relief from the stolid competence of Clarence Brown!

Queen Christina had a mixed reception. Superb reviews for Garbo, surprisingly admiring ones for Gilbert, but this was the first of her films that did better business overseas than in America, where regular moviegoers outside the big cities proved to be not so interested in the subject and in a Garbo who was only secondarily a lover. (Even so, it netted a profit of over $630,000.) She had been off the screen for a year and a half, and when she returned now, it was more as a sacred icon, less as a mere star. Mark Vieira got to the heart of the matter: "Irving Thalberg's formula had been replaced by Salka Viertel's influence. This was the first film in which Garbo was not offered as someone to be desired, but as something to be revered, a jewel in a grand setting . . . *Queen Christina* was the turning point in Garbo's career. After 1933, she would reach the heights of her artistry, but she would never again reach the average movie fan."

O'NEILL AND PIRANDELLO CERTAINLY WERE CLASSY. So was Queen Christina. And to many people—especially in Hollywood—Somerset Maugham was too. He also represented money in the bank: Probably more successful movies were based on his work than that of any other writer. Among the best known: *Of Human Bondage* (Bette Davis), *Rain/Sadie Thompson/ Miss Sadie Thompson* (Gloria Swanson, Joan Crawford, Rita Hayworth), *The Letter* (Davis again), *The Moon and Sixpence* (George Sanders), and *The Razor's Edge* (Tyrone Power and Gene Tierney), in which Maugham

The Painted Veil: with husband Herbert Marshall . . .

. . . and lover George Brent

himself is a character played by Herbert Marshall, who would now be star-ring opposite Garbo in the first of three film versions of Maugham's *The Painted Veil*.

There were critics who liked the movie, and *The New York Times'* critic began his review, "Pettish folk, out of an evident spirit of wish-fulfillment, are forever discovering that Greta Garbo has outlived her fame. They are knaves and blackguards and they should be pilloried in the middle of Times Square. She continues handsomely to be the world's greatest cinema actress in the Oriental triangle drama, *The Painted Veil*." Yes, but he also allows that the film is "insincere in its emotions" and that its narrative "carries lit-tle conviction or suggestion of depth."

Maugham's novel, and the play he fashioned from it, center on fading London debutante Kitty Garstin and the doctor-scientist she marries out of boredom. He takes her to Hong Kong, where she both enters into a liaison with a sexier married man and is forced by her husband to accompany him to inland China, where cholera is raging and where he hopes she will die. No such luck—it's *he* who succumbs, leaving Kitty a wiser and more gen-erous woman, prepared to dedicate her life to the child she is soon to bear. Its father? "I don't know."

Swedish Garbo cannot be English Kitty so she becomes Austrian Ka-trin, and the movie opens in Graz, where her beloved younger sister is get-ting married. One of the wedding guests is Walter, her doctor-father's favorite ex-student, and soon they are married and off to the Mysterious East. But Walter—somewhat stiff though genuinely in love and played by the excellent but also stiff Marshall—is more interested in his scientific work than in his restless wife. Which is where dashing (if you care for the type) George Brent comes into the picture as a young married diplo-mat who casually seduces Katrin. It's the old Garbo story—neglected wife, ardent lover, tragic or happy ending depending on the whim of the writers.

The best scenes are the early ones, in which Garbo is light-hearted, witty, humorous—kissing her sister again and again as she leaves for her honeymoon, teasing Walter as she makes him a midnight cup of tea. It's when she gets to the Orient that both the movie and Garbo turn heavy. To pep things up, into the story is plopped a great deal of Orientalia, most egregiously an extended street festival celebrating the Sun's marriage to the Moon. There are dragons shooting flames, lithesome Chinese dancing girls, choreography by the famous Hubert Stowitts. The whole thing, as Garbo biographer Robert Payne put it, might have been "invented by a drunken nightclub owner after seeing the New Year ushered in in San Francisco's Chinatown."

The costumes are all too often equally absurd—Adrian at his most "creative," particularly in regard to what Garbo has on her head, ranging from a bizarre something that looks like a trowel to a perky pillbox hat to a white turban that Garbo concocts by swiftly winding a strip of white cloth around her head to the white wimple-like object she has on when she's got up as a nursing sister assisting the French nuns of Mei Tan Fu in tending to cholera-infected Chinese children. (She's redeeming herself.) No wonder Alexander Walker said, "At over a million dollars, *The Painted Veil* was an expensive example of eccentric millinery."

Although in the novel Walter dies of the cholera, in the movie he *almost* dies, after having been stabbed by an enraged "coolie" because he has ordered the town's infected huts to be burned to the ground. When he emerges from his coma among the nuns, he sees wimpled Katrin leaning over him with love in her eyes. "I was a million miles away," he murmurs, "a million miles." "Don't go back," she pleads. "I won't." "I *love* you." She has come to understand and worship his noble nature, having scornfully rid herself of the *ig*noble George Brent.

Not in real life, though. Greta and George enjoyed a romantic interlude for a while—she even moved in with him. In fact, they all got along with

Herbert Marshall is stabbed by an enraged "native"; Garbo rushes to his side; true love (in a wimple) prevails.

each other. Marshall would report on how "kind and considerate" Garbo had been: "I have never met a more natural woman." Director Richard Boleslavsky, a Stanislavsky acolyte, was a positive and liked figure. Everyone was happy—except the audience. *The Painted Veil* barely made a profit. Why? Because despite its fire-breathing dragons and epidemics and stalwart nuns and stabbings, it's low-key and ponderous. Just compare it with the two outstanding films, also set in Asia, made from Maugham's *The Letter*—the first version with Jeanne Eagels, the second with Bette Davis. Garbo, of course, is more beautiful and subtle than either of them, but beauty and subtlety aren't the meat of successful melodrama.

WHAT NEXT? The brilliant David O. Selznick, whom Garbo was glad to have as her new producer, strongly believed that she should do something contemporary and American—in particular, a Broadway play, starring Tallulah Bankhead, called *Dark Victory*. For a moment, it looked as if she might agree, but then the lure of Art (and the urgings of Salka) swayed her back to her original idea: *Anna Karenina*. (We would have to wait four years for *Dark Victory* with Bette Davis.) *Love*, Garbo's first stab at Anna K., was based on the novel by "Lyof N. Tolstoi." *Anna Karenina*, eight years later, in 1935, is by "Count Leo Tolstoy." And that is not the only difference between the two movies, even apart from the basic difference that one is a silent and the other is in sound.

Garbo has matured, and given that she always looks somewhat older than her real age, her looks and manner are now exactly right for the tragic woman she is portraying. Watching her opening scenes, you're utterly convinced that this is a role she was born to play—she's an extraordinarily beautiful and aristocratic woman, not a lovely girl got up as a grown woman with a ten-year-old child. She's Anna Karenina. She's also an actress who has outgrown the fakey melodramatics that came with the silents territory. But the cards were stacked against her.

First, and worst, is her Vronsky—the dreadful Fredric March, who had been and would go on being a major Hollywood star. His "Dr. Jekyll" won him his first Oscar in 1931, and fifteen years later he'd win another for *The*

Anna Karenina

Best Years of Our Lives. He was Robert Browning in *The Barretts of Wimpole Street*, Jean Valjean in *Les Misérables*, Anthony Adverse in *Anthony Adverse*. He was in *Design for Living* and *Nothing Sacred*, and he was "Mr. Norman Maine" in the original *A Star Is Born*. On Broadway he would triumph in *The Skin of Our Teeth*, *A Bell for Adano*, and as the first American James Tyrone in *A Long Day's Journey into Night*. He could have been the first Willy Loman but turned down the role. (He didn't, however, turn down the movie.)

The trailer for *Anna Karenina* hails him as "the dashing, flashing, gay-

est, maddest . . . most tempestuous sweetheart of [Garbo's] career." Alas, in
the movie itself his Vronsky is dull, flat, unappealing, unattractive, and
with absolutely no sexual charge—Garbo is playing their love scenes with
herself. He has some kind of faint American accent, not unlike Gene Kelly's,
and he's about as Russian as Gene Kelly. There isn't a believable or interesting moment in his performance. Richard Corliss wrote, "To his love scenes
March brought the sort of sappy conviction you might expect from Merv
Griffin singing 'Summertime.'" Alistair Cooke: "He brings to this very
pre-War, elaborated Russia the manner of a West Point cadet entraining
for a Junior prom."

What was the problem, apart from the fact that March's reputation
(and salary) had always been inflated? Did he hate the fact that he was
second-billed, playing opposite the greatest of stars, and that this was the
actress's film? To give him credit, he hadn't wanted to make the movie—he
was tired of appearing in costume dramas and knew he wasn't really right
for them—but he was talked into it.

March isn't the only thing wrong with *Anna Karenina*. Its production is
grandiose, a reflection of Selznick's grandiose impulses. From the beginning, everything is big, heavy, ornate. And Russian, Russian, Russian,
with Russian choral singing (in the Cathedral at Easter), Russian specialty

Anna, with her husband (Basil Rathbone), meets Vronsky (Fredric March)

dancing, Russian music—Tchaikovsky's "None but the Lonely Heart" sounds behind the actors at moments of highest emotion. (Even so, one commentator noted that the only one in the movie who seemed Russian was Garbo.) The supporting actors disappoint, including the famous Freddie

Anna and Vronsky watching a game of croquet

Anna and her son (Freddie Bartholomew)

Bartholomew as little Seresha—the mother-son scenes lack the emotion that Garbo generated with Philippe de Lacey in *Love*. But then Garbo didn't like the famous Freddie Bartholomew, who one day dared to ask her for her autograph.

Anna and her niece (Cora Sue Collins)

This version of the novel does give Anna her suicide, subtly staged by Clarence Brown, and a family circle. Kitty (an over-eager and over-acting Maureen O'Sullivan) and Levin are restored to Tolstoy, and so are Dolly and Stiva (a surprisingly effective Reginald Owen). And the Karenin, Basil Rathbone, is an improvement on his brutish silent predecessor, even if he's more British than Russian—at least he's human. But *Anna Karenina* with an Anna and Vronsky who don't even like each other is a doomed *Anna Karenina*.

The critics were generous to Garbo, and she's so luminous, how could they fail to be? (Cooke again: "Tenderness is a prickly word, but it's nothing short of tenderness that has happened to Garbo. She has suddenly and decisively passed out of her twenties . . . And this quality of gentleness, a gift usually of women over fifty, is an overwhelming thing when it goes with the appearance of a beautiful woman of thirty." A late convert to Garbo, Cooke now celebrates "the way Garbo looks at people these days, the way she implies that the least you can do for people in this stupid, brawling world is to keep them warm and give them a share of comfort before the end comes.")

Some critics liked the extravagance of the production—the audience surely did: It was a big financial success. But what an opportunity missed! We should have had *Anna Karenina* with Garbo, not Garbo without *Anna Karenina*.

Let Garbo have the last word about her *Anna Karenina*. Behrman reports: "I drove out with Mr. and Mrs. Selznick, Mrs. Viertel and Miss Garbo to Riverside for the preview. The delicacy and distinction of Garbo's performance affected me as it did the audience; I felt as I always did watching her, that she is the most patrician artist in the world. Mr. and Mrs. Selznick were pleased. But on the way home, in the car, Garbo sat silent, speaking only once, in reply to a query from Selznick as to how she felt about the movie. 'Oh,' she said, 'if once, if only once, I could see a preview and come home feeling satisfied!'"

FINALLY THINGS WENT SUPREMELY RIGHT. Pauline Kael: "Like parents crowing over baby's first steps, M-G-M announced 'Garbo Talks!' (in *Anna Christie*) and 'Garbo Laughs!' (in *Ninotchka*), but they missed out when they should have crowed: 'Garbo Acts!' That was in *Camille*."

The consensus is that Garbo is at her greatest in *Camille*, and the consensus has it right. Everything came together for her. To begin with, *La Dame aux camélias* is a superb vehicle—not a superb play, but a superb setting for a sensitive yet extravagant talent like Garbo's. Which is why Bernhardt and Duse and untold numbers of other actresses have insisted on playing it—on the stage from Modjeska to Tallulah (in London, in 1930) to Susan Strasberg in 1963 (the only stage performance I ever walked out of in the middle of a scene); on the screen from Bernhardt herself to Nazimova (with Valentino) to Norma Talmadge to Isabelle Huppert. There have been

With Robert Taylor as Armand in *Camille*

at least twenty movie versions. And let's not forget *La Traviata*, the opera Verdi composed only a year after the play had its premiere—and Maria Callas, whose interpretation is the only twentieth-century one to rival Garbo's in acclaim. (Another famous Violetta at the Met was Licia Albanese, whose performance Garbo went to see a number of times, always sitting in the first row.)

George Cukor, who directed the M-G-M version—veteran of *Dinner at Eight*, *Little Women*, *David Copperfield*, and, most recently, the Norma

Shearer *Romeo and Juliet*—had both the vision and the tact to help Garbo bring out the best in herself. He appreciated "the wantonness, the perversity" of the way she played Camille, "usually a sobbing part," he said, but she played it with "enormous eroticism and boldness." He got along well with her on the set; like all her better directors he appreciated her intelligence and discipline. "I think you watch very carefully what she's doing. You make suggestions, but you let the impulse come out of her." Irving Thalberg, in charge of the production, said to Cukor when they were watching the rushes, "George, she's awfully good. I don't think I've ever seen her so good. She's relaxed. She's open. She seems unguarded for once." And Thalberg, as usual, knew what he was talking about. Of all her films, *Camille* is the one in which she seems most at ease.

The atmosphere on the set was easy, too—at least at times. Rex O'Malley, who is convincing and appealing as Gaston, the most loyal and generous of Marguerite's friends, reports, "We had lots of fun discussing our aches and pains and symptoms together." He also observed that "she doesn't act; she lives her roles. She was 'Camille' during the entire filming of the picture. Beautiful beyond words of description." Garbo was less at ease with her costar, Robert Taylor, who had just emerged into stardom—much the way Gable had six years earlier when he partnered her in *Susan Lenox*. She declined to get to know Taylor before shooting started: "Garbo didn't take much to Robert Taylor," Cukor said. "She was polite and distant. She had to tell herself that he was the ideal young man, and she knew if they became friends she'd learn he was just another nice kid." Years later she pronounced her verdict on him to a friend: "So beautiful—and so dumb."

The one thing about Taylor that everyone agreed about was that he *was* astoundingly beautiful. And young. (Twenty-six while *Camille* was shooting; Garbo was thirty-one.) But she had looked like a woman even when she was a girl, and Taylor looked like a boy even though he was a man. He was terrified at the prospect of playing opposite her, and he does a heroic job, considering that he's not very experienced and that "Armand Duval" is basically a sappy role. He seems appropriately besotted with "Marguerite," and Garbo is very generous to him in their scenes together. There are two problems, though—his diction isn't very refined, and there's no electricity

(*above*) With fellow courtesans Lenore Ulric and Laura Hope Crews; (*opposite top*) with the exigent Baron (Henry Daniell); (*opposite bottom*) with her true friend Gaston (Rex O'Malley)

between the two of them. It's love, love, love, but not much sex. Maybe he was too in awe; maybe Garbo wasn't turned on by puppies, however good-looking.

Robert Payne was particularly critical: Taylor, "grotesquely painted to resemble a male mannequin, pretty enough to decorate a chocolate box, was a pathetically insubstantial lover." I wonder, though. Going over the list of M-G-M's other male stars, you don't spot anybody who would have been as appropriate. And though he may not have *acted* Armand very well, he looked and felt like an Armand. Nor is a romantic film damaged by having a gorgeous male lead. Richard Corliss judges that Taylor is "a superb personification of the impossibly sweet Armand. Instead of imitating romance, as Fredric March had done [in *Anna Karenina*], Taylor embodies it. He helps us understand that Armand is less an archetype than an archangel—a kind of abstraction of Marguerite's last chance for love. Taylor always seems to be inhaling the fragrance of her beauty; any other air would be too polluted. If he sometimes suggests a choirboy in a bawdyhouse, it's because he's too intensely romantic to have a worldly sense of humor."

Their idyllic happiness in the country . . .

. . . interrupted by Armand's father (Lionel Barrymore)

M-G-M had done what it could to help Taylor prepare for Armand (and Garbo), assigning their leading dramatic coach to him to help pave the way. But we learn from Victoria Wilson's epic biography of Barbara Stanwyck that Taylor had another coach: Stanwyck herself. They were living together, though not yet married, and Barbara's nephew Gene, who was on summer vacation from Notre Dame and staying with her, "watched as Barbara sat with Bob, night after night, talking over the scenes, telling Bob how to say each line, [giving him] the phrasing, the emphasis, the small gestures for the next day's scenes." "What she's done for me," Taylor said, "can't be measured in ordinary terms. She's taught me more with her knowledge than I would have learned in a lifetime."

Need we say that Lionel Barrymore was his usual hammy self as Armand's father? Robert Payne again: He played the role "as though he were delivering speeches to Rotarians." Those old troupers Laura Hope Crews and Lenore Ulric (sometimes over-trouping) convey the frivolity and hardness of Marguerite's demimondaine world, and Henry Daniell (also terrified of appearing with Garbo) is a real success as the ruthless baron. M-G-M was flexing its depth of talent. Adrian, too, went all the way with his period costumes—Garbo's so various, so ornate, so heavy that she nearly fainted after being under the lights for less than an hour: They had to bring in a special icebox and wind machine to keep her going.

This was the least of the problems that beset the filming. Garbo was unwell—the assumption is that she was experiencing serious gynecological issues. William Daniels went on a three-day binge, waking up in Chicago not knowing how he had got there. And then—calamity. Suddenly, without warning, the physically fragile Irving Thalberg died, of pneumonia. He was thirty-seven. Hollywood was devastated. Cecil B. DeMille: "The passing of Irving Thalberg is the greatest conceivable loss to the motion-picture industry . . . I have long considered him the most competent and inspired producer in the business." Another competitor, Samuel Goldwyn, called him "the foremost figure in the motion-picture industry—and an inspiration." David O. Selznick: "Beyond any question the greatest individual force for fine pictures." Darryl Zanuck: "More than any other man he raised the industry to its present world prestige."

M-G-M was plunged into grief and fear—nobody knew what would happen. Another producer, Bernard Hyman, was brought in to supervise *Camille*, and he immediately demanded rewriting and reshooting that was highly costly and deeply destructive. Fortunately, wiser heads prevailed, and at great expense of time and money, the damage was undone.

Garbo herself was moved enough by Thalberg's death to actually attend his funeral, the kind of thing she almost never did. (Unless she didn't: Reports vary.) Her condition during the shooting was as usual exhausted and depressed, and Hyman's tampering made things worse. "I have never worked under conditions like these before," she wrote to Hörke Wachtmeister. "I sometimes start crying from tiredness . . . My writing's a bit confused, but what can you expect from a lady of the camellias?"

How, then, do we explain the miracle of her performance? From first to last she is exquisitely *right*. Her charm as the glittering demimondaine; her tolerant amusement at the impetuous Armand; her rapture when she acknowledges her love for him ("My heart is not used to being happy"); the loveliness of the pastoral interlude in the country; the contained despair and muted heroism when she realizes she must give up Armand for *his* sake; the wound to her heart when he publicly humiliates her; and of course the sublime death scene, when she fades away so simply and joyously in his arms—it is a seamless progression of mood and feeling, every moment subtle, true, moving. This is movie acting unmatched except by Lillian Gish (her generous mentor in her first months at M-G-M) in her greatest roles. Clearly Garbo had filled her mind and soul with Marguerite Gautier, combining impeccable craftsmanship with profound intuitive understanding; everything calculated, then forgotten in the moment when she encountered the camera and it revealed her essence.

Commentators get high-flown writing about her performance. Corliss: "Great acting such as this cannot be parsed. It can only be perceived, from a mortal distance, and treasured." Frank Nugent in *The New York Times*: "Greta Garbo's performance is in the finest tradition: eloquent, tragic, yet restrained. She's as incomparable in the role as legend tells us Bernhardt was. Through the perfect artistry of her portrayal, a hackneyed theme is made new again, poignantly sad, hauntingly lovely." Howard Barnes in the

Irving Thalberg and George Cukor

Herald Tribune: "With fine intelligence and unerring instinct she has made her characterization completely credible, while giving it an aching poignancy that, to me, is utterly irresistible . . . It is likely that Miss Garbo still has her greatest role to play, but she has made the *Lady of the Camelias*, for this reviewer, hers for all time."

And from the revered Otis Ferguson: "It is more than the distant shimmer of beauty, or a resonant husky voice, or a personal dignity wide enough for the demands of both humility and arrogance. It is more than can be measured in any of the dimensions through which we receive it, because sound waves and planes of light are only a medium of reflection for the regions of the spirit concerned here. Greta Garbo has the power of projecting not only the acting moods of a play but the complete image of her own person; and seeing her here, one realizes that this is more than there are words for, that it is simply the most absolutely beautiful thing of a generation."

There were dissenters, or at least one—the highly intelligent (and skeptical) Cuban critic G. Cabrera Infante, writing in 1956 under the heading "Camille Coughs": "*Camille* is the same banal tearjerker over which our mothers cried . . . For Garbo—too tall and too strong, with a voice more imperious than clamorous, at times elegant like a Swedish peasant girl dressed by Dior, at others like a man in drag—it was not the appropriate role." Yet "*La* Garbo succeeded toward the end of the film—in the first part she limited herself to gurgling with her guttural laugh and to showing her

long neck of a robust swan who dies hard. But beyond the cough and the falsely muted voice there is the mask of tragedy: the death of Marguérite is an affecting arpeggio and her fall has the silky mourning of a shroud."

William de Mille—Broadway playwright, Hollywood writer and director, brother of Cecil—had a more practical take on things: "A proof of Garbo's conscientiousness in all matters concerning her work is to be found in one of her more recent films, 'Camille.' In this film the lady deliberately lost twenty pounds during the course of its shooting, in order to make more convincing the heroine's decline in health. Here, at least, is one advantage the screen has over the stage, as no 'Camille' in the theater's history has ever been able to die at eleven o'clock weighing twenty pounds less than she did at eight-thirty; and even if she could, the lost displacement would have to be regained by the following evening. Under such circumstances the very thought of a matinée-day is staggering."

Another staggering thought: From Wilson's Stanwyck biography we learn that "the actors and crew set up a softball team, called the Camillas.

(*opposite top*) Armand bitter and angry; (*opposite bottom*) Armand and the faithful Nanine (Jesse Ralph) supporting her; (*above*) dying in his arms. (These are post-production shots, not stills.)

Garbo was their sponsor and stood at the baseline coaching her players and telling them how they should play their positions. Taylor played second base." Garbo coaches!

FROM THE HEIGHTS of *Camille* the only direction to go was down. Among the many things wrong with *Conquest*—and there *are* many—the most risible is the matter of accents. Garbo ("Countess Marie Walewska") talks with her now standard modulated Swedish/European. (She's supposed to be Polish, but who knew the difference?) Her equally Polish husband, Count Walewski, is played by the quintessentially upper-class British Henry Stephenson. Her callow Polish brother is played by the quintessentially all-American Leif Erickson. Napoleon is played by Charles Boyer with a French accent so thick that at times you can't make out what he's saying, although his mother, the formidable Madame Buonaparte, is acted by the very British Dame May Whitty—the unforgettable Miss Froy of Hitchcock's *The Lady Vanishes*.

For accent connoisseurs, the icing on the cake is the count's ancient sister, the Countess Pelagia, as rendered by the ultra-Russian over-the-top-of-the-top Maria Ouspenskaya, who knew only one language—Ouspenskaya-speak—and deployed it whether she was meant to be Russian, Austrian, French, Indian, Chinese, or Gypsy, as in her chef-d'oeuvre, *The Wolf Man*. It doesn't really matter, because the message is always the same: "Don't fuck with Ouspenskaya!"

What else went wrong? First things first: the story, such as it was. (Actually, it was a concept more than a story.) Patriotic Polish nobles convince Madame Walewska to give in to the emperor's importunate advances so that she can then convince him to liberate Poland. ("The Destiny of Poland is in your hands.") She resists and resists, but—even more a patriot than a loyal and loving wife—she finally consents.

Of course she and Napoleon fall in love, and she bears him an illegitimate son, but before too long she grows disillusioned over what she had managed to believe were his democratic impulses. He has sacrificed his noble ideals for the sake of POWER! ("Power has conquered you!") And to secure the Royal Succession, he has married the Hapsburg Archduchess Maria Louisa, daughter of the Empress Maria Theresa, setting up the only witty line in the movie: "The liberator of Europe has become a son-in-law." Even so, when Napoleon is exiled, Marie rushes to Elba with her little boy. Waterloo soon intervenes, however, so their reunion cannot be permanent.

The opening scene is effective—drunken Russian troops invade the Walewski chateau, slinging priceless furniture and art into the fire, smashing chandeliers left and right, and terrifying plump servant girls. But that's it for exciting action. It is after this that, in the snow, the emperor first spies Marie, who is hovering around determined to catch a glimpse of her hero. "Are you real," the emperor wonders, "or born of a snowdrift?"

Since Napoleon is always off to another triumph and/or residence, and Marie is always following him for another touching reunion, the movie is inescapably episodic: Title cards announce, "Two years have passed" or "Four years have passed." There are extended ballroom scenes, beautifully dressed

Conquest: in the snow, where Napoleon first sees her

in the grand M-G-M manner, but we don't get to see the emperor at war except when he's trudging back from Russia with his defeated army through yet more snow. Waterloo itself is represented by a pen falling on a map.

Various commentators have remarked that for the only time in her career, Garbo in *Conquest* is overshadowed by her leading man, but I don't see it that way. Boyer is certainly the finest actor she ever played with apart from Barrymore, but he doesn't dominate the screen, and though they liked each other very much off-camera, their love scenes have no electricity. He, very much a Frenchman, was extremely nervous about portraying Napoleon, and the writers didn't give him a very coherent Napoleon to portray. Of course Boyer is always intelligent and usually interesting, but although he was nominated for an Oscar (she wasn't), this is not his finest hour. S. N. Behrman, one of the countless writers on the film, wrote, "One may study

With Charles Boyer as Napoleon in a (rare) happy moment

even the final shooting script and see that the Emperor is not fully or satis-factorily developed, not as the Countess is. What Charles Boyer accomplishes in his portrayal is the issue of his own intelligence and his own magic. He didn't have a lot of help from the script, although he had help, or inspiration, from Garbo."

With the dread Maria Ouspenskaya

Garbo herself is generally languid, radiant in her rare happy moments but without a real character to embody or arc to follow. She was ill through much of the endless filming, missing nineteen days of work, and she was confused, having told a friend that "she didn't have the slightest idea of what this story is all about or who the hell Marie Walewska is." When she was on the set she was, as usual, good-natured, even playful, and her focus never dissipates, but the reality is that she had nothing to play. "Madame Garbo's elegant anemia, I fear, can pall a little here," is the way *The New Yorker* put it. Barry Paris put it another way: "The script, the censors, and Clarence Brown's direction had combined to achieve the impossible: to make Garbo uninteresting." Graham Greene, then a film critic, chimes in with his usual acuity: "She has been badly served, of course, by writers and producers. They seem to feel that the films are unworthy of so superb an actress, and in compensation they treat her with deathly reverence . . . So we are given *Queen Christina*, *Marie Walewska* [*Conquest*]: fake history, masquerades in fancy-dress, dialogue written in the conventional rhetoric of the middlebrow historical novelist. But there's no satisfactory half-way house between poetic and realistic drama: if you can't give Garbo poetry to speak, you ought to give her prose. 'I kiss the hand which refused to sign away our country's independence'—that isn't prose."

Conquest, deploying seventeen writers (including Behrman, the clever poet/screenwriter Samuel Hoffenstein, and, officially, Salka) dragged on through 127 days of shooting and cost M-G-M more than any movie had ever cost before: $2.7 mil-

With Charles Boyer

lion, half of which the studio failed to recoup, despite the large Garbo market in Europe, where it was called *Marie Walewska*. (Among the countless other titles considered: *The Woman Before Waterloo*, *Less than the Dust*, and *Sands of Glory*.) It was the only real money-losing film of Garbo's career. In a letter to the *Motion Picture Herald*, an exhibitor in Columbia City, Indiana, pronounced its epitaph: "The costliest picture Metro has produced, and I credit that they poured the jack into this epic. But the film did not do any business here. It died here, and the bankers will be moving in on Metro. It is a super colossal magnifico—but a dog at the box office."

WHAT NEXT? When Garbo was interviewed in Sweden in early 1938, she reported, "No, I am not going to play Joan of Arc . . . I am tired of period pictures and I want to do something modern now. My next film is to be a comedy." When the reporter asked whether, as usual, the film would have a sad ending, she responded, "Will I be allowed to keep my lover in it? Certainly I am hoping so. Don't you think it is high time they let me end a picture happily with a kiss? I do. I seem to have lost so many attractive men in the final scenes."

Before she could get to that kiss, however, there would be many paths not taken. Salka, always urging the high road, was convinced, and convinced Greta, that she should play Madame Curie. A script was commissioned from Aldous Huxley—even classier than Somerset Maugham!—but the studio nixed it. (Five years later, M-G-M would triumph with *Madame Curie*, with Greer Garson and without Huxley.) Garbo had told Huxley that she'd like to play St. Francis of Assisi. "And do you wish to enact the part of St. Francis himself?" "That is correct." "What! Replete with beard?" After endless palaver, she and the studio settled on *Ninotchka*.

To think about *Ninotchka* clearly, you have to get past all the hullabaloo surrounding "Garbo Laughs!" It made for a great ad campaign, but it was baloney—Garbo had laughed in many of her films, both silent and sound. Even so, there was (and still is) dispute over whether the laugh we hear when "Leon" tips over backwards in his chair in a Paris bistro is really her own or was patched in by the studio after the event. Cynics say you can tell it was a fake from the imperfect lip-synching. *I* say that (a) Garbo could do anything she wanted to for the camera and, besides, was known as a hearty laugher, and (b) if M-G-M was clever enough to lip-synch her, they were clever enough to do it right. (Billy Wilder, one of the scriptwriters, commented years later that the idea was absurd. "There was no need. Her real laugh was wonderful.")

In fact, M-G-M got just about *everything* right in *Ninotchka*, starting with bringing Garbo and Ernst Lubitsch together for the first (and, alas, only) time. They had been circling each other forever. In 1929—almost ten years earlier—after seeing Lubitsch's wonderful *The Love Parade*, Garbo impulsively drove to a florist, bought a huge bunch of roses, and delivered

GRETA GARBO in "NINOTCHKA"
An ERNST LUBITSCH Production
with Melvyn Douglas · Ina Claire
Screen Play by Charles Brackett,
Billy Wilder and Walter Reisch
Based on the Original Story by
Melchoir Lengyel · Directed by
Ernst Lubitsch.

GARBO GETS THE LUBITSCH TOUCH!

See it and you'll shout from the house-tops!

Garbo flirts—Garbo dances—Garbo drinks—Garbo howls—Garbo romances—Garbo kisses—Garbo hits the Paris hot spots, laughing, loving in the saucy, racy Lubitsch comedy of Paris in the wonderful days when a siren was a brunette and if a Frenchman turned out the light it was not on account of an air raid. Start telling your patrons now and don't stop!

"NINOTCHKA"
— don't pronounce it — SEE IT!

214

(*previous spread*) *Ninotchka* trade ad that appeared in the *Motion Picture Herald*; (*above*) she is a commissar from Russia, Melvyn Douglas is a French count; (*opposite*) with the three feckless Soviet functionaries who have preceded her to Paris: Alexander Granach, Sig Rumann, and Felix Bressart

them herself to Lubitsch's house. Three years later, she dropped in again to introduce Mercedes de Acosta to him. "Mein Gott, mein Gott, Greta! Greta, Greta, sit down and never go away. Greta, why don't you tell those idiots in your studio to let us do a picture together? Gott, how I would love to direct a picture for you!" "Ernst," she replied, "*you* tell them. I am far too tired to have a conversation with any studio executive." And so it went.

By 1938, once it was resolved that it was time for her to do a comedy, the question was, What comedy? A screenwriter named Melchior Lengyel was asked to come up with a notion for one, and a day or two later he scrawled on a piece of paper, "Russian girl saturated with Bolshevist ideals goes to fearful, capitalistic, monopolistic Paris. She meets romance and has an up-roarious good time. Capitalism not so bad after all." "I like it. I will do it," said Garbo. M-G-M gave Lengyel fifteen thousand dollars for the idea and got him started on a script. He was only the first of many credited (and uncredited) writers, including Behrman, Salka, Samuel Hoffenstein, and the team of Ben Hecht and Charles MacArthur, before Lubitsch—who had signed a two-movie deal with M-G-M (the second would be *The Shop Around the Corner*)—took over with his writing team of Charles Brackett, Billy Wilder, and Walter Reisch. With lots of input from . . . Ernst Lubitsch.

In the time-honored tradition of Hollywood, there had been many bad ideas floated and false starts made and inadequate scripts written before what we now see as inevitable took place: the happy marriage of Garbo, Lubitsch, and *Ninotchka*. First of all, he knew how to treat her, almost paying court to her on and off the set to help her overcome her nerves—this, after all, was her first comedy. He understood her, he was patient with her, and after she hinted to him that he was just a little too noisy and excitable for her, he calmed himself down. And, of course, his ideas were dazzling.

Garbo and stage star Ina Claire spar over diamonds and Melvyn Douglas.

"I love to work with her," he told a reporter. "She's got no phoniness, no star allures. She is the only star I ever worked with I did not have to drag away from the mirror." When he was asked why he had wanted Garbo in a comedy, he said, "Because she was funny. You couldn't see it? You didn't know how funny she was off the screen? . . . Some of them are so heavy. Heavy! But she was light, light always, and for comedy nothing matters more." And, he went on, "She had the most beautiful smile—what am I saying? She had a whole collection of smiles—warm, motherly, friendly, polite, sexy, mysterious."

None of them turns up in *Ninotchka* for a long time. Garbo herself doesn't turn up for a long time—her three renegade colleagues from Moscow first have to be seen in their swank Paris hotel, leading the life of Riley. When she finally enters the movie (at the train station; think *Love* and *Anna*

Karenina, think *Flesh and the Devil*) she's so commissarish that you can't imagine her smiling, let alone laughing. Paris, Melvyn Douglas, champagne, a frivolous hat, *love* will change all that. What makes *Ninotchka* so enchanting is the way Garbo depicts that change, delicately revealing the loving heart beating inside the commissar.

One also has to salute the contribution made by Melvyn Douglas as Leon (Count Leon d'Algout), the suave half-conman, half-gigolo, all-lover who falls for her. They had hoped for Cary Grant, but that would have skewed the picture badly: It would have been about Garbo and Grant. Whereas the story is about Ninotchka, not Ninotchka and Leon. Douglas is exactly right—a superb leading man but not a true star. He's a strong presence, though, and he handles the dialogue perfectly. Leon: "Am I repulsive to you?" Ninotchka: "No, your skin is good. The whites of your eyes are clear and the cornea is excellent." Leon: "*Your* cornea is terrific!" And he's masculine, which makes you believe that he can help her be feminine.

Slowly, inevitably, Ninotchka melts. She is loyal to her country, to her training (she's been a sergeant in the cavalry, with a wound to show for it), but she can't help it—she's in love. You see her blossom. You see her bloom.

Happy—and a little tipsy

You see her start to care about how she looks. (Gorgeous, even in her severe Bolshevik outfits—maybe *more* so than in her later French fashions.)
You see her tipsy! When the plot thickens, you see her retreat, regroup, and
walk away from love. She's more moving in these scenes than she is in most
of the tragic dramas she'd been decorating all those years. "Comrades!
People of the world! The revolution is on the march, the wars will wash
over us, bombs will fall, all civilization will crumble—but not yet, please—
wait, wait—let us be happy—give us our moment!" Corny to read, maybe,
but not as spoken by Garbo.

Garbo and her three comic colleagues from Russia are in Paris to sell a
trove of imperial jewels in order to raise money to feed the starving masses.
(It was Lubitsch's brilliant choice to replace some less sexy transaction with
these jewels. "The nice thing about jewels is that they are photogenic. You
can photograph them sparkling on a woman's tits.") Also in pursuit of the
jewels is their previous owner, the Grand Duchess Swana—the previous
owner of Leon, too. Here we have the sophisticated Broadway star Ina

Claire, famous for her class and wit—and, as it happens, the woman John Gilbert married on impulse when Garbo refused him. How would the two women deal with each other on the set? The official story is that they got along very cordially—hard to believe—although in the script they're only one step away from a catfight. Watching their showdown, you're observing two radically different kinds of acting: Garbo, with her intuitive and apparently simple approach, and Claire, with her polished technique flashing like her jewels. This clash of styles seems appropriate, though—because, remember, Claire is a Grand Duchess and Garbo is a Daughter of the People.

Essentially what happens is that Swana gives up her claim to the jewels in exchange for Ninotchka giving up her claim to Leon by returning to Moscow, going back to her old drab but purposeful life—no champagne, no frivolous hats. No Leon. But a romantic comedy has to end happily, and in a final twist of the plot, she is reunited with him with the connivance of her three rascally Russian stooges—or are they Russian Marx Brothers? Or Ritz Brothers? The denouement (in Constantinople!) takes place so quickly and preposterously that it's clear that neither Lubitsch nor anyone else took it seriously for a moment. It's pure convention, since all we actually need is a final clinch between the count and the commissar: the kiss Garbo had been waiting for. As one commentator put it, "If the film had ended on an iceberg floating in the South Pacific, we would not care and we would be equally happy."

The response to *Ninotchka* was more or less ecstatic: huge box office—more than four hundred thousand people saw it during its three-week run at Radio City Music Hall alone. The critics were euphoric, too. Howard Barnes in the *Herald Tribune* wrote, "The great actress reveals a command of comic inflection which fully matches the emotional depth or tragic power of her earlier triumphs. It is a joyous, subtly shaded and utterly enchanting portrayal . . . She floods the production with her timeless and ineffable beauty, giving a rich and haunting quality to the romantic scenes and a moving intensity to the few passages of straight drama."

Richard Corliss: "It took Garbo's artistry to find wistful wisdom in the scenarists' wisecracks and deep feeling beneath the Lubitsch touch, translating the genial aura of a superior thirties comedy into the substance of

The count falls . . .

acting and cinematic genius. The laughs we may credit to the filmmakers; the sympathetic tears we shed are for Garbo alone."

And the astute Robert Payne would point to a crucial element of *Ninotchka*'s artistic success: "It was a satire, wildly funny, totally improbable. What it satirized was Garbo herself, or rather her legend: the cold northerner immune to marriage, solemn and self-absorbed." Indeed, the script is punctuated by deliberate references to her—the way she dressed in private, the famous phrases like "I want to be alone!" "The film was gay, polished, and civilized," said Payne, "and had no message except that love-making and good food are the essential ingredients of life . . . It offered no solutions, raised no problems, asked no questions. Yet it touched one of the most unfathomable of life's mysteries—the childlike gaiety that lies somewhere at the heart of the universe."

Parker Tyler, perhaps the most elaborate (pretentious?) of film critics, summed it up this way: "How timely Hollywood was—connecting its greatest star with the destiny of hats on the eve of a war which isolated Paris from the fashion world!"

From important critics in England, two radically conflicting reactions. Pro: Dilys Powell.

Garbo at the beginning of this film is winter-bound. Love, she says, is a chemical reaction. Then in a flash the ice breaks and dissolves in a swift river; the martinet, the ex-sergeant in the Russian army, becomes a young girl, laughing at a remembered joke during the austere conference, edging shyly into her lover's room in a new hat, dancing, drinking too much champagne. This release of tenderness and warmth and gaiety is among the most moving pieces of acting I have ever seen in a film . . . I know the public today likes its favourites to be under the age of consent. Here is a last chance for audiences to show that after all they prefer a grown woman and a great actress.

. . . and Garbo Laughs!

And con: James Agate.

> I have always thought that Garbo was a great screen actress . . . Judge,
> then, of my surprise when on going to the Empire I found my hopes in
> Garbo disappointed, and my colleagues' dithyrambs wildly unfulfilled!
> For in my view, Garbo gives no performance at all. For half an hour she is
> glassy in the stereotyped Garbo fashion. And then she is supposed to
> laugh, and doesn't. She opens her mouth wide and goes through the mo-
> tions of laughing. But it is mirthless laughter, like the yawning of a
> horse . . . Then she has a long and totally unfunny drunken scene, after
> which she spends the rest of the time looking like Norma Shearer's mother!
> In my view this is the worst performance I have ever seen Garbo give.

History suggests Dilys Powell was right—today, even people to whom
"Garbo" means nothing have a great time with *Ninotchka*. As for Garbo
herself, when Lubitsch asked her what she thought of her performance she
said that she didn't know if she was bad or good. She was more definitive—
and more typically self-deprecatory—in a letter to Hörke Wachtmeister:
"My film is finished, and I'm afraid it doesn't amount to much."

EVEN SO, GARBO HAD BEEN HAPPY (FOR HER) making *Ninotchka*, but had
later turned against Lubitsch and everyone connected to him—thanks to
Salka Viertel, at least one observer believes, in revenge for her having been
dumped from the film.

It was two years before she made another movie—no one knew what to
do with her, except to put her in an American comedy, since her overseas
market was gone with the war. And where did they eventually find one? In
a play written in 1901 by the Berlin playwright Ludwig Fulda that had been
filmed (with Constance Talmadge) in a 1925 silent called *Her Sister from
Paris*. It was Salka who dug this one up when no one could think of anything better, and when she was exercising almost complete control over
Garbo's career. The credited writers were Salka Viertel, S. N. Behrman,
and George Oppenheimer—in that order.

Garbo shocks the world in *Two-Faced Woman* by doing the "chica-choca."

Poor old *Two-Faced Woman*, having had to take the blame all these years for ending Garbo's career! Well, it *wasn't* what ended Garbo's career, although she never made another movie after it. Yes, it had a mixed reception—famously, *Time* magazine said, "Its embarrassing effect is not unlike seeing Sarah Bernhardt swatted with a bladder. It is almost as shocking as seeing your mother drunk." But the severe Otis Ferguson emphasized its virtues: "It is the kind of thing whose success depends on a light touch, humor in and between the lines, and considerable invention. The invention

is there, in both situation and little touches that surprise laughter and divert attention from improbability . . . In spite of defects, the laughs keep coming. Unless you are determined to be grumpy you will probably enjoy it." Nor was it a disaster at the box office—the very small amount of money it lost was due to frantic retakes, not that they helped much.

Far more relevant than *Two-Faced Woman* to Garbo's withdrawal from the screen is the dateline of Ferguson's review: December 15,

(*above*) Uncomfortable in Melvyn Douglas's arms; (*below*) trapped in a hideous bathing suit

1941—eight days after Pearl Harbor, deep into the European war. The world had changed, foreign markets were practically gone, and Hollywood was adjusting. What could Garbo's place be in this new world that was both frighteningly grim and demanding frivolous entertainment—a world of Betty Grable and Carmen Miranda? M-G-M had done its best, successfully steering her into

romantic comedy with *Ninotchka*. But *Two-Faced Woman* wasn't romantic comedy, it was farce, and as one of her early biographers put it, "Garbo has a sense of humor but not a sense of the ridiculous."

Watching it coolly today—not in relation to Garbo's fate but as just another movie—your heart sinks. Gratifying as it would be to be able to chal-

Roland Young, Robert Sterling, Garbo, and Ruth Gordon hover over a supine Melvyn Douglas in a scene cut from the movie.

lenge history's judgment and proclaim it a misunderstood masterpiece—or even a well-made example of its genre—you can only concede that it's a ghastly mess, its only virtue: Garbo. George Cukor, who had done so well for her with *Camille*, was absurdly outside his comfort zone. *David Copperfield*, yes; *The Women*, yes; *The Philadelphia Story*, yes; coming up, *Gaslight*, *Born Yesterday*, *My Fair Lady*, and on and on. But not farce, not slapstick.

And the leading actors in support of Garbo are uniformly dreadful. Constance Bennett grimacing, sulking, bitching, yelping, clearly trying to put Garbo in the shade and undermining her in every possible way;* Melvyn Douglas, so sympathetic in *Ninotchka* just two years earlier, here reduced to

---

* She cannot have been amused that Garbo was enjoying a good-natured flinglet with her long-term lover and soon-to-be-husband, Gilbert Roland.

With Constance Bennett trying to steal the show

double-takes and pratfalls—you can't bear to see him making love to Garbo in either of her avatars, the skiing instructress Karin or her invented twin, Katherine; Roland Young with his trademark wry sophistication exaggerated until you want to kick him. And buried in the detritus, Ruth Gordon—one of the most acerbic actresses of her time—reduced to being a sweet, understanding secretary with absolutely nothing to do except be filler for a plot that doesn't hold together for a minute. (Plot: An unworldly nature-loving young woman, at home only on skis, invents a twin sister and morphs overnight into a flirtatious, champagne-loving, coutoured-up glamourpuss whom no man can resist. You see, she's fighting for her man!) As one critic put it, "Two Garbos for the price of one is none."

Since the movie doesn't know what it's doing, it keeps doing it—scenes disastrously over-extended, like the one in which "Larry" has to fakily tumble down a snow-covered mountain on skis, flailing and somersaulting for what seems an eternity. But then nothing about Larry is credible, starting with his being a successful magazine editor and notorious rake-about-town (that's where Constance Bennett comes in) who falls instantly in love with the ultra-athletic skiing instructress and marries her overnight. Adding insult to injury, the Breen Office and Cardinal Spellman (!) insisted that a scene be inserted indicating that Larry has caught on to Karin's pretending to be her own sister, so that when he takes her to bed he knows that it's really his wife he's having it off with, not her imaginary sister. Even faux-adultery is a no-no!

And Garbo? She looks great on skis and plunging into a pool in her (hideous) bathing suit, but these early stretches of the movie, when she's Karin, are forced and boring. This part of the story is designed as a reprise of Garbo-as-commissar in *Ninotchka*, but all it does is make you long for Lubitsch. Things look up momentarily when we get to New York (substituting for Paris) and Karin-as-Katherine breaks loose, dancing, getting tipsy, being sexy. You don't believe it for a moment, but it's fun seeing Garbo give it her all.

The notorious scene in the nightclub in which she dances the "chica-choca" is to my contrary mind the most appealing scene in the movie (although it, too, goes on too long). Garbo is utterly game here, even managing to suggest that she's never had a better time in her life than bumping and grinding in a tight dress. It's an Irene Dunne moment in an Irene Dunne role, the Irene Dunne of *The Awful Truth*, but Garbo's work, as always, is honorable. She's been betrayed, though—by the script, the style, Cukor, the times. Only the great Adrian took action. When he saw how badly Garbo was being dressed, he just quit: An M-G-M presenting a Garbo without real glamour was an M-G-M he wanted no part of.

Cukor plus Garbo created a masterpiece in *Camille*. Cukor plus Garbo created a disaster in *Two-Faced Woman*. He should have known better, she should have known better—after all, she chose her own vehicles (and directors). But she was thirty-six and beginning to register that she, and her face, were aging. The ignominy of *Two-Faced Woman* gave her an excuse, conscious or unconscious, to withdraw: Older-woman roles (Joan Crawford or Bette Davis roles), mother roles, cameos, were not for her.

Her mystery, her dignity, her fame intact, she removed herself from us, this late aberration of her career quickly forgotten. She would always be Camille, Mata Hari, Queen Christina, Grusinskaya, Anna Karenina, Ninotchka. And if she got a little drunk and did the chica-choca, I say hats off! After all, her first movie, *Peter the Tramp*, was a slapstick farce too—and if she didn't do a rhumba in it, she did prance around in a bathing suit.

The end of *Two-Faced Woman*—and of Garbo's career

10

GARBO GONE

S HE DIDN'T ANNOUNCE THAT SHE WAS RETIRING. She didn't *think* that she was retiring. She just stayed home. Late in 1942 she made a deal with M-G-M for a single film—she was to play a heroic nurse during the Russian-Finnish war—which was to have been titled *The Girl from Leningrad*. A few months later, however, it was called off by mutual consent. Garbo had already been paid $70,000 and was due to receive $80,000 more on completion of filming—money that under the terms of her contract she was to receive even if the movie wasn't made. When Louis B. Mayer summoned her to his office to hand her the check, she dropped it on his desk, saying, "No, Mr. Mayer, I did not earn it." Just that swiftly, her eighteen years with Metro were over, and Mayer gave orders to empty out her dressing room and get it ready for his young new sweater girl, Lana Turner. Lana, Greer, Judy, Hedy, Kate were in; Greta, Joan, Norma, Jeanette, Myrna were on their way out. No actress who began there during the silent era would survive at M-G-M.

Garbo could have survived, but probably not within the studio system. And not with her sense of who she was—and wasn't. She knew she had great beauty on the screen, and now she was sensing that her "perfect" face was beginning to lose its perfection. Elsa Maxwell reports (maybe even accurately) having observed her in a powder room "staring so intently into the mirror that she did not hear me enter. I have no idea how long she had been studying her reflection, but she shuddered suddenly and buried her face in her arms. Only she could have found a flaw in that exquisite face. Only a woman with a morbid fear of age could have failed to see that time would enhance the beauty of her classic features and magnificent bone structure. She was thirty-five and all she could see were middle-aged roles in her future." And yet anyone who goes to YouTube and looks at the camera tests she made in 1949 can see that she was still ravishing at forty-four, and that she still had the most natural and charming smile in the world.

Project after project was put before her—the profusion and variety are bewildering. A Salka Viertel script called *Women of the Sea* about a female captain of a ship in the Norwegian merchant marine? Almost, but not quite. Anna Lucasta? *The Emperor Waltz* with Bing Crosby? If not waltzing with Bing, why not Mary Magdalene in *The Scarlet Lily*? George Sand was in constant play. And Peter Pan. And Dorian Gray. And Elizabeth of Austria, for Alexander Korda. What about Blanche DuBois? The Madwoman of Chaillot? Or Clytemnestra in *Mourning Becomes Electra*, in which, at forty-two, she would have been playing the mother of Rosalind Russell, thirty-nine, who was married to Freddie Brisson, the son of her early crush Carl Brisson. And speaking of mothers, what about *I Remember Mama*? David O. Selznick wanted her for Hitchcock's *The Paradine Case*. (She's said to have sent her agent a telegram saying "No mamas. No murderers.") Clarence Brown had the notion of remaking *Flesh and the Devil* in sound, but M-G-M was not amused. Selznick proposed *Lady Chatterley's Lover*, to be made in Sweden to avoid censorship problems. Her old director G. W. Pabst wanted her for *The Odyssey*—she would be both Penelope and Circe.

One completely sensible and appropriate idea was the title role in *My Cousin Rachel*, from Daphne du Maurier's tremendous bestseller. She said yes, and the next day changed her mind: "I could never be Cornish." (Olivia de Havilland could, opposite Richard Burton.) Then another big bestseller: *Not as a Stranger*, Stanley Kramer presiding. (De Havilland again.)

Orson Welles tells us he wrote a screenplay for her and Chaplin to be called *The Loves of D'Annunzio and Duse*—"two crazy monsters, degenerate hyper-romanticism . . . but neither would do it." And speaking of Duse, Somerset Maugham was approached to "do" her for his friend Greta, but he "had too much work on hand" and suggested André Maurois. Salvador Dalí wanted her to be St. Teresa of Avila. An adaptation of *Death Be Not Proud*, John Gunther's memoir of his late son. George Sand (yet again), with Liberace to star opposite her as Chopin. ("Liberace?" she asked. "What's that? It's a restaurant?") No to Darryl Zanuck, who was determined to have her star in *Anastasia*. No to $100,000 to play Catherine the Great on TV. And then there was the idea of a film biography of Tchaikovsky, with G.G. as Madame von Meck (for a million dollars) and—guess!—Leonard Bernstein as the composer. Are we surprised that it never happened?

Tennessee Williams wrote a script called *The Pink Bedroom* for her, and in her suite at the Ritz—well-fortified with vodka—he told her all about it. "I got a bit high and began to tell her [the story] . . . She kept whispering 'Wonderful!' leaning toward me with a look of entrancement in her eyes. I thought to myself, She will do it, she'll return to the screen! After an hour when I had finished telling her the scenario, she still said 'Wonderful!' But then she sighed and leaned back on her sofa. 'Yes, it's wonderful, but not for me. Give it to Joan Crawford.'"

It was Walter Wanger—he had produced *Queen Christina* back in 1933—who came closest to bringing Garbo back to the screen. The film was to be based on the Balzac novella *La Duchesse de Langeais*, in which an obsessed general tries desperately—and futilely—to seduce a beautiful noblewoman who had evaded him years before and has now retreated to a strict Spanish convent. The story had already been filmed four times—in 1942 it starred the superb French actress Edwige Feuillère, and a 2007 version, directed by Jacques Rivette, featured Guillaume (son of Gerard) Dépardieu as the general.

Contracts had been signed, a script had been written, and in Hollywood Garbo made camera tests, including one with the superb cinematographer James Wong Howe. "I can do my own makeup, fix my own hair," she announced. Howe remembered, "The minute the cameras started rolling, she took on, oh, a wonderful feeling. You could see this creature just come alive." They worked for about an hour, and then she said, "Sufficient now?" When he nodded yes, she said, "Good. I think I go home." (In another version, "Thank you. I go back to the beach.")

Also in California she met with James Mason, who was to play opposite her, and whom she had approved. (And he, her—in 1949 he was by far the more popular of the two, and was being paid more than she was.) After the usual fumblings over script and director, it was decided that Max Ophüls would polish the Sally Benson script and direct. Ophüls, coming to America as a refugee before the war, had made the beautiful *Letter from an Unknown Woman* and, with Wanger and Mason, *The Reckless Moment*, and later would make *La Ronde*, *Lola Montès*, and *The Earrings of Madame De . . .* There couldn't have been a more suitable director for *La Duchesse* and La Garbo.

Garbo went to Rome, where the indoor scenes were to be shot and where the Italian magnates who were putting up the money wanted to meet her. And then it all began to unravel. The particulars of the financial entanglements grew more and more strained and frantic, not helped by the presence of George Schlee, the businessman who had become Garbo's constant companion and adviser, and who knew nothing about the film industry and offended everybody. Filming was postponed. Mason backed out, and Garbo nixed Errol Flynn and Louis Jourdan as possible co-stars. The Breen Office nixed the script. Sally Benson sued. Most important, the money melted away in a welter of recriminations. The Italians essentially jumped ship, and when outsiders were approached, Howard Hughes among them, and wouldn't or couldn't come to the rescue, it was over: The Duchess of Langeais was dead. Back in America, tears in her eyes, Garbo told a friend, "It was a fiasco. I will never make or try to make a motion picture again. This is the end." And, of course, it was.

Even so, offers and suggestions kept pouring in. The most intriguing was the idea of her filming a single scene—a cameo role—as the queen of Naples in Luchino Visconti's production of *In Search of Lost Time*. Alas, the money for that project also evaporated, and as Barry Paris put it, "Visconti's Proust went the way of Wanger's Balzac."

There are many theories as to why Garbo, at the age of thirty-six, stopped working. To get as far as she could from the limelight? She had no way of knowing that fans and paparazzi would continue to torment her until her death. The safety net that M-G-M had provided was gone, and *Two-*

Faced Woman had shown that she couldn't fit into standard Hollywood fare. She had no need for money, unlike so many other fading stars who *had* to keep going. And then she was *Garbo*—and a Garbo movie had to be about Garbo. She lacked that desperate drive to keep going and going; she wasn't Dietrich or Crawford or Davis. In fact, as we know, she may have loved her actual work in front of the camera, but she hated the public side of it. When she was offered a role in *Airport 1975*, her response was, "What could be worse than playing a movie star?" She knew what she was talking about: She had resisted playing that role for her sixteen years at M-G-M.

Mark Vieira explains her abdication this way: "What she chose to do at this crucial point in her career was nothing. Her resolve was frozen by a combination of sloth, dread, and narcissism. Her gifts had not enriched her emotionally; they had drained her. Now they had become a burden. She could not define them or control them. At last, in an effort to find peace, in a world that only valued her for these gifts, she abandoned them."

Her own explanation? When one day David Niven asked her, "Why *did* you give up the movies?" she "considered her answer so carefully that I wondered if she had decided to ignore my personal question. At last, almost to herself, she said, 'I had made enough faces.'"

11

GARBO ON HER OWN

FROM THE EARLY THIRTIES ON, Garbo was no longer ruled by M-G-M—she made the choices and set the rules. By this time, everyone knew that she didn't play the Hollywood game, either professionally or privately. As her fame grew, her aversion to public exposure grew as well and she went into hiding. Except when she *wasn't* hiding. She was at home, and at ease, at Salka's. She went to dinners, although her hosts never knew whether she would turn up, or when, or in what mood. One meticulous biographer, Norman Zierold, tells us, "The number of gatherings attended by Garbo was in fact astonishing. It is hard to find anyone who was in Hollywood during the thirties who doesn't have a story to tell about Garbo at a large party, or an intimate dinner, or a spontaneous drop-in-affair." She was, as one wit put it, "a hermit-about-town." She went to the movies, although usually she had her driver let her out of the car a few blocks from the theater and would slouch into it with her hat pulled down over her face. She went riding, she swam at the beach. Once in a while she did whatever she did with old pal Borg. Every few years she went back to Sweden and spent time with her friends—Mimi Pollack, the Wachtmeisters, Max Gumpel, Wilhelm Sörenson. (These trips, of course, ended in 1939, when war broke out, by which time she had transplanted her family to America. Not that she spent much time with them.)

She was frequently in New York, for some time living in an apartment in the Ritz, sneaking into theaters, going out to dinner and to parties (if they didn't involve meeting a lot of strangers). Richard Rodgers reports her presence at a gathering at the Waldorf: "She was exactly the opposite of everything we'd all heard about her." He played songs of his on the piano, she sat next to him and "sang along with the other people." She took little trips—to the country, to the beach. She stayed with (rich) friends. And she struggled to stay out of the limelight until, eventually, hiding from photographers, reporters, curious citizens, ducking in and out of buildings and restaurants and taxis, became a way of life.

How did the state of the world affect her? Hardly at all, apart from the years she couldn't get to Europe. Robert Payne tells us that one of the survivors of the Lincoln Brigade "described his surprise when he returned to Hollywood and discovered that Garbo insisted on giving clothes and money to all the survivors of the brigade who reached California. She entertained them, fed them, accompanied them to the Farmer's Market, asked them interminable questions." This, Payne remarks, was her only political act, although we know that in 1939 she donated $5,000 to the Finnish Relief Fund (anonymously). Was her concern for Finland a salute to Stiller's country of birth? Certainly she didn't do what just about every other Hollywood star was doing—go out on the road to sell war bonds or to entertain the troops. (What would she have done? Sing? Perform skits with Bob Hope? Kiss a lucky soldier who won a lottery?) She was often criticized in the press. (Can it be true that she refused an autograph to a soldier in uniform standing on crutches with an autograph book? Yes, it can, claimed Orson Welles, who says he was present at the occasion.) Finally, Salka to the rescue: "If anyone has made the suggestion that Garbo isn't selling bonds because her sympathies are on the wrong side, it's too preposterous even to be discussed. There are some people who just cannot face crowds, no matter for what cause. Garbo is such a person. Instead she buys many bonds herself [and] has done her utmost to help me in my work of rescuing anti-Fascist refugees from Europe."

And then, as if to counter the slander that Garbo was not wholeheartedly on the Allied side, there is the story that she was a working spy. In *A Man Called Intrepid*, William Stevenson's book about the great British spymaster William Stephenson, there are two mentions of her. Garbo, whom Stephenson knew, "had reported high-level Nazi sympathizers in Stockholm." And, Stephenson told his biographer, when he was on a mission to Stockholm he "had legitimate reasons to visit his Swedish associates and friends of Greta Garbo." Charles Higham, a notoriously less-than-reliable source and obsessed by conspiracy theories, tells us that she had become involved with Britain's secret service through Alexander Korda and "served as go-between for the British with shipping magnate Axel Johnson and members of the Swedish royal family." Higham also credits her with "helping obtain the release of physicist Niels Bohr from occupied Denmark"— so completely far-fetched a notion that it undercuts anything else he has to say. To begin with, Bohr wasn't "released": *A Man Called Intrepid* tells the gripping story of how he was extracted first from German-occupied Copenhagen to Sweden, then—at considerable peril—from Sweden to America.

Higham also wrote that Garbo "would risk her life involving herself in the mass rescue of Jews from Denmark." (If you believe that, you'll believe anything.) But it is David Bret who spins the most extended (and debatable) account of the brave actions of Mata-Garbo. He has her, among other things, telephoning Bohr to persuade him to convince the king to help save Denmark's Jews. But it's when Bret says that "capturing Bohr would have been an immense scoop for Hitler," we know we're in the realm of total confusion, given that Bohr was *in* occupied Denmark and could have been carted off to Germany at any time.

It seems likely that Garbo was useful in identifying Nazi connections in Sweden, since her world there included leading industrialists, and she would have had the cooperation of Max Gumpel and the Wachtmeisters. Beyond that we can only speculate. She did, however, tell her friend Sam Green, "Mr. Hitler was big on me. He kept writing and inviting me to come to Germany and if the war hadn't started when it did, I would have gone and I would have taken a gun out of my purse and shot him, because I'm the only person who would not have been searched." Not even her "Mysterious Lady" or her "Mata-Hari" went *that* far!

What she did do, finally, was apply for American citizenship, although that was, in biographer Karen Swenson's view, for pragmatic, not patriotic reasons—she was anxious about her (considerable) Swedish investments should the Cold War lead to Soviet aggression in the Baltic region, and she decided that "American citizenship would protect her interests best." On her forty-fifth birthday, in 1950, she signed a preliminary Petition of Naturalization, describing herself as an "unemployed movie actress." Two months later, in the Federal Building in downtown Los Angeles, she had to face a barrage of serious questions in regard to any inclinations toward Communism, and specifically about her "friend" Salka Viertel, whose left-wing views and activities were well known to the FBI. The record reports: "Miss Garbo states she does not know anything about Mrs. Virtel [*sic*] and her political beliefs, and only has dealt with her in connection with possible stories for picture making."

This less-than-loyal assertion, and the testimony of friendly witnesses, did the trick, and on February 9, 1951—wearing a spotted black veil—she took the oath of allegiance, along with 150 other applicants. Hardly necessary to say, the scene was swarming with photographers, for whom she actually agreed to pose: "All right, go ahead." Soon she would sell her Los Angeles house, pack up her belongings, and make the move to New York, which would be her home until she died.

12

GARBO AND SOME MEN IN HER LIFE

H ER PRIVATE LIFE was also going through changes. Her most publicized romantic relationship since John Gilbert began when in
1937 she met the famous conductor Leopold Stokowski, who had
asked Anita Loos to introduce them. "Stoki didn't waste much time on the
overture," Loos reported. "He got straight down to business, laying on the
charm. He told Garbo that they were destined to have a history-making romance, like Wagner's with Cosima. It was written in the stars. There was no
use their trying to escape it. The gods had made their decision. Mere mortals
could only obey." (Five days later he called Loos "to ask her a favor." Would
she "please take Garbo to Bullock's Wilshire and buy her some decent
clothes?")

Soon the destined pair were together in Italy, in Ravello, and quickly
beset by the press in the villa in which they were staying: "Four policemen
with dogs were stationed at the gates to keep invaders at bay. For the next
three weeks the couple lived like prisoners, unable to set foot outside the
grounds." Desperate, acting on Stokowski's advice, Garbo made a deal with
the reporters: If they would back off, she would give them an interview.

Their main interest was in whether Greta and Leopold were getting
married. She gave a thoughtful response: "There are some who want to get
married and others who don't. I have never had the impulse to go to the altar. I haven't many friends and I haven't seen much of the world. My friend,

Mr. Stokowski, who has been very much to me, offered to take me around and see some of the beautiful things. I optimistically accepted. I was naïve enough to think I could travel without being discovered and without being hunted. Why can't we avoid being followed and examined? It is cruel to bother people who want to be left in peace. This kills beauty for me." If she

HUNDREDS OF INTIMATE PICTURES!

Modern Screen

JUNE
10
CENTS

THE LARGEST
CIRCULATION
OF ANY SCREEN
MAGAZINE

**GARBO
FINDS
LOVE!**

GRETA GARBO
and
LEOPOLD STOKOWSKI

didn't know why, she was indeed naïve. She was the most famous woman in the world, and the most elusive; he was practically as glamorous a figure as she was, a musical giant known for his amours.

Soon they were gone from Ravello—to Capri, Naples, Tunis, then north across Europe to Sweden, where they spent a number of weeks enjoying the privacy that had evaded them in Italy, secluded on the estate called Härby that Garbo had bought two years earlier and which her mother and her brother, Sven, with his family were occupying. And then—separately—they sailed home. Stoki had had more than enough seclusion. In a surprising shipboard interview on her arrival back in New York, Garbo told the reporters who wanted to know whether she and "Stoki" were already married, "You would know all about it if we were." Would she ever marry? "If I could find the right person to share my life with, perhaps I would." So Stokowski was clearly not the right person. After they made their separate ways back to America, they seem never to have met again.

As usual, there are conflicting versions of the Greta-Stoki "romance." Maybe they didn't meet at Anita Loos's but on the set of *One Hundred Men and a Girl*, the movie he was making with Deanna Durbin, although Garbo's turning up on the Universal lot seems beyond unlikely. The more interesting question was whether the romance was sexual and their trip abroad some kind of honeymoon. Not according to those who believe the relationship was purely platonic. After their return home did they really never see each other again, or were there sporadic encounters in New York and California? We'll never know. All we do know is that after those ten months together, it was over. Stokowski went on to *Fantasia* and to marry Gloria Vanderbilt (she was twenty-one, he was sixty-three). Garbo went on to Gayelord Hauser.

They met through Mercedes. Hauser was a highly successful dietician, nutritionist, and health expert who specialized in stars. (His book *Look Younger, Live Longer* would be a tremendous success—the number-three nonfiction bestseller of 1950, and number one in 1951.) Six foot three, handsome and virile, he had lived in L.A. and Palm Springs for decades with his "manager," ex-actor Frey Brown, and soon he had revolutionized Garbo's eating habits, weaning her from her fanatical vegetarianism, adding to her diet reasonable amounts of such extravagances as bits of chicken. (She had always had stomach problems, as well as her anemia problems and ovarian problems.) It wasn't only her eating that he changed: He got her out and about—they had *fun* together. The two pairs (Gayelord and Frey, Greta and Mercedes) even did some double-dating! Greta and Gayelord traveled together—to Florida and the Caribbean, to Europe—and spent a lot of time with each other in New York. Yes, there were public rumors of a "relationship," even of marriage—rumors that suited them both, since they covered a lot of tracks and there was no danger of anything serious coming of them.

With Gayelord Hauser

The attachment to Hauser was one of the most wholesome and beneficial of Garbo's life. Naturally, he helped her in many practical ways—that was a sine qua non of Garbo friendships. For one thing, he introduced her to his own highly effective business manager and partner, Anthony Palermo, who went on handling her investments and financial affairs for years. (And for no recompense—like Harry Edington years before. Why pay?) Always cautious, always suspicious, Garbo had found in Hauser a completely disinterested, trustworthy companion; a *friend*. They remained close until his death, late in 1984. Garbo had come to spend Christmas with him, and the next day she was at his bedside when he died. He was eighty-nine, and alone—Frey had died seven years earlier. She was seventy-nine, and also alone. But then she always had been.

Well, there were moments when she wasn't *entirely* alone. For instance, on New Year's Eve, 1941, at a party in New York, she met Erich Maria Remarque, the world-famous author of the World War I novel *All Quiet on the Western Front* and, as it happens, one of Marlene Dietrich's highly publicized lovers. They spent time together in town—Julie Gilbert in her biography of him and his wife-to-be Paulette Goddard says, "He found her accessible, caring, and candid. She would call him if she wanted to see him, and then they would go off and explore New York—the galleries, the Empire State Building—and she would advise him to cut down on alcohol, to stay away from nightclubs and out of Harlem. He promised her he would try."

Erich Maria Remarque, with Billy

They met again in Hollywood, and soon they were some kind of couple, dining together, walking his Kerry Blue terriers on the beach. "They laughed, talked, hugged, kissed, and to top off the walk, Garbo would do a handstand in the middle of the road." ("Every dog in the road knows her," he would remark.) Remarque was handsome, glamorous, amorous, and straight. That he drank was really irrelevant; that he was cultured was not. Here was a man who could talk to her about literature and, more important, about art. (His famous collection included three Cézannes.) Dietrich was furious. Did that add to Garbo's fun?

In his journal, Remarque described their first sexual encounter. After a candlelit dinner at his place they went upstairs: "She entered the bedroom, the light of the dressing room behind her, softly flowing over her shoulders, enchanting her outline, the face, the hands, the trembling, something imperceptible shook her, then the voice . . . the absence of any form of sentimentality or melodrama—and yet full of warmth." Well, he was a novelist. The relationship slowly petered out. Happy memories, though apparently he told Paulette that Garbo was "lousy in bed." A novelist, but not a gentleman.

It didn't matter. Garbo was too involved by this time with another man, a man who would dominate her life from 1942, when they met, to 1964, when he died. George Schlee, born sometime between 1895 and 1901, had fought with the White Russians after the Revolution and then had to get out of Bolshevik Russia. The story goes that in the railway station of Sevastopol, in the Crimea, he came upon the young and beautiful Valentina Sanina, also fleeing (with her jewels), who had been born sometime between 1901 and 1904. (Or a lot earlier. Scrupulous biographer Hugo Vickers thinks she might have been considerably older than that: "One document suggests she was born on 18 April 1889—someone crossed that out and put 1899. When I saw her a lot in Venice in 1983, she must have been 84 and it would not entirely surprise me had she been 94.") Valentina and Schlee joined forces, she telling him, "I can't give you love, but if you want friendship, then I'll marry you." Presumably she couldn't give him love because her preference was for women, Mercedes undoubtedly one of them.

Having arrived in New York in the early twenties, the Schlees (if, indeed, they were legally married; no one really knew) rapidly established themselves in society, and Valentina began her American life first as an actress, then as an ultra-fashionable couturière. She opened her first salon in 1924 and four years later launched Valentina Gowns. One thing that's certain is that she was an exceptionally talented designer, and George skillfully attended to the business side of things. Valentina dressed Gloria Swanson, Katharine Hepburn (she did all the clothes for *The Philadelphia Story* on Broadway), the Duchess of Windsor, Queen Marie of Romania, Lynn Fontanne, Norma Shearer, Rosalind Russell, Vivien Leigh, Mary Martin, and Gertrude Lawrence, as well as women from a different stratum of New York Society: Mrs. John Hay Whitney, for one, and according to Karen Swenson, "The names Astor, Vanderbilt, Mellon and McCormick could also be found in her appointment book." "There was nothing grander than a simple Valentina dress," said Irene Selznick.

It was Gayelord Hauser who brought Garbo to Valentina's showroom in January 1942, determined to improve her public look. At the first fitting session, apparently, Schlee walked in from a back room to find a completely naked Garbo. Maybe. When they did meet, with or without clothes on, it was love at first sight, or at least a powerful and irresistible connection. Valentina was a sophisticated woman—a caustic wit as well as a famous designer. (Among her legendary pronouncements: "Mink is for football." "Ermine is for bathrobes." "Children are for the suburbs.") Certainly she was delighted to add Garbo to her clientele.

At first the Schlees and Garbo were a public threesome—sometimes with George walking in the middle and the two women wearing identical Valentina gowns. That ended when Schlee essentially took Garbo over. He

(*above*) Valentina Schlee; (*opposite top*) Schlee and Valentina; (*opposite bottom*) Schlee and Garbo

arranged her life for her, making plans and carrying them out. They were everywhere together, after the war traveling incessantly, Garbo his passport into the world of international celebrity and money. Probably with her money he bought an elaborate villa called Le Roc in Cap d'Ail, a few miles from Monte Carlo, where they stayed for long stretches of time every summer. Unfortunately, he not only oversaw her finances—successfully—but tried to manage her film career: disastrously, as when he interfered with the professionals during the *Duchesse de Langeais* fiasco. Among the many people who disliked him was Truman Capote, who told Hugo Vickers, "George Schlee was an absolute bastard. He was so unattractive, so grotesque, he was extremely ugly. I could not understand what it was all about, yet he had a hold on Valentina and Garbo."

Schlee was domineering, possessive, jealous, but Garbo was clearly relieved to have a worldly and capable man take care of her affairs, escort her everywhere, plan her life, protect her. A friend of hers, Nicholas Turner, said, "He had absolute control. When he didn't want to do something, they didn't do it. No matter how she felt about it . . . She liked very much to get compliments from men. This made Schlee very upset. He was as jealous as the devil. I don't think he could tolerate having her exposed to other people, especially interesting or attractive men. Whenever that happened—and it happened several times [on the cruise they had all been on together]—he would invent some excuse for

Garbo's home in New York

cutting the trip short . . . so we would put into a port, and they would hire a car to take them back to their place. She never objected, never said a contrary word. Schlee dominated her completely." Some people felt that she found in him an echo of Stiller, whom he even slightly resembled. And the consensus is that they weren't lovers—another echo of her relationship with Stiller.

Their life together grew more complicated when in 1953 she finally settled down in a permanent home, buying an apartment in New York at 450 East Fifty-Second Street, a cul-de-sac between First Avenue and the East River— the building in which Schlee and Valentina lived. ("I had a hard time getting this apartment. They don't like actresses in this building.") She was on the fifth floor, they were on the ninth—a convenient arrangement, no doubt, although in 1947 Noël Coward in his diaries wrote, "Drinks with Valentina, who bared her soul a little over George and Garbo. Poor dear, I am afraid she is having a dreary time." But war didn't break out between the two women until George's death, years later. Garbo and Schlee were in Paris, at the Crillon, after their annual stay at Cap d'Ail. Late one evening in October 1964, George, whose health had been deteriorating, felt restless and went out for a walk, was struck by a heart attack, and was dead when he arrived at the hospital. Greta received a call from a man whose French she could not understand and had him call her great friend Cécile de Rothschild, with whom she and George had just had dinner. It was Cécile who broke the terrible news to Greta, and she who spirited Greta out of the Crillon and into hiding.

Valentina—the grieving widow—arrived at once from New York and

The Villa Le Roc at Cap d'Ail

told Greta to disappear. "He's my husband, what are you doing here?" Her rage, long bottled up, expressed itself in highly dramatic (you might say demented) ways. She insisted that the groundskeepers at the Westchester cemetery where George was buried prevent Greta from visiting his grave, not that there is a record of her ever attempting to do so. She not only wiped all traces of Greta from the Villa Le Roc but had the grounds and building exorcised, and then put on the market. A Russian Orthodox priest was also summoned to the Schlee Fifty-Second Street apartment to exorcise "that vampire." (He even exorcised the fridge, into which Garbo in the old days would reach for a can of beer.) And for the next twenty-five years the widow and the vampire tormented each other (and the building's employees) with their elaborate ruses to avoid bumping into each other in the elevator or the lobby. When occasionally they did cross paths, apparently Valentina stared and Garbo shrank away.

In the immediate aftermath of Schlee's death, Garbo was inconsolable and kept herself isolated. Eventually she managed to go out for a walk, accompanied by her friend Raymond Daum. "At one point," he would report in his 1991 book, *Walking with Garbo*, she "sighed deeply, and her eyes filled with tears. 'Everyone I love dies.'"

❖13❖

GARBO, MONEY, AND ART

GARBO, WHO HAD GROWN UP IN SEVERE POVERTY, spent the rest of her life anxious about money. Although her earnings grew to astronomical levels, she remained parsimonious—ungenerous, really—in small matters. One example of her obsessive behavior can stand for all. Just back in New York from Sweden, she had some Swedish money left over that she wanted to convert and asked her old M-G-M publicist pal Hubert Voight to take care of it for her. But "when I reported that the only way I could cash it at that time of night, was to lose one-twentieth of its value," she chose to stay in New York over the weekend in order to get the full value of her currency during regular banking hours on Monday. The difference, Voight tells us, was about four dollars. Nothing changed as she grew richer and richer: Her annual Christmas tip to the doormen at Fifty-Second Street stayed twenty-five dollars for thirty-seven years.

She was equally cautious about large financial matters, except when she decided to splurge, as she did when she bought Härby (though Härby was also a practical solution for dealing with her mother and brother) or when she dived into the art market. Stories proliferate of how she dickered with tradespeople, of how she avoided paying admission fees. And of how she used experts like Harry Edington and Anthony Palermo to transact her business affairs without compensation, and benefited from advice on investments and real estate, both in America and Sweden, from her rich and astute friends and connections.

Even after she won her salary battles with M-G-M she felt financially under siege, and at least once with cause. In the early thirties, when she had something between $300,000 and $400,000 in the bank, she was badly hurt when the supposedly rock-solid First National went under. Mercedes de Acosta tells us that she and Greta sneaked into the bank's vaults and made off with securities that were hidden in Greta's safe-deposit box. Not only that, but Mercedes sent a long telegram to President Herbert Hoover:

> please forgive me for bothering you at the moment when you have so much on hand but much is at stake. as you no doubt know the first national bank of beverly hills closed last week in which the film star greta garbo had all her money. i consider much grave dishonesty surrounds her. she is a child and incapable of taking care of herself. i have wired the swedish ambassador mr bostrom to protect her and hope you will communicate and advise him.

This message was actually passed along to the State Department; we are left to imagine its reaction, as well as Ambassador Boström's.

The timing of this disaster was particularly tricky, since Edington was deep in negotiations with M-G-M and didn't want them to know that Garbo was in a vulnerable situation. But with her salary raised to $250,000 a movie, Garbo was soon back on solid financial ground—in 1932 her earnings were $312,000, at a time of low taxes and, in her case, modest expenses. To her credit, despite her anxieties about her finances she never deviated from certain principles, never, for instance, cashing in on the endless potential sources of extra income—like sponsoring commercial products, from soap to cigarettes—that almost every Hollywood star indulged in.

In 1941 she bought a house—she had been renting house after house for fifteen years as she obsessively sought greater and greater privacy—and then three years later she bought a grander one, on Bedford Drive in Beverly Hills. But by then she was spending more and more of her time in New York, where until she acquired the apartment on Fifty-Second Street, she stayed either in apartments belonging to friends like Sam Behrman or in apartments friends found for her in which she could stay rent-free. Or she lived in hotel suites. Berthold Viertel angrily described what she endured at the St. Moritz.

> The lobby, all exits, the surrounding streets were occupied every day and night hour by storm troops—admirers and reporters—who chased the artist everywhere. There was no lack of noble and discreet sympathy . . . even among the hotel personnel, although all of them—elevator boys, newsstand vendors, florists, ticket agents, room service waiters and telephone operators—had been induced with large tips to be private detectives. It is impossible to take this incredible affair lightly or as being humorous. Impossible to negotiate or pacify. Only one thing remained: flight, head over heels, through secret corridors, over back stairs, through side doors as in a mystery novel.

It was in New York, in the early forties, that Garbo plunged into the art world (or art business). Barbara Barondess MacLean claimed to be the person who, in November 1942, masterminded her first purchases: two important Renoirs. Barondess had been a minor Hollywood actress who had appeared in a minor role in *Queen Christina* and apparently had resented Garbo ever since. ("I think she was the dullest woman I ever met." "She used people and never gave anything back.") Giving up on the movies, she became a highly successful interior-decorator-to-the-stars in Hollywood who then moved to New York. Despite MacLean's claim, according to a Sotheby's expert Garbo just walked into a gallery and asked about a painting on display, Renoir's *Enfant assis en robe bleu*, whereupon the great collector Albert Barnes turned up and said to her, "Young lady, you won't go far wrong with that painting." And then, we're told, he took her to Philadelphia and showed her his private gallery of Impressionist art. "In two days," as Karen Swenson puts it, "she learned most everything she needed to know about buying art."

Within a month she bought three Renoirs and a beautiful Bonnard, though since she as yet had no permanent home in New York in which to hang her new purchases, she stored them in a closet back in Beverly Hills. Later she would acquire two Rouaults, a Kandinsky, and a group of violent paintings by the Expressionist Alexej von Jawlensky that she described as "horror things." "I don't know who the hell else would buy [them] . . . I'll probably regret it. No. They're my colors. I do like it: they're my colors."

Art on view before the Sotheby's Garbo sale

And indeed color seems to have been her chief criterion for art. As Barry Paris says, "She loved salmon, pink, and rose, of which there was a great preponderance not only in her paintings but in her living quarters. Walls, curtains (often drawn over the Renoirs), Savonnerie carpets, upholstery— everything was coming up rose or shades thereof . . . Blues and greens, by and large, need not apply."

According to Cecil Beaton's diaries, she said to him about the Renoirs and the Bonnard and one of the Rouaults, "I bought them as an investment before I knew anything much about painting. They're rather boring ones, I think." She explained to Sam Green that many of her paintings were wrapped up in cheesecloth because "I would just have to wrap them up again when I go away."

Clearly, by this point Garbo did not have to worry about money. With Palermo's help, her money was safely tucked away in real estate, investments, and art. And these investments were providing her with a considerable annual income—from property she had bought on Rodeo Drive in Beverly Hills alone she was receiving $10,000 a month. She had money and/or securities sequestered in various places, and much of the time as she progressed around the world she was living at other people's expense. Even so, she would hesitate over buying a sweater that might prove unnecessary. You never knew . . .

When she died, in 1990, her estate was estimated to be worth $55 million. (At the highly publicized auction of her effects held at Sotheby's, her paintings and all the rest brought in $19 million.) Another estimate was $32 million, plus hidden trusts, et cetera. Everything went to her niece, Gray Reisfield, who had looked after her in her final years—Garbo specifically cut out "any and all children and their descendents" of her brother, Sven, except of course for Gray. This was to thwart any possible claims from the illegitimate son Sven had fathered when Greta was a girl, plus a second one who came along years later. Among the people who were bitter about being excluded in the will was Anthony Palermo, who had dealt not only with her investments but with her banks, brokers, and insurance agents. It was practically a full-time job. "I worked for her for fourteen years for nothing because I was promised to be in the will." Barbara MacLean complained bitterly as well, asserting that she had received no commission for her role in introducing Garbo to Renoir. With Garbo, in the end, only family mattered.

⇥14⇤

GARBO AND BEATON

T
HE THREE LONGEST-RUNNING RELATIONSHIPS in Garbo's life—
her friendship with Mimi Pollack was primarily epistolary after
Garbo left for Hollywood, and by the mid-thirties was essentially
pro forma—were with Salka Viertel, which never soured; with Mercedes
de Acosta, which was both tragedy and farce; and with Cecil Beaton, the
famous British society photographer. How to describe it? On-again, off-
again? Her weakness, his fantasy?

He was born in 1904, a year before Garbo, into a modestly well-to-do
English merchant family, went to Harrow and Cambridge, and quickly established himself as a fashion (and fashionable) photographer in both England and America, where he was on the payroll of both *Vanity Fair* and
Vogue. He was handsome, gay, a fashion plate, snobbish, ferociously ambitious, and his greatest ambition, almost from the start, was to know, photograph, befriend—and marry—Greta Garbo.

Cecil was in Hollywood in 1930, taking pictures of the stars and writing
about them, and trying as hard as he could to meet Greta. No go. Even so,
he wrote a sketch of her that appeared later that year in his *The Book of
Beauty*. Two years later he was back and futilely trying again to meet her
until one Sunday afternoon she turned up at the house of Edmund Goulding (who was directing *Grand Hotel*), where he was a weekend guest.
Quickly he changed into one of his chicest outfits: white kid jacket, white

shirt, sharkskin shorts. "But you are so beautiful," she said to him (he reports in his journal). Instantly they were best pals ("We talked nonsense as if we had known one another forever"), and soon they were upstairs in his bedroom, where he was showing her pictures of his lovely house in the English countryside (later owned by Madonna). He kissed her, he told his journal. Then he was off to England and she was off to *As You Desire Me*.

Several years later he wrote about her again, in a long profile that appeared first in *The Sketch*, then, in 1937, in his *Cecil Beaton's Scrapbook*. It was, of course, highly flattering, but it also cut close to the bone.

> She has a sense of humor, a sense of fun, but she is unhappy, neurasthenic, morbid, for she has become, by accident, something she never wished to be. A healthy peasant girl has been publicized as an exotic spy. She must lose weight, not even touch carrots—so that not even her health but her nerves have suffered from the worries of publicity. If she is seen hurrying down a side alley, she is chased for a story, and this perpetual hunting so haunts her that, being highly strung, she starts to cry and will lock herself away from even the maid for days on end. She is even too nervous to read.
>
> For these reasons she cannot develop as a person. It is well and good to safeguard herself against the bad influences of Hollywood life, but Garbo has now become unreceptive to anything except herself, so that even when she takes her periodical holidays they are not experiences for her. She is not interested in anything or anybody in particular, and she has become as difficult as an invalid and as selfish, quite unprepared to put herself out for anyone; she would be a trying companion, continuously sighing and full of tragic regrets; she is superstitious, suspicious and does not know the meaning of Friendship; she is incapable of love.

He must have known Garbo would see these words—she was a devout reader of anything written about her—and they are hardly the words of a wooer. Here speaks a spurned lover. And yet he persisted, more ardently than ever, after the war. In 1946, in New York, she asks him to photograph her for the passport she was hoping to receive as a new American citizen. "At first she stood stiffly to attention, facing my Rolleiflex full-face as if it were a firing squad. But, by degrees, she started to assume all sorts of poses and many changes of moods. The artist in her suddenly came into flower."

The following year, she comes to his rooms at the Plaza and "her practical side came out when, touring his suite, she suddenly drew the mustard velvet curtains. I was completely surprised at what was happening & It took me some time to recover [from] my bafflement. Within a few minutes of our reunion, after these long & void periods, of months of depression &

With Cecil Beaton

doubt, we were suddenly together in unexplained, unexpected and inevitable intimacy."

Unexplained intimacy? What, in fact, explains anything at all about this peculiar relationship? Beaton's mania about marrying her must have involved a large measure of physical appeal, at least on his side—and he is quick to quote (or invent) things she said to him reflecting a strong physical attraction to him. Truman Capote, in a telephone conversation with Hugo Vickers, Beaton's official biographer, said, "He was in love with her. He certainly was. Or infatuated. A better word really. Curiously enough, Cecil was one of the few people who gave her any physical satisfaction." Vickers tells us that Cecil was aware of his sexual hold on her, and attributed it to the fact that "I am so unexpectedly violent and have such unlicensed energy when called upon. It baffles and intrigues me and even shocks her. May this last a long time." His true feelings, it seems to me, are revealed in his referring to this time with Garbo as "My greatest triumph"—it's a celebration of a victory, not of requited love. All this goes into his journals.

Cecil's obsession with Garbo over the decades suggests a serious mental imbalance. He pursues her back and forth over the Atlantic and across the continent, declaring his deathless passion and his dreams of marrying her; she skitters back and forth, at times using him almost as an errand boy— the way she used almost everybody. He's furiously jealous of George Schlee, and frightened of him—sympathetic to the more and more needy and bruised Mercedes de Acosta. Finally, in the fall of 1951 he persuades Garbo to come for a long visit to Reddish House, his beautiful place in Wiltshire. She enjoys it there, gets along well with the housekeeper and staff (does not get along well with Cecil's mother and sisters, who refer to her as "that woman"), accompanies Cecil on a round of visits to local luminaries like Augustus John and Clarissa Churchill (soon to be Eden). The distinguished biographer James Pope-Hennessy comes to stay and writes to a friend, "She has the most inexplicable powers of fascination which she uses freely on all and sundry; but whether it is deliberate or not nobody knows . . . she is only explicable as a mythological creature. And then it gradually dawns on one that she is entirely uneducated, interested in theosophy, dieting and all other cranky subjects, has conversation so dull that you could scream . . . Cecil Beaton guarded her like an eagle and nobody was ever allowed alone with her."

Their "friendship," or whatever it was, proceeded in flurries. He still nourished hopes that she would settle down with him in the Wiltshire countryside, but Garbo, it now appears inevitable, would never (*could* never) settle down with anyone. After a while we begin to recognize a pattern—he pursuing, she encouraging his advances, retreating, re-emerging, tantalizing, disappointing; he protesting bitterly that she didn't take him seriously;

THREE
VERSIONS OF
GARBO
BY
CECIL BEATON

she dredging up resentments about what he had written about her in the 1930s. To the world, however, they were some kind of couple some of the time. Certainly they were seen together in New York, London, Paris, even California. But were they more to each other than a glamorous convenience punctuated, occasionally, by sexual excitement? In fact, were they even that? Garbo certainly never revealed whatever there was to reveal. As for Beaton, Vickers has concluded that the affair really did happen—that Beaton's sufferings over it were all too real, and that he had three honest ambitions for her: to get her back into films, to design her costumes, and to marry him. On the other hand, Sam Green bitchily told Vickers, "He was too star-struck to star-fuck."

Inevitably, the relationship withered away. Cecil was caught up in work, and of course he got fed up in Paris wanting to do interesting things while she mused about which coat to wear. She had nothing of consequence to do, and he was not only busy photographing the great and the near-great (including—frequently, and to his immense gratification—the royal family) but also designing for the stage and screen, climaxed by his triumphs with *My Fair Lady* and *Gigi* (Oscars for both), as well as conducting his many friendships and romances. Greta, in any case, was increasingly taken up with her life among the international set: Onassis (outings on his famous yacht), Churchill, a variety of Rothschilds.

Through the 1960s Cecil was preoccupied with the ongoing publication of his journals, which he had been obsessively writing since childhood. The first volume, *The Wandering Years*, had appeared in 1961. Then, in 1965, came *The Years Between* (the war years). Now he was preparing *The Happy Years*, which would carry him into the late 1940s—the period of his feverish affair (if that's what it was) with Garbo. How could he publish his journals without acknowledging the relationship—without, he being Beaton, boasting of it? Yet how could he expose her to his account of it? No one knew better than he the depth of her feelings about her privacy. Hadn't he witnessed her apply the guillotine when Mercedes published her mild indiscretions in *Here Lies the Heart*?

In 1968 he signed a contract for the book and then tortured himself about it. He withdrew the manuscript, went back to it, and finally couldn't resist—publish and be damned! He decided to become mortally offended when she wouldn't answer his calls—then took the line that since she obviously didn't care, he had nothing to lose. When excerpts began to appear in print, however, panic set in. "The awful feelings of guilt and anxiety continued to dog me. I had headaches and felt very rotten. I couldn't sleep without waking to think of some further detail of my diary as published in *McCall's* that would offend Greta or a great number of friends." Then in the heat of the turmoil came news he had been hoping for and anticipating for many years: a knighthood! But this glorious affirmation was tainted for him by the fear, amounting to paranoia, that the scandal of what he had done to Garbo would cause the powers-that-be to rescind the honor. At last, on New Year's Eve, it was officially announced, and soon afterwards he was knighted by the queen at Buckingham Palace.

When *The Happy Years* was finally published, in 1972, his anxieties proved to have been justified. There were close and loyal friends—Lady Diana Cooper, for one—who deplored his disloyalty. There were mixed reviews: Some hailed his chronicle of the times as revelatory; others either doubted his veracity or condemned his tattling. Auberon Waugh—an enemy, as his father, Evelyn, had been—reviewed it somewhat measuredly in England but went for the jugular in the *Chicago Tribune* when the book appeared in America:

> The saddest and most bizarre part of the Beaton story comes in the description of a love affair which apparently blossomed between himself and Greta Garbo. As these two social and emotional waifs act out their chosen parts—he as the flamboyant but sensitive extrovert in the throes of an ideal passion, she as the startled fawn—we see the Beaton predicament in a hideous, cold light: first we see that beyond the affectation and the false values there is an emotional desert of sadness and loneliness; then we see that beyond the sadness and loneliness there is an object of the cruelest and most unutterable comedy.

Predictably, there were awkward moments, as when Cécile de Rothschild, Garbo's new tigress protector (and slave), cornered him and de-

Election night party in London, 1951: with Anthony Head and Beaton. Behind Beaton's head, Somerset Maugham

manded to know how much money, including fees for photos for *Vogue*, he had made out of Garbo in the preceding twenty years. When he tells us in his journal that he estimated the amount at four thousand pounds, she said, "'Not bad is it? I mean I wouldn't mind being given four thousand pounds to spend on the kitchen.' She laughed that nasal choking voice. 'Not bad, eh? For someone who didn't need the publicity. Even Stokowski didn't sell his story to the papers.'"

Why would Beaton humiliate himself by recounting this story? Why, as he also tells us, did he begin hallucinating Garbo figures in airplanes, in the street? He knows, he tells us, that he had done wrong—and insists that he would do it again, if given the chance. When in 1968 he wrote about her in his journal, it's like an echo of what he had written for *The Sketch* thirty years earlier: "All the nicest things about her are lost in a haze of her selfishness, ruthlessness, and incapability to love." And yet, although she had wounded him countless times, he cannot bring himself to say outright how angry at her he was. Through all the drama of "to-publish-or-not-to-publish," there is no indication that he understood just how aggressive as well as indiscreet it would be of him to unleash what you don't have to be Freud to recognize as an act of punishing if unconscious revenge. But then Cecil Beaton was a genius of surfaces—self-knowledge was not one of his conspicuous attributes. Frederick Ashton once summed up the Beaton-Garbo relationship to Hugo Vickers: "For Cecil, 'getting' Garbo was like every candle on the celestial altar lighting up simultaneously, whereas she was more Scandinavian in her approach—sex is good for the skin."

Garbo, of course, never reacted publicly to his treachery, but there would be a final scene to this dispiriting saga. In his early seventies Beaton had suffered a seriously debilitating stroke from which he only partially re-covered. He had been a close friend of the young American, Sam Green, who had become Garbo's chief facilitator back in New York, and Green was determined to bring about some kind of rapprochement between the two of them. Begging, nagging, importuning, chiding, Green took advantage of a moment when he and Garbo were both in England to convince her that she should go to see Cecil as a gesture of reconciliation. "I figured it would do him good," Green told Vickers, "and she wouldn't suffer from the experience either."

At the appointed hour she hesitated, frightened that it was all a trap—that Cecil would have photographers in the trees outside his house in Wilt-shire waiting to ambush her. But no. "Cecil was delighted to see her," Vickers tells us, and "she snuggled up to him sitting on his knee . . . but as Cecil made his slow progress to the dining room, Garbo turned to his sec-retary, Eileen, and commented, 'Well, I couldn't have married him, could I? Him being like this!'" The next day, as she was getting ready to leave for London, Cecil made as if to hug her, saying, "Greta, the love of my life!" Deeply embarrassed, Garbo spotted the visitors' book. She shunned the embrace and broke the rule of a lifetime, signing her name in full. She made sure she never saw Cecil again.

Nor, when he died several years later, did she send flowers. Even so, Sam Green remarked that her visit to Cecil, even though she was more or less forced into it, was the most generous act of her life.

⇒15⇐

GARBO AT HOME AND ABROAD

THERE WOULD BE NO FINAL SCENE to the drama that was Garbo's relationship with Mercedes de Acosta. No one had loved her more fervently or served her more slavishly, but as the years went by Mercedes grew more exigent and less useful—more of a burden. And sadder. "She's done me such harm, such mischief, has gossiped so and been so vulgar," Garbo said to Cecil Beaton in 1947. "She's always trying to scheme and find out things and you can't shut her up." But it was the publication of *Here Lies the Heart*, in 1960, that brought about the final break, with its implications of a highly emotional relationship between the two women. Greta never again acknowledged her existence, while Mercedes struggled more and more desperately against both a brain tumor and real penury. Beaton and Sam Green, both of them fond of Mercedes, tried to intervene, but Greta was implacable. Mercedes sold her apartment, her jewels, her personal papers to pay her hospital bills; friends gave her money for food. She died, forlorn, in 1968.

Things were different between Garbo and the other great friend of her Hollywood years, Salka Viertel. Their bond never frayed—Salka had been Greta's ambassador to Mayer and Thalberg, her intellectual and cultural lodestone, her literary adviser, her best friend and surrogate mother, her refuge. When the post-war political climate in America brought an end to Salka's already tenuous film career, she returned permanently to Europe and established herself in the then unexploited Swiss resort town of Klosters, where her son Peter was living with his second wife, Deborah Kerr. Every summer Garbo went there to be with Salka, until she became not exactly part of the community—Irwin Shaw, Gore Vidal—but comfortable with it, and particularly fond of Kerr. She lived simply and economically, staying in a small rented apartment or a modest hotel where no one fussed over her, taking her usual long walks, and spending hours at Salka's bedside as the older woman slipped into dementia.

Sam Green recalled his one sighting of Salka when he was in Klosters with Garbo. "We walked about half a mile up the road to a little chalet and, without knocking, went in through a side door. I followed her up to a second-floor balcony where a wizened little lady with flying white hair was sitting wrapped up in a lap robe. She couldn't speak and I don't think she could comprehend, either, but Garbo still made small talk with her, and there was a sense of communication between them." Salka died in 1978, having outlived Mercedes, her great rival, by a decade. Back in the old Hollywood days, people believed that Salka used her great influence over Garbo to further her own career as a screenwriter, but her son Peter had a different view, bitterly remarking in an interview with biographer Scott Eyman, "Garbo would never go to bat for anybody, especially for money. She was very cowardly, a narcissist. Charming, certainly beautiful, but not that great a friend. Actually, she used my mother more than my mother used her, which sounds funny, because she was a star and my mother was an oarsman in the galley."

Klosters was far from being Garbo's only foreign destination during the latter part of her life. She traveled widely, perpetually restless, always under an assumed name—usually "Harriet Brown"—and inevitably the object of intense curiosity from the press, especially photographers. Often, though, she was out of their range: Her world had expanded to people who could protect her privacy. Her closest friend for many years was the Baroness Cécile de Rothschild, who accompanied her everywhere and tended religiously to her needs. Cécile was a bluff, outspoken bulldog of a woman with a deep, nasal voice, who after George Schlee's death became Garbo's chief facilitator. (Given her immense fortune and her fierce devotion, this was not difficult for her to do.)

Cécile's niece, the distinguished biographer and cultural historian Anka Muhlstein, told me that her aunt was, alas, not very charming, not very amusing, and was always worried—when not clinically depressed. She never married, and it was understood but never mentioned that she was a lesbian. Nor was Garbo ever discussed with her family, except, Anka recalls, on a single occasion when Cécile suddenly remarked that if you ran into Garbo in the street, no matter how close you were to her, you were not allowed to greet her or acknowledge her existence. "An unhappy woman," is how Anka remembers Cécile sadly; a "poor little rich girl." Her role in Garbo's life gave *her* a life.

With Cécile de Rothschild

The two women traveled together everywhere, and there was considerable speculation about whether their relationship might be sexual, but their closest friends were convincing in their denials: Apart from anything else, Garbo was no longer interested in sex. "Once when we were wandering around Paris," Sam Green said, they came upon a sex shop and "she said she'd never been in one before and was curious. It was crowded with horny men, but she went in and took a long look around." Then, outside, she said, "Ah, the sex thing. I'm glad that part of my life is over." She was then in her late sixties.

But what had it been before it was over? Certainly when she was young she had a variety of men in her bed, from Max Gumpel to Borg to Gilbert, and why not? Later there were Remarque, Stokowski (maybe), Schlee (maybe not), Beaton, and doubtless many more—there was, for instance, a single unsatisfactory encounter with Baron Élie de Rothschild (brother of Cécile), whom she saw frequently in Paris and New York. As for women, it has always been rumored that Garbo was bisexual or even predominantly lesbian, but with whom? Not, it would seem, with Mercedes: When the letters Mercedes sold at the end of her life were opened in 2000, there were no sexual revelations.

What we do know is that Garbo had always enjoyed cross-dressing, from her early years of commandeering Sven's clothes through dressing as men for costume parties (Hamlet, for one) to some of the roles she hoped to play: Dorian Gray, St. Francis. And of course she went around in what were essentially men's clothes, and from childhood on often spoke of herself as a man or a fellow or a boy. Simple cross-dressing, or gender confusion? How ironic if the "Most Beautiful Woman in the World" really would rather have been a man.

It seems to me that what interested her more than sex was being taken care of. Which is where Sam Green came in. It was Cécile who, having decided her pal Sam would be good for Greta, had introduced them in 1970, and the three of them had happy times together—in Paris, New York, on a yachting cruise to Corsica. Green told Barry Paris that Cécile could actually be fun to be with: "Nothing standoffish about her at all. If G and I decided to throw peanuts, Cécile would throw one back." (Further hijinks among the rich and famous: Garbo reported to a friend that Aristotle Onassis, whom she knew quite well, "loved practical jokes and I was there [on board his yacht, the *Christina*] when he shoved Niarchos and some other people who were fully dressed into the pool. Oh, how he laughed. He didn't dare have a go at me.")

In New York Sam Green would be at Garbo's beck and call for a dozen years, and the two of them, sans Cécile, traveled together too—all over Europe, to Henry McIlhenny's Castle Glenveigh in Ireland (Sam pretended they were cousins, but they weren't), to Fire Island, to his home in Cartagena, Colombia. In London, Green told Barry Paris, Garbo received an embossed invitation: "Thursday, the seventeenth of October, you are requested for tea at Buckingham Palace at 4:30." And underneath, in ballpoint ink, was written, "You will be alone, E.R." Impossible to go, of course: "I have nothing to wear." Later in the day she elaborated: "Once the royal family gets the scent of greasepaint in their nostrils, they'll never let up." Did she really not have a respectable dress with her? "A dress?" Green exclaimed. "She hadn't worn a dress in forty years. She travelled with two pairs of pants—one on, one for the laundry. That was it. She had two cashmere sweaters—one dirty and one on, period." A good story, but one that Hugo Vickers assures us is "utter rubbish. This is not how such an invitation would be issued."

She had been less cavalier some years earlier when, having rejected several formal approaches from the White House, she accepted a personal invitation from Mrs. Kennedy—through a friend in common, the fashion designer Princess Irene Galitzine—to dinner there. It was understood that the dinner would be very small and very private. There were only three other guests, she told Sam Green years later: "a lady," presumably Galitzine; Lem Billings, a close friend of the president's; and "some other lady, a princess or somebody." Lee Radziwill. The evening went smoothly, the president staying with his guests far longer than he usually did. There was even a tour of the White House. "I went on top of Lincoln's bed. Took my shoes off. My, I was very careful." The date was October 21, 1963. The murder of Kennedy only a month later, Green reported, "upset Garbo terribly. She wrote his widow a letter of condolence—in Garbo's life a rare instance of reaching out."

Sam Green was an intelligent, handsome art dealer and museum curator—pal of Andy Warhol and the Lennon-Onos—who had also been a longtime friend of Beaton's. (Small world, isn't it?) As *The New York Times* wrote about him when he died, in 2011, "Judging his background too banal to make a great story (he was one of three children raised in an academic family in Connecticut), the man born in 1940 in Boston and christened Samuel McGee Green would later rejigger his ancestry and style himself Samuel Adams Green, claiming descent from a founding father and two American presidents." When Cécile Rothschild brought him and Garbo together, he was thirty, she was sixty-five, and they formed an intense bond. During the nine months of the year that Garbo spent in New York, Sam would call her every morning for a long, long conversation. What had Sam done the night before? What was Greta thinking she just might—or maybe not?—do today? Certainly a long walk. Shopping? She was still in search of the perfect pullover, the perfect shoes. Of course she had a vast wardrobe of clothes in her apartment, including her superb Valentina gowns, but she almost never touched them. Why bother to dress up?

It's not clear whether she understood that Sam Green was taping their phone calls—he says she was but preferred not to think about it. (Highly unlikely, given her mania for privacy.) When Barry Paris was working on his biography of her, soon after Garbo's death, Sam made the tapes available to him, and Barry played some of them for me, until I was so bored I couldn't bear to go on listening. Typical was a discussion over whether they should set out for a shoe store where she thought she might find a certain model in brown. But it was raining, but not hard, but it might get worse, but did she really need these shoes after all . . . In his book Paris gives us extended examples. One should suffice:

> I have tax that hasn't been paid and the government is drowning me with
> letters . . . I don't have any secretary. I don't want any secretary. I'm going
> to try to arrange things differently. This way is too nerve-wracking. I
> can't stand it. My apartment is a mess, and I'm a mess. I couldn't face hav-
> ing a stranger come here . . . I loathe my handwriting so, and I had to write
> out some checks by myself here. I made these poor little checks, and they
> look like a chicken has been walking on them. I have a new [bill] this
> morning. Maybe I'll wait till Friday and let somebody else do that one.
> That is Edison, Con Edison. Is that electricity?

She had other men prepared to drop everything and accompany her on her endless walks. One was Sven Broman, a middle-aged Swedish journalist she had met in Klosters in 1985 and whom she forgave for having co-written a book about her some years before. Garbo was always happy to have people she could speak Swedish with, and she maintained a warm connection with Mr. and Mrs. Broman through the final years of her life. The three of them shared long walks and talks in Klosters, and she understood that he would set down what she told him and produce the book that be-

AT HOME IN
NEW YORK . . .

(*top*) In Corsica, with Sam Green, Caral Gimpel, and Cécile de Rothschild; (*middle left*) in Paris; (*middle right*) in Rome; and (*bottom*) in Portofino

. . . AND ABROAD

came *Conversations with Garbo*, in which she is remarkably open about herself, though always discreetly. She welcomed the appealing Bromans when they came to New York, but her acceptance of them was probably triggered less by the Bromans themselves than by her deep feelings about Sweden, from which she felt unhappily cut off—she couldn't bear the relentless attention paid to her whenever she went home, and her final visit there had been in 1975. Speaking Swedish to nice people released her inhibitions about discussing her mother, her childhood, her relationship with the Wachtmeisters; in fact, the Wachtmeisters' daughter, Gunnila Bernadotte, was very helpful to Broman when he was writing his book, even allowing him to read and quote Garbo's many letters to her.

Another "walker"—this one a New York walker, not a Klosters one—was Raymond Daum, a film and television producer for the United Nations, who met her in 1963 at the annual New Year's Day party given at the home (in the Dakota) of Ruth Ford and Zachary Scott. Daum had grown up in the movie world—his father was a Los Angeles building contractor who in his youth had built sets at Paramount—and he was a friend of George Schlee's. At the party Garbo was sitting isolated on a hassock, with everyone in the room too nervous to approach her, but when Schlee introduced Daum to her, mentioning that he worked at the U.N., "she made room on the hassock and said, 'Sit down, Mr. Daum, and, Schleeski, get me another vodka.'" She was very interested in the United Nations and was amused to learn that Daum lived only a few blocks from her, on Beekman Place.

He offered to give her a tour of the U.N., but it would be five months before Daum received a call from Schlee, saying, "She'd like to come today." She came, and George was left waiting an hour in the Delegates Lounge while Garbo and Daum took their tour. That, Daum reports, was the only time he ever saw her in a skirt—"a gray pleated one, which she wore with a navy blazer." The first thing she commented on was the stretches of blue carpet in all the corridors. When I told her it was a gift from the United Kingdom, she said, "Imagine all those English girls working like mad at their looms—and imagine how little they were paid for their labor."

After George Schlee died, Garbo and Daum fell into an easy pattern of quiet visits and long walks—a routine that extended itself for eighteen years until Daum left New York in 1983, during which time she never gave him her telephone number: She would summon him or drop in on him when it pleased her to, and he never met any of her friends and acquaintances. "She kept us all in compartments. Like Commie cells—one didn't know the next." Whenever they were together, Daum went home and quickly transcribed everything he remembered of their conversations, and when he decided to write his book, "I apprised Garbo of my plans to publish." Her response was silence.

He leaves us not only many remarkably frank reminiscences and opinions but a telling portrait of what she was like at this time:

> As she entered a room, she presented a striking figure, even in these later years. Garbo had a noble head, honey-colored skin, clean salt-and-pepper hair in bangs, and the weathered face of an outdoor woman, lined with age and offset by sad and searching blue-green eyes. She was taller than might be expected, five feet seven, and at 110 pounds, she remained boyishly slim. [When she stopped by to see him] her decisions to leave were always unpredictable. A quick nod of the head signaled an end to the relaxed conversation we had shared—nothing especially profound, but sprinkled with good-natured laughter. "Well, well, well," she would say, concernedly, "look at the time. I should have gone home ages ago." She would put on her coat, not wishing to be helped, and, with a quick kiss on the cheek, she would go, leaving the impression that she was keeping to a tight schedule. In reality she had nothing more pressing than a solitary evening in her spacious fifth floor apartment, watching television, cooking for herself, and dining alone.

A more intimate friendship developed between Garbo and the once-famous radio singer Jessica Dragonette, who began on the airwaves in 1927 and went on singing for decades: as popular in her classical/semi-classical way as the equally famous Kate Smith. Dragonette, five years older than Garbo, had been raised in various Catholic institutions and remained deeply religious all her life. She was living with her sister, Nadea Loftus, in 1939 when Gayelord Hauser, a close friend, brought Garbo to Sunday brunch at their apartment, and Garbo was completely at ease—here was a kind of family life that, since coming to America, she had only enjoyed with Salka Viertel. Jessica was vivacious, fastidious, cultured, and—after a while—in no way in awe. "I shall never know," she wrote in her memoir (*Faith Is a Song*), "what induced her to come, to shed the shroud of her life's inevitable mystery, to loosen her disinclination to show herself, for however much I had desired it, I had never asked Gayelord to bring her"—another example of Hauser's affectionate intuition about Greta, and his disinterested generosity.

In the mid-forties Dragonette married Nicholas Turner, a handsome veteran of the armed forces, fifteen years her junior, who had been pursuing her for some time. They were married by New York's Cardinal Spellman in his private residence in St. Patrick's Cathedral, and he was there at the elaborate wedding breakfast Nadea had arranged back in the sisters' apartment. "Nikki" Turner—variously referred to as a lawyer, an accountant, and a businessman—became an integral part of Jessica's friendship with Garbo; they remained friends even after Jessica's death, in 1980. In fact, he would suggest that Garbo had been interested in *him*. "Garbo was hot after me. *I* was the guy in New York. She cooked boiled beef for me. I made lemon sole for her." Boiled beef? No, Nikki: Garbo Talked, Garbo Laughed, but Garbo didn't boil beef. It's hard enough to accept—even with more than a few grains of salt—Turner's assertion that she was at the Dragonette-Turner home "three days a week, nine months a year, for twenty-three years." Almost certainly Turner was seriously exaggerating, but this was probably as close to a normal domestic friendship as Garbo ever had.

And then there was Jane Gunther, the second wife of the famous best-selling reporter John Gunther—*Inside Europe*, *Inside U.S.A.*, although his most celebrated book, about the death of his teenage son, was *Death Be Not Proud*. (As we have noted, Garbo had been approached to play the first Mrs. Gunther in a filmed version, a role eventually played on television by Jane Alexander.) Jane Gunther, a decade or so younger than Garbo, was a distinguished woman, educated at Vassar, writer, editor. The two women

FRIENDS

CLOCKWISE FROM TOP: With Aristotle Onassis; John and Jane Gunther; Jessica Dragonette; in New York with Philippe de Rothschild

formed a very close friendship that never eroded: Gunther was as discreet and private as Garbo, and they came to have total confidence in each other, not unlike the best-girlfriend relationship Garbo had had with Mimi Pollack and with no one else since. Soon after Garbo died, Gunther spoke publicly about their first meeting, in 1947: "She surprised me by being perfectly simple, without the slightest pretension, affectation, or theatricality. Here was a human being direct, gracious and unforbidding." They were good friends almost from the beginning, and the deaths of John Gunther and George Schlee brought them still closer together. Jane Gunther:

> She was certainly the most beautiful woman I have ever seen, or even imagined. Her features were perfect, but the wonder of her beauty came from something within. There was a strange melancholy in her, which led one to believe that her marvelous face revealed the secret of life—both the sorrows and joys. What was she like? She was Scandinavian, quite matter of fact, brave, accepting of disaster . . . How can I describe her? She was elusive, oblique. She did not talk about her relationships—the important things that happened to her. She was totally secretive. She did not lie ever but would evade a direct question . . . It was her nature to be private. What a fascinating creature, many-faceted. Profundity and mystery were almost contradicted by her gaiety, her delicious sense of humor, her sense of the ridiculous. She was responsive and funny, mocking and full of wit and jokes. A clown-like, childish delight in all sorts of things quite belies her public image, but it was a huge part of her. She was compassionate about people who were ill to an unusual degree.
>
> What I miss personally, of course, is not the public figure, but a friend I loved and do not want to be without, the person I want to speak to on the telephone about something as insignificant as the seagulls on my raft in Vermont. In the last years we used to talk about nothing in particular several times a week. I suppose that is what friendship is about, and G.G. was that sort of friend.

In 1983, Garbo was awarded Sweden's highest civilian decoration and was made a Commander of the Royal Order of the North Star. The award was presented by the Swedish ambassador, and the presentation took place in Jane Gunther's East End Avenue apartment. Three years later Garbo received another Swedish decoration (as Barry Paris remarked, "Swedes love to give and receive medals"), this one for "her contributions to the art of film acting." This ceremony, too, took place in Jane's apartment. Now *that's* friendship.

Jane and G.G. lunched together, went to shows together, shopped together—in fact, behaved the way many non-working New York women of means do. The reality is that Garbo's New York life in the years after her retreat from movie-making was far from the lonely, pathetic existence that has been ascribed to her. She was, in fact, all over the place: going to dinner parties, going to the movies, going out of town to stay with friends, and of course walking. And when she was out walking on her own, she would drop in on this or that person as the mood struck her—on Katharine Hepburn on Forty-Ninth Street, on Gunther on First Avenue, on Dragonette or the Brian Ahernes or Raymond Daum.

She was also known and made welcome by the many antiques dealers in the neighborhood, in whose shops she would browse, inquire about prices, and rarely buy anything. She was, for instance, a regular visitor at the elegant Dalva Brothers store, for sixty years located on East Fifty-Seventh Street, only blocks from her apartment. My friend Leon Dalva remembers frequently hanging out in his parents' store as a kid when she would come in late in the afternoon, sit down in "her" chair, observe the comings and goings, chat with his parents, and give him a fond pat on the head, a reminder to us that Garbo was always at her best with children and young people. Michael J. Arlen, son of the Michael Arlen who wrote *The Green Hat* and himself a first-rate writer, remembers that when at sixteen he was introduced to her at a cocktail party being given by his parents, she took him aside and earnestly urged him not to smoke.

More or less every morning she would slip out of her Fifty-Second Street aerie (after doing her exercises next to her balcony overlooking the East River) to do her shopping for the day—at a favorite Swedish delicatessen, where she once jokingly offered to work behind the counter; at the upmarket grocer Gristedes; at the best local bakery; at a favorite fruit stand; at the florist, although she tended to visit it late in the day when the owner was throwing out whatever flowers wouldn't keep and she could wheedle him into "donating" them to her—as parsimonious as ever. The shopkeepers in the neighborhood knew her and liked her, and worried if she didn't turn up for a while. In other words, she had a life.

As time went by, though, that life grew more and more circumscribed— people died or just drifted away, as people will. And her health grew steadily more precarious. She got cancer on one of her nipples, and it had to be removed, leading in 1984 to a partial mastectomy. She tripped over a vacuum cleaner in her apartment, suffering a severely sprained ankle, and never regained her ability to walk and walk and walk—nor did she replenish her stockpile of walkers once the Sam Greens and Raymond Daums had disappeared. She found it harder and harder to find food she could bear to eat. "You know," she had said to Sam, "I'm getting more and more ill. I can't stand food anymore. I don't know what to eat, and it's a panicky thing. I feel panicky." In 1988 she had a mild heart attack. But more serious was a fast-worsening kidney condition, combined with a serious gastrointestinal condition: By 1990 she was being taken three times a week by limousine service to New York Hospital for dialysis treatments. She was failing fast, and on Easter Sunday of that year—on April 15, 1990—she died, at just short of eighty-five, after only four days in the hospital. Gray Reisfield, her niece and heir, was with her at the end.

Aunt and niece had grown closer over the years, Garbo turning to Gray when she needed her. And they went on holiday jaunts together. After Sven and his American wife, Peg, had died, Gray was Garbo's strongest link to her past—to her family and to Sweden. And she had accepted Gray's family: her gynecologist husband, Donald Reisfield, and their four children. For a while, Gray would come to East Fifty-Second Street once a month to help with bills, papers, et cetera, but beyond that there wasn't much she could do, given the demands of her family and the nature of Garbo's life. Gray had gone to Bryn Mawr and eventually to Columbia Law School, from which she graduated in 1957, although she never practiced. Since her father hadn't been very successful in America (or in Sweden, for that matter), presumably Garbo had helped fund Gray's education. Greta may not have wanted to spend much time with her mother and brother after bringing them to America just before the war, but she took her financial responsibilities to them seriously.

In their early years, the four Reisfield children, three boys and a girl, had no idea of the history and fame of their great-aunt—they learned about it when one of them, at the age of twelve, came upon a picture in a magazine of his mother and great-aunt vacationing together. According to an interview given in Sweden by Derek Reisfield, the oldest son (who would grow up to make a fortune from a financial information website), and his sister, Lian Gray Horan, Garbo would frequently join the family at Christmas or Thanksgiving, and on very hot days in the summer she might drive out to New Jersey to enjoy the family swimming pool. She would, Derek tells us, often be there with Peg when the kids got home from school—in her early sixties she taught them how to turn cartwheels. (These things undoubtedly did happen—at least once.) "She was extremely funny and liked practical jokes and gadgets and things like that," said Derek. "She was an extraordinary person, but you just did not think or worry about what she or who she was. She was my great-aunt." (We should note that according to Sam Green, she once remarked to him, "I have a family in New Jersey. I would not recognize them.")

The Reisfield kids would also visit her on Fifty-Second Street when they were spending a day in New York, somewhat in awe of the apartment and the opulence of its furnishings and art. They were welcome, but it sounds as if they were welcome more as guests than as family. Certainly Garbo was guarded with them: Gray Horan reports that her longtime boyfriend, later husband, was not permitted to come to the apartment to meet her until well after they were married, though eventually "he was fully embraced."

After their great-aunt died, there was trouble in paradise—two of the nephews, Craig and Derek, had ugly altercations, one of them over ownership of Garbo's honorary Oscar and a piece of scrimshaw—a carved whale's tooth—that President Kennedy had given her on the night of the dinner at the White House. (In his memoir, *Palimpsest*, Gore Vidal tells us that Jackie complained, "He never gave *me* a whale's tooth!") And who knows what further complications there were in regard to Garbo's estate.

One crucial decision was put off for almost a decade after Garbo's death: where to bury her ashes. Given the ghoulishness of a certain kind of fan, and remembering the hysteria surrounding the deaths of such worshipped stars as Valentino and Judy Garland, as well as an ugly incident involving Chaplin's grave, Gray Reisfield was properly concerned that her aunt's remains be protected against marauders. It wasn't until 1999, nine years after Garbo died, that she was finally interred: in a quiet corner of the Stockholm cemetery where her parents and her sister were buried. The entire Reisfield clan was on hand (and was filmed) for the ceremony. There is a simple red-slate marker on the grave, on which the only words, engraved in her distinctive handwriting, are "Greta Garbo."

One of the things Derek Reisfield said in that interview he gave in Sweden is "My grandfather [Sven] was the person closest to her for the first two-thirds of her life and my mother was the person closest to her in the last third of her life." The facts dispute this assertion, though. Sven was seven when Greta was born and was already a father (of an illegitimate baby) by the time she was leaving school. And once she left for Hollywood, in 1924, they saw each other infrequently. Even after Greta brought him and his family to America just before the war, they were not together a great deal— apart from anything else, she had been seriously upset when Sven, trying to become a movie actor, took the name Garbo. As we have seen, she met her responsibilities to her family but did not choose to live with or near them. And her very real closeness to her niece, Gray, did not develop until she was growing old.

The person she *was* closest to for the last thirty-one years of her life was a Swiss woman named Claire Koger who was her uncomplaining (and poorly paid) maid, cook, and companion, a year younger than her employer, who resisted all requests to talk about her until, four years after Garbo died, she allowed Barry Paris to visit her in her tiny walk-up apartment on East Sixty-Sixth Street and spoke openly about herself and about Garbo. She was then just a few weeks short of her ninetieth birthday, and frail, but her mind was clear, as was her conscience: Although she was living in severely reduced circumstances, she had refused countless offers to sell her story—and Garbo's—to the press.

That she had been able to keep living independently, however modestly, was due to an extraordinary man, a respected painter named Richard Schmidt who lived close to Garbo's apartment, had frequently passed the two old ladies in the street, and had a nodding acquaintanceship with them. When he heard that Garbo had died, it occurred to him to write a letter of condolence to Claire, which led slowly to a friendship and eventually to his becoming her legal guardian—her only relative was a niece in Switzerland.

Over the next few years, as Claire grew weaker and more in need of help, Schmidt did his best to convince the Reisfields to come to her assistance: After her thirty-one years of service—and friendship—Claire received no financial consideration from the family except for $3,500 left her in Garbo's will, somewhat less than six months' worth of her weekly salary of $150. Gray Reisfield, as we know, benefited by $19 million just from the auction of Garbo's effects in 1990, and the total estate totaled $32 million. I have seen copies of the letters addressed by Schmidt to Reisfield and her lawyers, pleading for relief so that Claire could be appropriately cared for, all to no avail; in fact, no answers were ever received. Fortunately, another benefactor—Garbo's doctor, Stuart Saal—volunteered to take care of her health free of charge, which he did until her death. Schmidt, of course, also did everything for no reward, except a rich friendship. A big story about Claire in the *Daily News* in 1995—headline: "Garbo's will leaves best pal in poverty"—points out that although Garbo's final estate-tax papers confirm that Claire received only $3,500 under the will, "Ironically, $25,000 is listed for Gray Communications" for "media relations." "Odd," remarks the reporter, "since Garbo's idea of a good relationship with the media was no relationship."

On the other hand, the family was soon commercializing Garbo's name, leasing it to various companies to be used to brand various lines of clothing and jewelry. (There are, for instance, countless Garbo mugs for sale on the web, and I'm looking right now at the "Certificate of Authenticity" that accompanies my "Greta Garbo as Grusinskaya in *Grand Hotel*" commemo-

Garbo's will leaves best pal in poverty

MYSTERY: Greta Garbo enjoys a good laugh in the early 1970s.

LINDA STASI

THE woman who served as Great Garbo's constant companion for 30 years is living in poverty after being virtually cut out of her famous employer's will.

Claire Koger, 88, sits day after day in her chair in her tiny fourth-floor walkup on E. 66th St., no longer even able to get out of her chair by herself, or carry on the simplest conversations.

It wasn't always like this for the tiny Swiss-born German immigrant. For 31 years, Claire Koger was the constant companion of Greta Garbo, serving as her seamstress, confidant and sometime live-in best friend.

Garbo always promised to take care of her when she died.

But she left Koger exactly $3,500 "separation pay" from her $30 million estate. The rest went to Garbo's niece, Gray Reisfield.

Koger is dismissed in Garbo's final estate tax papers as $3,500. "Household Employee." Ironically, $25,000 is listed for "Gray Communications" for media relations." Odd since Garbo's idea of a good relationship with the media was no relationship.

Now Koger's alone, and before the year is out she will be out of money, according to her legal guardian, artist Richard Schmidt, who is not poet. Schmidt refers to himself simply as "a huge admirer of Garbo," and has taken on the financial dealings and emotional well-being of the person who knew Garbo better than any other human.

He only wants, he says, to keep the wolf from the door.

"I promised Claire that I would never send her to a home. She's always loathed the idea, and she's independent and also extraordinarily private.

He has implored Gray Reisfield and her husband, Dr. Derek Reisfield through their attorney, Theodore Kurz of the law firm of Delafonse-Warzer and Plimpton, for help. He would like the estate to pay half of Koger's monthly expenses, and make provisions so that he can arrange to pay for occasional outings for Koger.

Ambulette services are quite expensive and will not carry the frail Koger up and down the four flights.

And since Koger is not quite destitute she is not entitled to Medicaid.

Schmidt's letters, like his phone calls to the attorney received no response. The Reisfields' home phone was

not answered.

Meanwhile the Reisfields, who moved into Garbo's luxury seven-room apartment overlooking the East River when the mysterious star died in 1990 of myriad problems — from cervical and breast cancer to failing kidneys — auctioned off the Renoirs, antiques and the carpets, and merchandised the Garbo name to a chain of restaurants, an upcoming perfume and a line of clothing.

"She only wore men's pants," scoffed Schmidt. "How do you make a line of women's clothing of men's pants?"

Me visited Koger in circumstances as far removed from the Reisfields' as possible the other day.

The front door of the building on which she lives leads to a small, dark hallway with the stairway to the left.

There are two little rooms with a kitchen that serves as a living room. There are a few sticks of furniture, and a TV. It could have been Alice and Ralph Kramden's apartment.

Koger has a hard time making herself clear but she says she has no complaints. Like Garbo she keeps silent about the past.

"Claire was quite depressed when I met her," Schmidt said. "She was someone but distant, but then she grew to trust and like me."

She yelled "Richie," when we met and motioned for us to pour some from a bottle of sweet claret she keeps on hand for occasions like this. Koger tried to communicate but became agitated when she was unable to make even the smallest sentence come out clearly. "The bed is good," she declared, somewhat embarrassed that she was unable to continue chatting.

Schmidt came into Koger's life shortly after Garbo died in 1990. He went her a sympathy note, and they became friends.

Koger was still very loyal, and had been Garbo's right hand, helping her until she died by screening calls, doing the laundry and helping the volunteer get about.

Schmidt said simply: "They were as close as two people can be. Garbo had a habit of speaking of herself in the masculine gender. And isn't it true that Richfield is very great man there is a great woman."

In a letter to attorney Kurz

SEE STASI PAGE 24

WELL-Y, WELL-Y: Greta Garbo left her pal Claire Koger just $3,500.

OPPOSITE: From the New York *Daily News*, August 21, 1995. The article continues: "Schmidt wrote: 'Miss Koger was 83 years old when Garbo died and had served her faithfully for more than 30 years. It seems inconceivable that you, as executor of the estate of Greta Garbo, did not recognize an obligation to provide security to Miss Koger . . . There surely was no reason to prevent you from following customary and humanitarian employer/employee business practices, even if you did not feel a moral obligation to do so.' Meanwhile, the time—and the money—are running out for Koger. Author Barry Paris, who wrote the definitive book, *Garbo: A Biography*, from Knopf, vouches for Schmidt's integrity. 'He really cares about Koger—and is trying very hard to help her.'"

rative plate.) Derek Reisfield explained in his Swedish interview: "We have certain intellectual property rights, the rights of publicity and then we own various trademarks and copyrights so we try to police those and have use of those so that we can enforce them. It's very expensive. We've gone after people and sued them to stop them. And that's not pleasant and not fun. We try to keep it as upmarket as possible." His mother, Gray, also emphasized that the family was very concerned to keep the Garbo brand classy. Perhaps they were not aware that from the beginning Garbo had fought tooth and nail all attempts to cash in commercially on her name?

Claire Koger, as we have seen, had steadfastly refused to exploit her Garbo connection. Her main concern when she spoke with Barry Paris, and also as reported by Richard Schmidt, was to honor her employer of so many years. Garbo was generous to her, she insisted—if not with a living wage, with countless gifts of cast-off or unwanted items of clothing, including shoes (the two women had the same foot size). And she proudly showed Paris a colorful little wooden bird Garbo had brought back to her from a trip to Sweden. What's more, when Claire's niece and nephew-in-law visited New York, Garbo actually came to Claire's apartment (which she had never seen) to meet them! One morning she called to announce her imminent arrival, giving Claire only a few nervous minutes to tidy up; arrived promptly in blue denim slacks and a jacket; and stayed for a quarter of an hour of agreeable chat in German. "That was nice," said Claire.

To the outside world, Claire and Garbo were simply employer and em-

WAYS IN WHICH GARBO'S
IMAGE WAS USED

ployee, but Schmidt, who knew Claire better than anyone, explained things differently to Barry Paris.

> There is absolutely no doubt about their supreme importance to each other. Those thousands of hours alone in the apartment—the trust and degree of intimacy were unparalleled in either of their two lives. Claire, of course, would never say it in so many words. You have to remember that both of them were basically unverbal, which is why they got on so well together all those years. Once, when I asked Claire directly if they were best friends, she said, "I suppose so." She didn't like to talk about it. Another time she told me, "We were very close—like sisters." I think that says it all. Their emotional dependence on each other was obvious.

Most telling, perhaps, is that although publicly Claire referred to Garbo as "the lady" or "Madame," when they were together she called her "G.G."—and on occasion even "Kata," the name her family used because when she was very little she couldn't pronounce "Greta" and "Kata" was the best she could do.

To the end, Claire was taking care of Garbo (or Greta, or G.G., or Madame, or Kata), although as time went by her arthritis grew so acute that Garbo had to do a lot of the heavy lifting. More and more frequently, Claire would sit with her boss watching the junky television Garbo preferred, but also late-night movies, including some of Garbo's own. ("A secret!") And more and more frequently she stayed overnight in the room reserved for her in the apartment. As Garbo's death approached, when Gray was not available Claire would accompany her to the hospital for her dialysis treatments, at home keeping her in clean clothes and tempting her to eat with a dish she had invented: a soufflé of boiled noodles baked with eggs, milk, cheese, and salt, plus grated cheese and dabs of butter on top. (Garbo had always had serious problems with her digestion, and her own cooking was of the most basic kind: broiled meat, vegetables she could just fling into boiling water, coffee made by throwing some water and some ground coffee into a casserole.) Throughout her final painful months Claire saw her cry only once.

Claire Koger died in 1996, having outlived her employer by half a dozen years. Whenever she could she went to her church on Fifth Avenue, where she had a circle of friends, but her movements were limited by both her arthritis and her inability to afford being carried down the stairs of her walk-up two-room apartment to an expensive ambulette. As for Garbo and church, I haven't come upon any references to her ever attending one, although perhaps she was tempted by Jessica Dragonette's Catholicism—if so, it didn't take. And at some point she did get interested in reincarnation. Sven Broman reports in *Garbo on Garbo* that she had said to him on one of their walks, "I would like to believe in a life after death, but the different religions have each got their own different solution. In America people go to church a lot, but I don't know if they're any more religious for all that. I know that there are many people who are convinced of life after death, but I haven't been given the capacity for belief. This is the kind of thing I spend my time brooding about . . ."

As she approached ninety, Claire's mind grew confused, but her sweetness survived. She remembered Garbo with awe and great affection—"There was never anyone like her!"—and she never complained to Richard Schmidt about the way the Reisfield family had behaved toward her. She did, however, acknowledge that she had been hurt when she wasn't invited to Garbo's private funeral at the Frank Campbell funeral chapel in Manhattan.

During the last period of her life, Garbo had succeeded in isolating herself almost completely. Apart from the Reisfields and Claire Koger, everybody was gone. Salka, Mercedes, Cecil were dead. Jane Gunther was in New England. The Wachtmeisters and Cécile de Rothschild had receded into the past. She had found an excuse for expelling Sam Green from her life. Her other walkers had drifted away, and after twisting her ankle she could hardly walk anyway. She had informed Mimi Pollack that she was no longer capable of writing, and so formally ended that already tenuous relationship of seventy years. Her mortal enemy, Valentina, for so many years an invisible presence four floors above her at 450 East Fifty-Second, beat her to the punch by dying just seven months before she did. Greta Garbo was finally alone.

GARBO

WHAT ARE WE TO MAKE OF THIS strange creature who, without trying, compelled the attention of the world in a way no other star had done? Chaplin and Pickford were great personal charmers—the Little Tramp, Little Mary; enchanting performers the audience could take to its heart, could adopt. They were cherished the way Dickens's great characters have been. No one ever wanted to adopt Greta Garbo. She stunned people with her beauty, her mystery, her glamour, her reserve; she offered the world intense emotion and great aesthetic pleasure; but she didn't offer herself. Somehow, instead, she imposed an *idea* of herself on the world. She was "The Divine Garbo," "The Swedish Sphinx," "The most beautiful woman in the world," and her mania for privacy heightened the world's sense of her distance from "real life." Maybe she wasn't really very interesting . . . who could tell? Her fame existed apart from her actual qualities, whatever they may have been. The only other Hollywood star who has had this kind of ongoing mythic power over the world is Marilyn Monroe—and Garbo actually had the idea of appearing in a movie version of *The Picture of Dorian Gray*, in which she would play the title character and Monroe one of his conquests.

Her life was a series of contradictions. Yes, she had wanted to be a great actress—but of the stage, and in Stockholm, which she loved. She insisted on being independent, on setting the rules both personally and professionally, yet it was not she herself who determined the course of her life but Stiller. And later, M-G-M, however much she balked. And then, for years, George Schlee.

She was certainly in love with John Gilbert, but she would not marry him, or anybody else. She chose to spend almost her entire adult life in America, yet she had no real connection to it—only to Hollywood, on and off, for professional reasons, and to New York, where she was conveniently situated between California and Europe; she had no interest whatsoever in the rest of the country and knew almost nothing about it. And she was not much interested in Americans: Her closest connections—Salka, Mercedes, Cecil, the Schlees, Cécile de Rothschild, et al.—were Europeans unless, like Sam Green, they were particularly useful. With the exception of Gilbert, even most of her (presumed) lovers, from Borg on, were European: Stokowski, Remarque, Beaton. Even Schlee.

She was spoken of as being austere, humorless, asocial, yet people who knew her well, going back to her childhood, talk about how much fun she could be, how she liked jokes, what a great laugh she had—when Garbo laughed, she *really* laughed. She was famous for her extraordinary movie costumes—setting fashions for women around the world in slinky dresses, preposterous hats—yet although she had closetfuls of outfits, she went around in slacks and men's sweaters. Of course she knew how beautiful she was, and suffered when she decided that her looks were beginning to fade, yet she apparently had no personal vanity, barely touching cosmetics when not made up for the camera and indifferent to mirrors. She hated being photographed, yet is the subject of thousands and thousands of ravishing photos. She was pleasant in her necessary day-to-day dealings with people, yet one day when a woman passing her in the street murmured "Good morning," she snapped back, "So what?"

Certainly she used people ruthlessly, but people *wanted* to be used by her: To know Garbo was a badge of high distinction. What she seemed to have needed most acutely from the outside world was not to be loved or admired—she was not your standard narcissist—but to be taken care of. Yes, she was like H. Rider Haggard's "She who must be obeyed," but she didn't like making decisions—often, *couldn't* make them. She resisted authority, defying Louis B. Mayer about her contract when she was only nine-teen, before having made a movie for him, but wasn't that a stubbornness based on suspiciousness rather than a deep aspect of her character?

A good deal of her public silence, it seems clear, came from the sense of inferiority she never lost over her lack of education. She took no public stands. Nor was she interested in what posterity would think of her—she left none of her millions for foundations or scholarships to be established in her name. (A friend said, "She wants her name to become extinct with her death.") After sixty-five years of working and living in America, her English, though fluent, remained imperfect, and her French was practically nonexistent. (She was comfortable in German, from her time living and working in Berlin.) Her reading? Certainly she read movie magazines, and she was surrounded by books—the usual leather-bound sets of classics supplied by decorators—but did she read them? The Norins say that she did read in bed during the days when she never left the house—"What else did she have to do?"—but her conversation, as reported by her walkers and on the hundreds of hours of the Sam Green tapes, reflects no intellectual curiosity. She was an accomplished athlete: Apart from the endless walking (often in the rain), she rode and played tennis (ferociously) and skied and swam. She liked drawing and designing things, and developed an eye for art. She very much liked the theater, but she had to be sneaked into and out of anything she wanted to see. And everywhere she went there were the infestations of paparazzi.

Could she have led a more "normal" life than the one she chose to live? A husband, or series of husbands? Children? After all, almost every great woman star of her time did marry and become a mother, from Gloria Swanson and Norma Shearer and Bette Davis to Rita Hayworth and Judy Garland and Ingrid Bergman and—notoriously—Joan Crawford Dearest. Not only did Sarah Bernhardt, with whom she was linked by *Camille*—Sarah played the Lady of the Camellias more than four thousand times!—have a son, but despite the vast extent of her amorous career, he was from first to last the center of her emotional life: We don't really know who his father was, but far from hiding his illegitimacy, she took him everywhere and proudly presented him to the world as Maurice Bernhardt. Even Bernhardt's great rival, the sublimely spiritual Eleanora Duse, had a (legitimate) daughter tucked away.

We'll never know whether Garbo had an abortion in her early Hollywood years, or whether her severe and recurring problems with her female organs would have made it impossible for her to bear children, but we do know that she stated emphatically that she had no intention of ever doing so. And yet, in the most pronounced example of her contradictory nature, she was not only drawn to children but was at home and at ease with them. Again and again we hear how she loved being with them—and how they loved being with her. Karen Swenson reports Max Gumpel's daughter, Laila Nylund, remembering, "She was always good with kids. It wasn't just that she related to you, but that she was a child within herself."

In fact, for a while she did have a semi-substitute daughter: the child actress Cora Sue Collins, who started in the movies in the early thirties. She played the child Garbo in *Queen Christina* (1933), and then, two years later, she was Anna's niece, Tania, in Garbo's *Anna Karenina*. As far back as *Christina*, Garbo had been interested in the little girl. A number of times, Cora Sue told me in one of our lengthy telephone conversations, she would notify the little girl's mother that she planned to pick up or send for her daughter, then take the little girl to her dressing room for "tea"—cookies and milk or hot chocolate. "When Cora is finished, I will take her to her dressing room. Thank you, Mrs. Collins." Otherwise, she never acknowledged Mrs. Collins's existence.

Most remarkable is that the relationship sustained itself as Cora Sue grew older: Even after she drifted out of the movies early in the forties (the same time, coincidentally, that Garbo herself drifted out of the movies), the two women maintained a friendship. Cora Sue went on to a rich life, much of it spent in Paris, where she and Garbo would occasionally meet, taking long walks together—Garbo had found a Paris walker! As always she attracted attention. "I don't understand it—how come they still recognize me?" Cora Sue now lives in California, where, in her mid-nineties, she is in full command of her life and her faculties—our only living witness, as far as I know, to Garbo in her working years.

The Garbo she remembers is a straightforward, generous woman, "one of the most down-to-earth people I've ever met. But she never liked talking about herself. She wanted to know all about *you—your* life, and the life around you. The starlets of *today*. She wasn't aloof or arrogant or anything like that, she simply didn't want to know anyone she didn't want to know."

What did they talk about? Nothing personal. The events of the day, the news, daily life. "She had a charming sense of humor," Cora Sue reports, "but not jokes! She didn't like jokes." On a deeper level? "I sensed that she had a bitter feeling of inadequacy," though of course that was never touched on. Nor did Garbo ever mention her family—her parents, her brother and sister, the Reisfields.

Finally, Cora Sue says, "I always remember how very warm she was. Not touchy-feely, but you always knew that she cared about you."

ONE WAY OF THINKING ABOUT GARBO is to contrast her with the figure often thought of as her great rival: Marlene Dietrich, who was born in Berlin in 1901, four years before Garbo was born in Stockholm. The relationship between the two women was bizarre, because it existed, and festered, only inside Dietrich's head. You can hardly blame her: She was an up-and-coming entertainer—in cabaret, revue, stage, film; she even performed on the musical saw!—when Garbo turned up in Berlin for the German premiere of *Gösta Berling* and soon was taken on by Pabst for *Joyless Street*. From then on Dietrich was relentlessly coupled with her in the German press as the German Garbo. But nobody thought of Garbo as the Swedish Dietrich.

Given Garbo's immense success at M-G-M, Dietrich was imported to Hollywood by Paramount as a rival glamour queen, made world-famous by *Der Blaue Engel* (*The Blue Angel*), directed by the imperious Josef von Sternberg. (He was born Jonas, not Josef, and, far from being a "von," was a poor Jewish boy from Vienna whose family had immigrated to New York.) The two of them made six spectacular if uneven movies for Paramount, beginning with *Morocco* and including the ravishing and tremendously successful *Shanghai Express*. We can think of von Sternberg as Dietrich's Stiller, but whereas Stiller strove to discover and release the true Garbo, von Sternberg turned Dietrich into a stunning artifact—the product of extraordinary costuming, lighting, photography. Her career in the movies went on for decades, subject to more than the usual ups and downs, but she remained a dazzling figure on both sides of the Atlantic, her fame enhanced by her heroic work entertaining Allied troops during World War II, by her countless liaisons with both men and women, her (non-romantic) palship with Hemingway, her proud assertion of her motherhood and then as the World's Most Glamorous Grandmother.

Along the way, she became a successful nightclub singer squeezed into glittering gowns and triumphing in Vegas, London, Paris—everywhere. She was desperate for audiences, for the spotlight. She was the ultimate performer. But was she an actress? That was her problem: She could never be Garbo. She was a show-biz legend, but she could never become a myth.

How this affected her is revealed by the things she said about Garbo—not in public but to her intimates, and over and over again. In my view, the finest of all Hollywood memoirs is the book about her by her daughter, Maria Riva—not a tell-all, like *Mommie Dearest*, but a scalding yet loving account of a complex relationship that lasted until Dietrich's death, in 1992. She had survived Garbo by two years. Riva's book is punctuated by vicious remarks her mother made about her "rival."

Letter to her husband, Rudi (Rudolf Sieber): "I had to go to that dinner at the Hearsts. Absolutely awful! The Child [Riva] will tell you. She laughed so when I told her all about it. Only one interesting man—one of Garbo's lovers. I don't understand how she gets them. He"—undoubtedly John Gilbert—"was drunk the whole evening but if you have to go to bed with Garbo, you *have* to drink."

And another: "Papilein, I saw Mercedes de Acosta again. Apparently Garbo gives her a hard time, not just by playing around—which by the way is why she is in the hospital with gonorrhea—also she is the kind of person who counts every cube of sugar to make sure the maid isn't stealing, or eating too well."

About the Oscars: "Those idiots . . . Look at Garbo. Didn't they want to give her one for that terrible *Grand Hotel*? Now, I have seen her be wonderful, but in *that* abortion slinking around mooning a fake Russian accent all over that awful ham, Barrymore—that was just *too* much."

(Garbo, as it happens, was nominated only three times for an Oscar—once, early on, for both *Anna Christie* and *Romance*, then for *Camille* and *Ninotchka*. Well, why would Hollywood repay her indifference to it with its highest tribute? In 1955 she was given an Honorary Oscar "for her luminous and unforgettable screen performances." She wouldn't come to the ceremony; she wouldn't be filmed making an acceptance speech. The statue was accepted by actress Nancy Kelly, then was kept by Minna Wallis, whom Garbo didn't know, for two years before it reached its owner, who stashed it away in a closet. When Sam Green suggested she take it out of the closet and make a lamp out of it, she said, "I have enough lamps.")

Back to Dietrich. Riva describes her mother narrating a scene that took place in the Thalbergs' kitchen during a party—Mercedes sobbing, Dietrich comforting and consoling. "This kitchen meeting," wrote Riva, "had many versions but always ended with the "cruel Swede" being replaced by the "luminous German aristocrat." (Not that Dietrich was an aristocrat, but she never forgot that she came from a far higher social class than the cruel Swede did, remarking to Joshua Logan, "She is a very clever woman, Garbo! She has the primitive instincts those peasants have, you know.")

About Mercedes writing a Joan of Arc for Garbo: "Papi, she is on again about Garbo doing 'Joan of Arc.' What stupidity! Can't you just see Garbo—hearing voices? Being so religious à la Swede?"

Garbo's eyelashes? "They put so many on, they look like featherdusters. They say they are her own. Nebbish!"

"The phone rang. 'Mercedes? Sweetheart! Rudi has kidney stones—I have to find a great doctor. Didn't Garbo have some trouble with peeing—or was that Stroheim when she made that awful picture with him, where she looked like a bleached chicken?'" And, years later, "Hear she has kidney disease . . . is going to Columbia Presbyterian for dialysis . . . *That* suits her! *That* goes with her character, smelly pee. She'll die of it like Chevalier."

Another witness to Dietrich's resentment (rage? envy?) was the famous Condé Nast writer and editor Leo Lerman, a close friend of hers, who recorded remarks of hers in his superb volume of journals, *The Grand Surprise*; remarks like, "That blankness, that beautiful blankness behind that face . . .

that was it . . . so touching. She was no actress . . . I was in the hospital with a strep throat, and she was in a room above me . . . with the clap. She got it from Mamoulian. And Mercedes was running between us with food. The hospital food was so bad . . . Mercedes said Garbo used everybody. She wrecked Stiller and killed Gilbert . . . She was a monster. When Stiller was dead, she thought she became Stiller—and she raped men. That is why she had queer men. She unzipped her fly and jumped on them."

Did the two women know each other? There are a few stories of casual encounters—in a nightclub, at parties, and several elaborate accounts of arranged dinners, all of which lack the ring of truth. Nobody has ever reported Garbo volunteering anything about Dietrich: That was not her way. But when a reporter once asked her about her supposed rival, she answered, "Who is this Marlene Dietrich?" As one commentator put it, "That is probably the wittiest thing Greta Garbo ever said."

But if she wasn't especially witty, it's incontrovertible that she had a considerable sense of humor—that she could, in fact, be very funny. Her schoolmates back in Stockholm confirm it. Co-actors confirm it. John Barrymore, for instance, who hadn't known her before *Grand Hotel*, said, "Do you know, she was always telling me some funny jokes on the set and she sees little things to laugh at. Little things other people wouldn't notice." Irene Dunne (who didn't know Garbo) found herself at a picnic with her and reports that she was relaxed, friendly, funny.

Katharine Hepburn, who never worked with her but knew her well, told Dick Cavett, "She's charming and sweet and nice and *funny*." And went on: "She had a real mystique, and a real, *real* gift for movie acting . . . She was mysterious, *is* mysterious . . . Photographically she had something that nobody else had. That's what made her. You don't become that famous for no reason."

What emerges from stories about her is that she was well aware of the effect she was making. Carey Harrison, son of Rex Harrison and Lilli Palmer (who had an apartment in the Garbo-Valentina building), remembers that Edna Hardt, a wonderful woman who helped raise him when she was working as his parents' assistant and who had previously worked for

Marlene Dietrich

Garbo, loved to recall her job interview with Garbo: "She asked me three questions. 'One: Can you cook?' 'Yes.' 'Two: Can you type?' 'Yes.' 'Three: Can you shoot?' Pause. 'Maybe.'" And she was hired.

And Leonard Stanley, who recently gave us the ravishing (and invaluable) book *Adrian*, aptly subtitled *A Lifetime of Movie Glamour, Art and High Fashion*—a book that celebrates the man who designed almost all Garbo's costumes for her M-G-M movies—generously shared with me what may be the ultimate Garbo story. As a young man, Stanley was a friend of the very rich Eleanor Aherne, wife of the movie star Brian Aherne, who had homes around the world, including one in Manhattan's Turtle Bay. One beautiful Sunday morning when Stanley was staying with her, she said, "I'm going to call up G.G. and get her to pull herself together and have brunch with us. It'll do her good." And then he listened to Mrs. Aherne's side of the conversation: "G.G., put something on and come on over. You'll have fun talking with the nice young man who's staying with me and the food will be great and it's a perfect day for one of your walks . . . ," and on and on, while clearly Garbo kept saying No. Finally, exasperated, Mrs. A. said, "*You* know you have nothing else to do and *I* know you have nothing else to do, so give me one cogent reason for not putting on your coat and shoes and getting up here!"—followed by a burst of laughter.

Garbo had said, "I haven't shaved."

And she came.

I can only conclude that not only did she have a sense of humor but that in some way that amused her, she was on to herself.

THE CLEAREST, MOST PLAUSIBLE CONSIDERATION of Garbo during her Hollywood years can be found in the unfinished memoir by Adrian—born Adrian Adolph Greenburg in 1903—that Leonard Stanley incorporated into his beautiful book. Before he was twenty-one he had been commissioned by Irving Berlin to design costumes for his *Music Box Revue of 1922–23*. Later, during his thirteen years at M-G-M, beginning in 1928, he designed costumes for two hundred or so movies, including twenty-eight for Joan Crawford, twenty for Norma Shearer, and eighteen for Garbo, although probably his most famous achievement was *The Wizard of Oz* (including those ruby-red slippers). As we have seen, after an angry disagreement about what M-G-M was doing to Garbo in the ill-fated *Two-Faced Woman*, he simply allowed his contract to lapse and left the studio in 1941, when she did.

Adrian: When I encountered her, she looked as ephemeral and remote as I had imagined. Her beautiful eyes and languid manner were elements of the image that M-G-M sold to the world, but I saw that they were real. After meeting her, I was not disappointed. To the contrary, I was fired by her personality more than by any I had known . . .

Miss Garbo's face is shaped like an egg. It forms a perfect oval, which is ideally suited to the new lines in millinery. Simplicity is the keynote to her smartness. Her natural aloofness and poise put meaning into simple clothes, and make it possible for her to handle formal wear without being clothes-conscious . . .

My imagination was never quiet when I approached her pictures. Ideas poured into my head with a liquid ease. I soared, because I knew she would be equal to anything I could conceive and that she would more than do it justice. This she did. No one on the screen has worn regal costumes or evening gowns with more ease. To put her into the costumes with the madness of my *Mata Hari*, the grandness of *Queen Christina*, or the elegance of *Camille* was a stimulating experience. She had a knack for wearing the most astonishing things with a total lack of self-consciousness. She turned the unconventional into a part of herself. A hat of pure fantasy could become a reality on her. Nothing surprised you if she appeared in it. It was simply Garbo . . .

When designing for Garbo, I worked from no mold, no formula. No existing fashion was of interest to me. Garbo was unlike anyone else; she should be dressed unlike anyone else. Thus I went about my task with no sense of limitation and with an almost religious fervor . . .

She disliked dressing up. She usually showed up in a gray sweater and slacks. Sometimes the sweater was long overdue at the cleaners . . . She usually wore white sneakers and they stuck out from under the skirts like duckbills . . .

It takes all the imagination I possess to visualize the glamorous finished costumes on this bedraggled woman.

As for Garbo the woman:

Garbo was incapable of directness. I could never go straight to any point with her or use a direct route. I had to zigzag. She was also capable of a guilelessness that was ensnaring. When you were with Garbo, you were sure you had never seen any one so enchanting in your life. When she radiated that magical glow, you were sure that you alone had the key to her friendship. But if you were so rash as to mention that you had seen a mutual friend the day before, Garbo would become a frowning, petulant abstraction. She would turn on you in anger and ask you why you were always bringing up this person's name.

A friendship with Garbo brought you into a world of secrecy . . . You were not to discuss her with your friends, and certainly not with mutual friends. You were not to disclose that you had seen her. If you were walking with her on the street, you should avoid greeting a friend; if possible, you would dart down a side street to avoid him.

You were never to make a definite date with Garbo, but if she wished to see you, you were expected to break any date you had. Upon her arrival at your house, she would immediately rush into the kitchen to look into the pots on the stove and charm the cook. You were invited to call but you never expected to be asked for dinner, lunch, or tea. Occasionally you were offered a carrot from her lunch box, but it was Garbo etiquette for you to graciously refuse. You could give her a gift, but you were not to expect a thank you in any form. Certainly you were never to know if she derived a moment's enjoyment from it . . .

Garbo was not unaware of romance. She left a long trail of heartbroken swains, although in truth they were not too heartbroken. Garbo did not bring out a sense of gallantry in a man. She made the rules. She tried to force him into her way of living, and too soon. No man was allowed to remain himself. He became a dog on a leash and the tugging did not lead to a pleasant walk . . .

Many of them were men of talent and offered much to her. She never hesitated to take what they offered, but she did so with the selfishness of a spoiled child and then turned away from them. Fortunately most of the men were more mature than she was, and they were patient with her rudeness and thoughtlessness until their good natures were eventually tried beyond repair . . .

Somewhere in early life, something very terrible must have happened to her, something very hurtful, for her to live in such a state of mistrust.

If Garbo can offer so much beauty to the world, what does it matter if she is difficult? It does not matter, unless you want to become her friend. Then you must not expect anything remotely like friendship. The experience has evaded Garbo. Her chameleon-like nature seems to defeat it. In the years I knew her, Garbo had a tendency to use a queen's approach to life. I often felt like crowning her, but not with a tiara.

The most unexpected glimpse of Garbo that Adrian gives us is of her arriving quietly at his studio and calling out "Hopsack!" Then, as he stood there, she would jump into the air and land with her arms around his neck and her legs around his waist. "Carry me! Carry me!" she would say. "If her mood was a merry one," Adrian wrote, "I was a pushover for her charm and would carry her around the studio with pleasure."

"Hopsack"? Garbo? Maybe adorable Mary Pickford, maybe saucy Gloria Swanson, maybe tomboyish Janet Gaynor—winner of the first Best Actress Oscar, and Adrian's wife—but Garbo? It's a reminder that she was not only convincing as a diva, a spy, or a commissar but equally convincing as a little housewife in an apron joyously riding around on Lars Hanson's shoulders in the single recovered reel of *The Divine Woman*.

The great success of the Adrian-Garbo collaboration is that she inspired him to extravagant fantasies of clothes and then wore them as if they were things she just happened to have pulled out of her closet and flung on. You forget they're costumes—they're her clothes. Which, not surprisingly, is the way she also wore her roles: Now she's Anna Christie; now she's Queen Christina; now she's Camille; now she's Ninotchka. These are not brilliant impersonations, as are, for instance, so many of Meryl Streep's performances: Garbo, despite her unique looks and voice, disappears into these women, leaving us to wonder whether she achieves this through artistic genius or self-abnegation.

Was Adrian right in assuming that something terrible must have happened to her early in her life? My own conjecture is that rather than having suffered from a specific trauma, she suffered from an absence of something—a childhood. She herself said that she had no talent for childhood and had had no time to indulge in one. From her earliest years she was always the leader, the strong one, the determined one, with a charming but somewhat feckless father and a mother who was clearly no match for her. What's more, she always knew what she wanted to be, and, unlike other little girls who wanted to be actresses, she pursued her goal with unremitting determination—she was her own stage mother. Given her beauty and drive, if Stiller had not intervened she undoubtedly would have become a successful stage actress and sooner or later drifted into the movies, first in Sweden, and eventually perhaps, like Ingrid Bergman (who was only ten years her junior), in America. But she would not have become "Garbo"—a role she did not seek and for which she was unprepared.

Consider: In 1925, when she arrived in Hollywood, uneducated, not yet twenty, she spoke no English, her hair was impossible, and M-G-M didn't know what to do with her. In 1926, her first American film, *Torrent*, was released—a personal triumph for her. In 1927, her third film, *Flesh and the Devil*, made her one of the most famous women in the world. And she was very young, on her own, trapped in a spotlight extreme even by Hollywood standards. She didn't understand what was happening to her—America, Hollywood, fame were outside her experience. She must have realized that her beauty was special, but she never really obsessed over it, although she hated seeing it begin to fade. She never found—never really wanted—a life partner; her sexuality was ambiguous; the wounds her family's poverty had inflicted on her never healed. And, again, she was never reconciled to her lack of education. "Garbo was shy, insecure," the director Jean Negulesco said of her. "She felt that as a person she actually had nothing special or unusual for others to make a fuss over."

Well before she was twenty-five, Garbo had lost the three people she was closest to: her father, her sister, and Stiller. And she was deracinated—Sweden was never her home after 1925, and although she became an American citizen, she never became an American. Although she loved children and, as we have seen, was at ease with them—entering into their childhoods, really—she was unable to, or chose not to, have children of her own. In many ways she became her own child—demanding, willful, needing to be taken care of. People often used the word "childish" about her.

In *Garbo on Garbo*, Sven Broman quotes at length from an article, published in Sweden in 1959, by Dr. Eric Drimmer, a well-known psychologist who spent the war years in Los Angeles, during which time he both married Eva Gabor and worked for M-G-M, trying to relieve the anxieties and stress of such stars as Clark Gable and Robert Taylor. In 1939, Garbo approached him wanting help for her nerves (in his casebook he noted her asking for "relief from nervous tension"), and he worked with her for six months, and later would write:

Garbo is a wonderful person. She is reserved and stand-offish, but once she has opened up you feel she is talking straight from the heart. This

With Adrian

makes a very strong impression on you. I saw her as a restless person, always looking for and never finding a foothold in life . . . As I became familiar with her problems, I grew increasingly convinced that Greta Garbo suffered from a shyness *vis-à-vis* the world around her that bordered on the pathological . . . People who describe Garbo's shyness as a pose do not have the faintest idea what they are talking about. I can assure you that the different ways she would react to various situations were as much a mystery to her as to anyone else. It was to find an explanation for all that she could not understand in her own personality that she consulted me.

If a normal human being is suddenly faced with a dangerous wild animal, that person will experience intense fear. That is exactly what Garbo felt when faced with a crowd of people. A few strangers pushing forward to get autographs, and even her colleagues, on occasion, could fill her with terror. Her sole impulse was to turn and flee. The more I came to know about her past and heard her story, the more convinced I became that Garbo was a normal, ambitious and cheerful girl when she left Sweden. Hollywood was solely responsible for her inhibitions. No matter how paradoxical it may sound, her life took a wrong direction just at the point at which her fame and wealth were created. At the beginning there was no more mystery surrounding Greta Garbo than around any other young girl who suddenly appeared in Hollywood and was thrust into the limelight.

Garbo remained friendly with Dr. Drimmer (and his post-Gabor second wife) long after he returned to Sweden, where she would see them whenever she was in Stockholm. "The last time was in 1962," Mrs. Drimmer would say. "Garbo was out walking on Djugården with Einar Nerman. Suddenly she felt like freshly baked waffles and jam. 'The Drimmers can fix that,' Einar said. So they came here, and having a guest as pleased as Garbo made being the hostess very gratifying. She ate her waffles with all the delight of a child."

Sam Green told Barry Paris that one day, alone in her living room, he dropped a few peanuts on the floor, and when he bent down to pick them up, he noticed a tiny figure peeking out from under the sofa he was sitting on. "It was a troll," he said. "You know, those little plastic dwarfs with the ugly, wild, magenta and turquoise Dynel hair? When I bent down further and looked underneath the sofa, there was a whole row of them—at least a dozen, a whole little community of them—in a kind of formation." From then on, whenever he had the opportunity, he would check, and there they all were, but in new formations.

Trolls, of course, are significant figures in the Scandinavian folklore Garbo grew up with, so, said Green, "Why not trolls? Children play with dolls. Garbo played with her trolls. They amused her. Alone late at night, when the Sandman wouldn't come—maybe she couldn't get to sleep, maybe she acted out little scenes or fantasies with them from some favorite fairy tale—who knows? You tell me."

WHY GARBO

✕

HAS THERE EVER BEEN anyone like her? Only one actress suggests herself: Setsuko Hara, who died in 2015 at the age of ninety-five and who has often been called "the Garbo of Japan." She began at fifteen, and within a few years she was a major star—and remained one until, in her early forties, she turned her back on the movies, isolated herself in the seaside town of Kamikura, and simply didn't emerge from her modest compound, having given a final press conference at which she said that she had never enjoyed making movies and had only done it to help support her large family. Certainly, Hara did resemble Garbo in her retreat from the public eye. But a more significant similarity lies in the effect she had on her audience, as captured by the renowned Japanese novelist Shūsaku Endō, who wrote of her, "Can it be possible that there is such a woman in the world?"

Her most famous role was as the noble daughter-in-law in Ozu's *Tokyo Story*—the film that several years ago the leading directors of the world chose as the greatest movie ever made. Hara's "Noriko" is a grave beauty with huge eyes and an exceptionally wide smile—like Garbo, she's an actress of extraordinary restraint across whose mobile face flicker emotions that reveal a woman of deep feeling and generosity.

And like Garbo, she transcends her roles and her dialogue—through her considerable technique and remarkable beauty, of course, but also through the mysterious way her soul has of suddenly seeming to be reaching out and touching not only her fellow actors but you who are watching her. Somehow—like Garbo—she is sharing her humanity with us all.

Setsuko Hara had Ozu and the other major directors of her time. Garbo had M-G-M, and mostly trashy stories, and inferior leading men, and pagodas on her head. Yet again and again—as her Anna bends down over her sleeping little boy, as her Christina stares ahead at the horizon from the prow of her ship, as her Camille slips out of life in the arms of her Armand—her eyes and her smile, her *self*, remind us that life is not only difficult and painful but also worth living.

OVERLEAF: Her living room overlooking the East River

A GARBO GALLERY

⤞⤝

S EVERAL OF THESE IMAGES—those by Arnold Genthe and Russell Ball—were shot in New York, before Garbo left for California. The others were taken in Hollywood, almost all of them in the photographer's studio the day after a film was finished when costumes and props were still available. Her preferred photographer was Clarence Sinclair Bull, who is responsible for fourteen of the twenty-two pictures in the gallery and, it's been said, shot four thousand images of her between 1926 and 1941. There is a tiny numeral on each page to help identify the photographer involved. Clarence Bull's work includes images numbered 1, 7–17, 19, and 22. Ruth Harriet Louise is represented in images 5, 6, 18, and 21. Number 2 was taken by Edward Steichen, number 3 by Arnold Genthe, number 4 by Russell Ball, and number 20 by George Hurrell.

19

Greta Garbo

Who knows why there was a magazine called *Television* in 1931, long before television really existed? But there was, and there were at least three issues. Garbo, of course, was on the cover of the first, Dietrich on the second (she would not have been amused), and Harlow on the third.

A
GARBO
READER

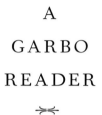

KENNETH TYNAN'S PROFILE OF GARBO

✥

The first line of Tynan's famous profile of Garbo—originally published in Sight and Sound *in April 1954—is probably the most famous and most frequently quoted thing ever written about her.*

WHAT WHEN DRUNK, one sees in other women, one sees in Garbo sober. She is woman apprehended with all the pulsating clarity of one of Aldous Huxley's mescaline jags. To watch her is to achieve direct, cleansed perception of something which, like a flower or a fold of silk, is raptly, unassertively and beautifully itself. Nothing intrudes between her and the observer except the observer's neuroses: her contribution is calm and receptiveness, an absorbent repose which normally, in women, coexists only with the utmost vanity. Tranced by the ecstasy of existing, she gives to each onlooker what he needs: her largesse is *intarissable* [inexhaustible]. Most actresses in action live only to look at men, but Garbo looks at flowers, clouds and furniture with the same admiring compassion, like Eve on the morning of creation, and better cast than Mr. Huxley as Adam. Fame, by insulating her against a multitude of experiences which we take for granted, has increased rather than diminished her capacity for wonder. In England two years ago she visited Westminster Abbey, early one morning when no one was about, and in this most public of places found a source of enormous private enchantment. A walk along a busy street is for her a semi-mystical adventure. Like a Martian guest, she questions you about your everyday life, infecting you with her eagerness, shaming you into a heightened sensitivity. Conversing with her, you feel like Ramon Novarro, blinded in *Mata Hari*, to whom she said: "Here are your eyes," and touched her own.

I half-believed, until I met her, the old hilarious slander which whispered that she was a Swedish female impersonator who had kept up the pretence too long; behind the dark glasses, it was hinted, beneath the wild brown hair, there lurked the features of a proud Scandinavian diplomat, now proclaiming their masculinity so stridently that exposure to cameras was out of the question. This idle fabrication was demolished within seconds of her entering the room; sidelong, a little tentative, like an animal thrust under a searchlight, she advanced, put out a hand in greeting, murmured something muted and sibilant to express her pleasure, and then, gashing her mouth into a grin, expunged all doubt. This was a girl, all right. It is an indication of the mystery which surrounds her that I felt pleased even to have ascertained her sex.

"Are you all things to all men?" someone asks her in *Two-Faced Woman*; to which the honest reply (I forget the scripted one) would be: "To all men, women and children." Garbo, Hepburn and Dietrich are perhaps the only screen personalities for whom such a claim could seriously be made. "She has sex, but no particular gender," I once wrote of Dietrich, "her masculinity appeals to women, and her sexuality to men"; which is also true of Hepburn. Yet Garbo transcends both of them. Neither Hepburn nor Dietrich could have played Garbo's scenes with her son in *Anna Karenina*; something predatory in them would have forbidden such selfless maternal raptures. Garbo alone can be intoxicated by innocence. She turns her coevals into her children, taking them under her wing like a great, sailing swan. Her love is thus larger than Hepburn's or Dietrich's, which does not extend beyond the immediately desired object. It was Alistair Cooke who pointed out that in her films she seemed to see life in reverse, and, because she was aware of the fate in store for them, offered the shelter of her sympathy to all around her.

Through the cellophane kitsch (how it dates!) of the Lubitsch Touch she pierced, in *Ninotchka*, to affirm her pity for the human condition. The words were addressed to Melvyn Douglas, but we all knew for whom they were really intended, and glowed in the knowledge: "Bomps will fall, civilisations will crumble—but *not yet . . . Give us our moment!*" She seemed to be pleading the world's cause, and to be winning, too. Often, during the decade in which she talked to us, she gave signs that she was on the side of life against darkness: they seeped through a series of banal, barrel-scraping scripts like code messages borne through enemy lines. Sometimes, uttering sentences which were plainly designed to speed the end of literature, she could convey her universal charity only in glimpses, such as, for instance, a half-mocking, half-despairing catch in the wine-dark voice. Round the militant bluster of M-G-M dialogue she wrapped a Red Cross bandage of humanity.

It is likely that too many volumes have been read into and written about her, and that every additional adulatory word reinforces the terror I am sure she feels at the thought of having to face us again and measure up to the legend. Possibly we exaggerated her intelligence from the beginning; perhaps she was perfectly happy with the velvet-hung, musk-scented tin lizzies which Salka Viertel and S. N. Behrman (among others) turned out as vehicles for her. Perhaps association with Lewis Stone and Reginald Owen, a stout pair of uncle-substitutes who crop up, variously bewigged, in many of her films, was vitally necessary to inspire her. Recall, too: that Carl Brisson and John Gilbert are known to have been high on her list of ideal men; and that we have no evidence that she has ever read a book. Except physically, we know little more about Garbo than we know about Shakespeare. She looks, in fact, about 34, but her date of birth is disputable; the textbooks oscillate between 1905 and 1906, and one biography ungallantly plumps for 1903, which may, of course, be the wound left by an embittered typesetter. Stockholm cradled her, and, like Anna Christie, she was the daughter of an impoverished sailor. She had a brother and a sister, left school at 14, entered the newly expanding Swedish film industry, and was discovered by Mauritz Stiller. After the completion of *Gösta Berling* in 1924 her life is a list of movies, 11 silent, 14 talking, and a file of newspaper pictures, catching her aghast and raincoated, grey-faced and weirdly hatted, on the gangplanks of ships or the stairways to planes. We often know where she is going, but never why. Occasionally a man is with her, a sort of Kafkaesque guard, employed to escort her to her next inscrutable rendezvous. Baffled, we consult the astrologers, who tell us that those born, as she was, between the end of August and the end of September are almost bound to be perfectionists; but what, we are left sighing, is she perfecting?

She changed her name from Gustafsson to Garbo, the Swedish word for a sprite. I used to think the Spanish "garbo" an insult to her, having heard it applied to matadors whose work seemed to me no more than pretty or neat. A Hispanophile friend has lately corrected me: "garbo," he writes, "is animal grace sublimated—the flaunting of an assured natural charm, poise infected by joie de vivre, innate, high-spirited, controlled, the essentially female attribute (even in bullfighters) . . ." In short, "garbo" is Garbo without the melancholy, with no intimations of mortality. The word describes the embryo, the capital letter invests it with a soul. It is the difference between *Gösta Berling* and *Anna Karenina*.

But here again I am acquiescing in the myth of gloom. Long before the fit of hoarse hysterics which convulsed her when Melvyn Douglas fell off his chair, Garbo had laughed, even if it was only "wild laughter in the throat of death," and made us laugh too. She was never wholly austere. Posing as a man in the tavern scene of *Queen Christina*, how blithely she made us smile at her awkwardness when asked to share a bedroom with the Spanish ambassador! A secret heart-smile, with the lips drawn back as if bobbing for apples, was always her least resistible weapon. Her gaiety coalesced, to the dismay of academic distinctions, with plangency. Her retirement is unforgivable if only because it means that now we shall never see her Masha in *The Three Sisters*, a part Chekhov might have written for her. It takes lesser actresses to express a single emotion, mirth or mirthlessness. Garbo's most radiant grins were belied always by the anxiety in the antennae-like eyebrows; and by the angle of her head she could effect a transition, not alone of mood, but of age. When it was tilted back, with the mouth sagging open, she was a child joyously anticipating a sweet; when it was tipped forward, the mouth still agape, she became a parent wide-eyed at her child's newest exploit.

Some of her impact, certainly, was derived from the exoticism of her accent; here was probably the first Swedish voice that many a million filmgoers had ever heard. Anglo-Saxons are notoriously prone to ascribe messianic characteristics to any stranger with a Slavic, Teutonic or Nordic intonation; Bergner and Bergman are examples that come to mind, and the history of the London stage is punctuated with shrieks of exultation over long-forgotten soubrettes with names like Marta Kling, Svenda Stellmar or Ljuba Van Strusi. Garbo was unquestionably assisted by the fact that she had to be cast, more often than not, as an exile: how often, to go about her business of homewrecking, she arrives by train from afar! The smoke clears, revealing the emissary of fate, hungrily licking her lips. The displaced person always inspires curiosity: who displaced her, what forces drove her from her native land? If it was Garbo's luck to provoke these enquiries, it was her gift which answered them. The impulse behind her voyage was romantic passion. Bergner might have left home to collect Pekes, Bergman to go on a hiking tour: Garbo could only have journeyed to escape or to seek a lover. Which is, as a line in *Ninotchka* has it, "a netchul impulse common to all."

Superficially, she changed very little in the course of her career; a certain solidity in her aspect suggested, at the very end, a spiritualised reworking of Irene Dunne, but that was all. She could still (and often did) fling her head flexibly back at right-angles to her spine, and she kissed as thirstily as ever, cupping her man's head in both hands and seeming very nearly to drink from it. And her appeal never lost its ambiguity. The after-dinner cooch-dance which drives Lionel Barrymore to hit the bottle in *Mata Hari* reveals an oddly androgynous physique, with strongkneed legs as "capable," in their way, as the spatulate fingers: nothing is here of Herrick's "fleshie Principalities." Pectorally, the eye notes a subsidence hardly distinguishable from concavity: the art that conceals art could scarcely go further. If this undenominational temple-dance is seductive (and, like the swimming-pool sequence in *Two-Faced Woman*, it is), the explanation lies in our awareness that we are watching a real, imperfectly shaped human being, and not a market-fattened glamour-symbol.

I dwell on Garbo's physical attributes because I think the sensual side of acting is too often under-rated: too much is written about how actors feel, too little about how they look. Garbo's looks, and especially her carriage, always set up a marvellous dissonance with what she was saying. The broad ivory yoke of her shoulders belonged to a javelin-thrower; she walked obliquely, seeming to sidle even when she strode, like a middle-weight boxer approaching an opponent: how could this athletic port enshrine so frail and suppliant a spirit? Queen Christina, reputedly her favourite character, is encased for several reels in masculine garb, and when besought by her counsellors to marry, she replies: "I shall die a bachelor!" And think of: "I am Mata Hari—I am my own master!" To lines like these Garbo could impart an enigmatic wit which nobody else could conceivably have carried off. Deficient in all the surface frills of femininity, she replaced them with a male directness. Her Marie Walewska was as lion-hearted as Napoleon himself, and I have heard her described as "Charlemagne's Aunt." Her independence (in the last analysis) of either sex is responsible for the cryptic amorality of her performances. In most of the characters she played, the only discernible moral imperative is loyalty, an animal rather than a human virtue—that "natural sense of honour" which, as Shaw says, "is nowhere mentioned in the Bible."

"Animal grace sublimated": I return to my correspondent's phrase. If it is true (as I think it is) that none of Garbo's clothes ever appear to be meant for her, much less to fit her, that is because her real state is not in clothes at all. Her costumes hamper her, whether they are stoles, or redingotes, or (as on one occasion) moiré, sequinned, principal-boy tights. She implies a nakedness which is bodily as well as spiritual. It is foolish to complain that, basically, she gave but one performance throughout her life. She has only one body, and in this incarnation that is all we can expect.

Through what hoops, when all is said and done, she has been put by Seastrom, Cukor, Clarence Brown and the rest of her mentors! She has gone blonde for them, danced "La Chica-Choca" for them, played a travesty of Sarah Bernhardt for them, stood straight-faced by for them as Lewis Stone warned her of "a new weapon called The Tank." Can we ask for more self-abnegation? A life of Duse was once mooted for her—what an *éducation sentimentale*, one guesses, she would have supplied for D'Annunzio! Later she hovered over, but did not settle on, a mimed role in Lifar's ballet version of *Phèdre*. And at the last moment, when all seemed fixed, she side-stepped the leading part in Balzac's *La Duchesse de Langeais*. The most recent, least plausible rumour of all insisted that she would film *La Folle de Chaillot*, with Chaplin as the Rag-Picker . . .

So it looks as if we're never to know whether or not she was a great actress. Do I not find the death scene of *Camille* or the bedroom-stroking scene of *Queen Christina* commensurate with the demands of great acting? On balance, no. The great actress, as G. H. Lewes declared, must show her greatness in the highest reaches of her art; and it must strictly be counted against Garbo that she never attempted Hedda, or Masha, or St Joan, or Medea. We must acclaim a glorious woman who exhibited herself more profoundly to the camera than any of her contemporaries: but the final accolade must, if we are honest, be withheld.

GARBO, THE HARRISONS, AND THE WINDSORS

The German-born actress Lilli Palmer tells us about the visit (on their separate yachts) of Garbo and the Duke and Duchess of Windsor to Portofino, where she and her husband, Rex Harrison, had a villa on the cliffs overlooking the harbor. From her charming and perceptive 1975 autobiography, Change Lobsters and Dance.

WE HAD MET THE WINDSORS in New York. In the middle of boisterous parties, he would seek out a quiet corner to recite German poetry with me. After all, his mother, Queen Mary, had been a German princess, Mary of Teck, and had spoken English with a slight Teutonic accent all her life. Windsor had learned to speak fluent German from her as a child, although he was obliged to forget it all during World War I. But he liked to excavate it whenever he had a chance . . .

For a few days every year, he liked to tie up at Portofino "for his German lesson." When he came up to the house to dine with us, it was certainly an honor but not an unmixed pleasure. Although it was twenty years since he had abdicated, he liked to see protocol observed, only you had to guess when to observe it and when to ignore it. Naturally you had to be punctual to the minute and stand up whenever he stood up; even if he was only going to the toilet, respectful attention was drawn to a function that common people prefer to attend to as inconspicuously as possible. When you greeted him, a little bob or rudimentary curtsey was appreciated. I only bobbed to him. His duchess got a firm handshake. (Benita Colman, our home guest, refused to bob to the Duke. "I only curtsey to what sits on thrones!" she said firmly.) He also had to preside at the head of the table, something Rex only reluctantly conceded. Before dinner, however, the Duke surprised me by gallantly relieving me of the tray of hors d'oeuvres I was passing and handed it around himself. This spoiled Rex's appetite. "I just don't like seeing my former king passing the sandwiches," he said . . .

He was a small, elegant man, hardly taller than I. From the back he looked like a boy. Facing you, he looked his age, fifty-five, although his blond hair was touched up. The face was still handsome, crisscrossed with tiny wrinkles, the nose sharp and pointed like a hunting dog's. His duchess wore a perfectly plain blue linen dress without pleats, pockets, or collar. Its cut alone made her look almost beautiful. Wallis Windsor, however, was anything but beautiful. Many people have puzzled over what it could possibly have been that so irresistibly attracted the King of England. I believe it was her defiant independence ("I'm at my best with enemies!"), her marvelous carriage, and her voracious vitality. If she had happened to be hungry, she might have taken a bite out of you . . .

One of their "courtiers" at that time was Jimmy Donahue, a Woolworth heir, who escorted them both everywhere. The Windsors were never alone, but always surrounded by a few people who had nothing better to do at the moment. Jimmy Donahue was a cheerful playboy who never did a stroke of work, never had a thought in his head, but knew everyone, remembered the first names of the *maîtres d'hôtel* of all the best restaurants, was good company, and amused the Duchess. But how did one amuse the Duke? That was more difficult. His sense of humor on the subject was disturbing. "You know," he once said to me with a smile, "I've got a low IQ."

"But, sir," I protested loyally, "just think of your book, *A King's Story*. That's a fascinating tale and very well written."

"Didn't write it myself."

ONE EVENING, while Windsor, his wife, and Jimmy Donahue were having dinner with us, there was a telephone call. Greta Garbo and her longtime companion, George Schlee, were in the harbor and wanted to know if they could come up. I told the Duke, and to my surprise he became quite animated. "Yes, tell them to come up," he said enthusiastically, "I've always wanted to meet her." The Duchess was equally delighted; she had never met Garbo in person either. Rex jumped into the jeep and drove downhill to pick them up.

It was a historic moment. The two women sat face to face and sized each other up from head to toe. Both knew they were legends of the twentieth century. Looking at them, I thought that life casts people in roles that a good scenario would never assign them. The woman for whom a man would be willing to give up his throne should obviously have been Greta Garbo, forever the world's most beautiful woman, unique and unattainable.

There's no need to have beautiful features in order to be beautiful. It is the overall arrangement and its particular harmony that gives the impression of beauty. But in Greta's case every single feature was not only boldly designed but perfect by itself. Nothing was small in her face. A broad, high forehead, a strong, chiselled nose, a wide mouth, and most impressive of all, enormous dark blue eyes set under eyebrows curved like butterfly wings. When we swam together, she would dive and reappear on the surface with drops of water clinging separately to eyelashes that looked as if they had been purchased at the drugstore. To me, though, the unique quality of her face showed at its best when she was displeased. In Greta's face, even her frown was a thing of beauty.

Yet, there she sat in old blue slacks and a faded blouse, a lonely woman. ("Why haven't I got a husband and children?" she once said, during one of our long walks through the olive groves. "Are you serious?" I asked. "A million men would have been happy to crawl on all fours to the marriage license bureau." "No," she said, "I never met a man I could marry.") And there, next to her, Wallis Windsor in something white and exquisite, with what were probably fabulous jewels around her neck. Greta's brown hair hung straight and shapeless, matted from seawater, around her face. Wallis, of course, traveled with her own hairdresser. The Duchess's voice was decisive and metallic. Greta's was husky, barely audible. Sweden's Queen Christina against America's splendid Nutcracker.

"I'd like to give a party for you aboard the *Sister Ann*," said Wallis benevolently. [The *Sister Ann* was the Windsors' rented yacht.]

"I have no dress," murmured Greta.

"Then it will be an informal party," said Wallis with a glance at her husband, who nodded eagerly. "All right. Tomorrow at eight in the harbor."

The general conversation languished. Greta never contributed much anyway, Schlee did his Russian best, Jimmy wasn't in form. And yet Wallis had brought up a subject that ought to have interested all actors and actresses.

"Who will portray us on the screen when the time comes?" she asked. "Because there certainly will be a film about us, won't there?"

No doubt.

"Well, then, who will play us? What do you think?"

We didn't know; we hesitated. This was slippery ground.

"My part is easy to cast," said Wallis, "because they won't show me as I was, forty years old and God knows no beauty. They'll choose some curly blond mooncalf or a vamp à la Theda Bara with a long cigarette holder, to make our story plausible."

One of us said, "Whom would you choose, if it were up to you?"

"Katharine Hepburn," said the Duchess without hesitation.

"And to play the Duke?"

Wallis didn't answer. But Windsor nodded politely in Rex's direction and said: "I think perhaps you would be the best choice."

Rex pulled hard at his nose and muttered something gratified, if inaudible . . .

Next day we collected Greta and Schlee from their yacht, which was tied up at night at the farthest, stinkingest end of the harbor, where they hoped, in vain as usual, to escape notice. Her entire life was devoted to finding some way to spend her days unrecognized and anonymous, as other people do. The harder she tried, the more persistently the press and the general public pursued her. Garbo hadn't made a picture in twenty years, but people still felt the urge to stare as closely as possible into her face. The rented yacht could dock only at night. During the day it drifted half a mile or so from shore, the deck shielded by canvas awnings, as though they were expecting a cloudburst. Photographers and reporters circled the yacht in rowboats and dinghies.

We went out to Greta's yacht in our small Cris-Craft, the *Lilli-Maria*, and quickly climbed aboard by the ladder their sailors lowered for us. Greta and Schlee were sitting, somewhat cramped, under the awnings. "Maybe if you'd pose just once for the photographers," I said, "give them five minutes, perhaps they'll leave you alone."

A cross Swedish frown appeared between Greta's eyebrows. "No use," she said. "They won't go away. I've tried everything." So we all sat under the canvas and sweated. From time to time I peeped through a crack to see whether the boats had finally given up. There were only a few left, their occupants green in the face, because the sea was rising. "Won't be long now," said Schlee, the voice of experience.

We waited. I wanted to wash my hands and climbed down the narrow stairs to the cabin. Looking for Greta's bathroom, I went into the first one on the right, attracted by all kinds of pleasant smells. The glass shelves were loaded with bottles of cologne and perfume, and there were soaps of all colors, bath salts, and oil beside the tub—and an electric razor. Wrong one. I thought, this is George's bathroom. I tried the opposite one. This was Greta's all right; her swimsuit was hanging on a hook. Otherwise the room was practically bare: a toothbrush, a comb with a couple of teeth missing, half a bar of Lux soap.

When I got back on deck, the last dinghy had disappeared. We all climbed into our motorboat and dashed back to the dock at top speed, trying in vain to tie up between two strange yachts without being recognized. The photographers were triumphantly waiting for us, surrounded by a crowd of people. Greta realized that it was hopeless, and climbed stony-faced behind me up the steps to the dock. At the top the crowd was waiting.

For the first time in my life, I was physically afraid. I thought that any minute I would be crushed, smothered, or at best thrown into the water . . . "*La Divina!*" yelled the frenzied crowd, surging forward. A minute more and we'd have all been in the water, with the photographers and the fans on top of us. Schlee had his arm around Greta, Rex was punching anyone within reach—but the rescue came from the photographers, who hit out at the crowd with their tripods, yelling wildly in Italian. Finally we made an opening and fought our way through to the jeep, kicking anyone who got in the way. For once, the jeep started immediately and we roared off, panting and completely unnerved . . .

Up at our house she was safe. Only the jeep could negotiate the path, and a high wire fence kept mountain climbers at a distance. We spent the days on the terrace, chatted, sat quietly in the sun, or went for Greta's beloved walks in the olive groves behind the house. Her daily walks were her religion; she withered when she was deprived of them. I once collected her from Onassis's giant boat and she moaned, "It is too small! I cannot go for my walks!" . . .

WE WERE EXPECTED aboard the *Sister Ann* at eight o'clock. That meant eight—not a minute later. I did my usual Prussian punctuality act and reminded everybody several times that it was time to get out of swimsuits and into slacks. No response. Everybody was on his third martini and feeling no pain.

By the time we finally got into the jeep it was half past eight. During the few minutes it took us to tear down to the harbor, we discussed possible excuses, couldn't find one, laughed a lot, and finally decided on the old story that the jeep wouldn't start.

Five minutes later we arrived, breathless, at the dock. The *Sister Ann* was all lit up. Crowds of people were surging around the barrier at the dock entrance, but Windsor had notified the harbor police and they saw to it that we got through safely. We made for the yacht's little saloon, hoping to mingle with the other guests without being noticed. But there were hardly any other guests. Apart from the hosts, who were sitting stiffly side by side on the sofa, there was only an elderly American couple, a former senator and his wife, who were morosely jiggling the ice in their drinks. Wallis's face was one dark thundercloud.

I bobbed to the Duke and murmured, "The jeep, sir . . . the damned thing wouldn't . . ."

But Wallis wasn't interested. "It's Jimmy," she said coldly, interrupting my stutterings. "He went ashore this afternoon and he's not back yet. He knows perfectly well that the Duke insists on punctuality. It's simply a question of manners, that's all."

At that moment, Jimmy appeared in the doorway, helloing exuberantly in all directions, his arms full of gardenias, which he deposited grandly on the Duchess's lap by way of a peace offering. She swept them to the floor, stood up, and said, "Do you know what time it is?"

Jimmy brought his wristwatch to within an inch of his eyes. "Well, well, what do you know!" he exclaimed. "I'll be damned!"

Head high, Wallis strode past him to the quarterdeck. The Duke, the two Americans, the four of us, and Jimmy followed in single file.

The quarterdeck, where the festive table had been laid, could not be hidden from the people on the dock. We were in full view, though at a distance of some fifty feet . . .

I sat between Windsor and Jimmy, and during the cold soup Windsor and I engaged in a "German lesson" on absorbing subjects like the weather, the swimming, and his three pugs. Gradually, however, we became aware of what was going on at the rest of the table. The senator appeared to be holding forth in what amounted to a monologue, since Wallis was gazing absently out to sea, Schlee and Greta were not interested, and Rex was in a brown study over his soup plate. Not only was the senator drunk, he was stubbornly and aggressively carrying on about his pet aversion, the British, who "over and over again had sacrificed innocent American boys to save their empire." Perhaps he was plastered enough to believe that Windsor shared this hostility toward his former subjects, which was a fatal mistake. The Duke lived abroad, but he felt no bitterness, let alone enmity.

The senator allowed his glass to be refilled. His face was already a dull red. Rex's was red, too, but for a different reason. Every critical remark about England affected him personally, and he stopped eating and looked murderously at the senator, who had just gotten onto the subject of the old destroyers that Roosevelt had sent to aid Churchill even before America entered the war. "That's where it began," he croaked, and I suddenly realized that we were dealing with a die-hard isolationist. "We've always had to pull the chestnuts out of the fire for the British. And what do we get out of it, I ask you? What do we get out of it?"

"The man's drunk, sir," I said quietly in German. "He doesn't know what he's saying."

"That's all right," said Windsor calmly. "These things happen. I just don't listen."

But Rex was listening and about to explode.

I turned to Jimmy, who was engrossed in modeling a battalion of little bread men, and whispered, "Jimmy, I beg you, change the subject this minute or something terrible is going to happen."

Jimmy nodded. "Say, fellows," he called across the table, forcibly interrupting the senator's tirade, "who's coming to San Fruttuoso with me tomorrow? I hear you can get marvelous lobsters there, right out of the sea."

The senator looked at Jimmy as if he were a lobster himself. He'd just got going on Roosevelt, his arch enemy, and how he'd been bribed by the British capitalists.

"Oh, well," said Jimmy, smiling at me, "we'll have to try something else." He stood up, pushed back his chair, strolled over to the rail, and casually vaulted over it into the water.

"Hurrah!" yelled the crowd on the dock, which had followed his every move with the same fascination we did. We all sat staring at the spot where Jimmy had vanished, as if he might reappear there, although we had plainly heard the loud splash when he hit the water some fifteen feet below . . .

Windsor was the first to recover his speech. He pointed to the empty seat beside me and said, "But there must be some protocol . . . !"

There sat the ex-King of England, his index finger raised like a suspended question mark. He had been brought up differently from ordinary mortals. In an interview shortly before his death, he said with disarming frankness, "I have never in my life picked anything up. When I take off my clothes, I simply drop them on the floor. I know there is always somebody behind me to pick them up." He was used to consulting an imaginary master of ceremonies, the chief of protocol, about all day-to-day events, but there was probably no regulation covering appropriate behavior when a guest jumped overboard in his dinner jacket.

No one moved. Even the German lesson had no guidance to offer. I glanced at Wallis. Her jaws were clenched and her nose white with shock and anger. "That boy has no manners," she finally managed to say. "I'd like to ask you all not to speak to him when he comes back. We'll act as if nothing's happened."

The shouting on shore suddenly redoubled. ("Three cheers for the brave swimmer!" "The company too hot for you, eh?") Jimmy must have been climbing out of the water. I could imagine what he looked like; the harbor was filthy, full of refuse, dead rats, and condoms. Before he jumped in, he'd been wearing an immaculate midnight-blue velvet dinner jacket over a pleated evening shirt, patent leather pumps, and diamond cuff links.

The senator was the only person who hadn't taken Jimmy's departure in. His wineglass was refilled and he was on the warpath again, with Roosevelt still the target. "A Bolshevik in disguise," he trumpeted, "America's ruination, destruction, perdition . . ."

Nobody contradicted him, because nobody was listening. The Duchess signaled to the steward, who distractedly handed the dishes around again, although our plates were still full. Suddenly Wallis said loudly and rudely, right into the senator's lecture, "Of course it's all his mother's fault. It's all Jessie Donahue's fault. On the one hand she pampers him, and on the other she keeps him so short of money that he doesn't care what—"

"And when he was elected for the third time . . ." said the senator.

"Elected?" said Greta in confusion. "Jimmy was elected?"

The senator demolished her with one look, but before he could get going on Roosevelt's fourth term, Jimmy appeared in the saloon doorway. He nodded pleasantly all around, as though he were seeing us for the first time that night, and walked to his chair. His hair was still dripping wet, but he had changed into a dark green velvet dinner jacket and a no less immaculate shirt.

"Well?" he said to me quite loudly. "Did it help? Are we on a different subject now?"

As if on cue, the senator bellowed, "Pearl Harbor would never have happened if Britain hadn't been in such a mess. To this day I'm convinced— and I wasn't the only one in the Senate who thought that way—that Churchill and Beaverbrook and the whole gang bribed the Japanese."

"Oh, for God's sake!" said Jimmy, patting me consolingly on the shoulder. "We'll just have to try again." He stood up and made for the rail once more. This time, however, he didn't bring off his vault quite so elegantly, because Greta had jumped up and was hanging onto his trouser leg. "Don't! Don't!" she pleaded. "Not again! You'll get sick. Stop! Ouch!"

He had given her a vigorous push, knocking her backwards onto the deck. Then he jumped over the rail, laughing, and disappeared into the black night.

Splash! The people on the dock broke into frenzied cheering, "Bravo! Hurrah!" or simply aboriginal screams of delight.

That did it. No hope of rescuing the party. Though the least concerned guest, the Russian George Schlee, made a brave try. He stood up, raised his glass a bit too high, and called out, "I propose a toast to the British Empire." Whereupon the senator could do nothing but struggle to his feet and empty his glass, muttering something unintelligible. The rest of us were already standing, glasses raised, repeating passionately, "To the British Empire." It was good to be able to stand up and do something.

Wallis didn't sit down again, so we got no dessert. She went straight back to the saloon, with us trotting behind her. There we stood around, because the coffee wasn't ready and the hosts and Jimmy had disappeared through another door.

"Let's go," said Greta.

"Without saying good-bye?"

"Without."

I felt I should make at least a gesture to cover our retreat and went to look for our hosts. Hearing voices from the library, I knocked and cautiously opened the door. Luckily they hadn't heard me, because all three were absorbed in a passionate "conversation."

I closed the door as noiselessly as possible. Then Schlee, Greta, Rex, and I tiptoed, crouching, down the gangplank and ran to the jeep.

"I need a black coffee," said Greta.

"I need a brandy," said Rex.

And the jeep roared off toward the security of the olive grove.

24 HOURS WITH GRETA GARBO

In 1931, Harriet Parsons—girl reporter, daughter of Louella Parsons (Hollywood's most powerful columnist), and eventually a respected movie producer (The Enchanted Cottage, Night Song, I Remember Mama, Clash by Night, Susan Slept Here)— *wrote for the fan magazine* Silver Screen *this riveting account of tailing Garbo for an entire day and night . . .*

G ARBO!
To the public she is a glamorous figure shrouded in mystery. To the press she's a framework on which to hang wild flights of journalistic fancy.

Garbo! If all the stories written about her were laid end to end they would reach from Hollywood back to her native Stockholm with enough stray adjectives left over to fill the Grand Canyon.

Yet no two stories are alike. Why? Because Garbo keeps her own counsel and much of the time her own company.

Now I, in common with some twenty million other movie fans, had thought about Garbo, dreamed about her, wondered about the hidden facts of her life. And also, I, like some hundred other writers, was dying to get a story on her that might reveal some of the facts about her—show the world the real Greta.

I was in Hollywood. Garbo was in Hollywood. If I was human—and I certainly am—so was Greta. She existed and had her being. She could be seen. When these bright ideas hit me, I got the big brain wave. Somehow, some way, I would stick by Garbo's side for a whole day—all twenty-four hours of it—all twenty-four hours when I was observing her but she didn't know she was being observed—and find out how she spent just one typical day of her lovely, glamorous life.

It wasn't an easy stunt—but oh, what a thrill!

I chose a Saturday night and a Sunday. I thought Greta would be free then, away from the studio and her art, most thoroughly herself. And, by a lucky chance I found out one salient fact—that Greta goes often to a little theatre in the Mexican quarter of Los Angeles, a theatre run by the Yale Puppeteers. I learned that on my particular Saturday there was to be an act burlesquing Hollywood and Garbo and I gambled that Garbo might go to witness it—gambled and won.

The theatre is on Olvera Street, a colorful segment of the angelic city, only a block long and barred to vehicles. It is more like a marketplace in the heart of old Mexico than a thoroughfare in the center of one of America's largest cities.

Next door to the theatre is a subterranean cafe—the Casa de la Golondrina. The menu is entirely Mexican and the people who dine there are interested in their food, not in sightseeing. It seemed to me just the type of place where Garbo might choose to eat before attending the puppet show. So I started my quest there.

I took no chances. The show didn't start till nine but at seven I was in the little cafe, seated alone with my hat pulled down over my eyes, at a table that overlooked every corner of the room. I stalled over my dinner, lingered over my coffee. Seven-thirty came, eight o'clock, eight-fifteen. I was just deciding this was my unlucky day when the door opened and a man and a girl entered quietly.

I caught my breath in excitement. It was Garbo! I sat breathless while she and her escort selected a table. It was the one next to mine, not four feet away. Garbo was dressed as no other girl in Hollywood would have been dressed—a grey suit, severely tailored, a man's grey shirt, a navy blue tie with white dots, a heavy grey topcoat and a dark blue beret with no hair showing from beneath it. Her pale, lovely face had a luminous quality and she was quietly very gay.

I dragged my fascinated eyes away from her to her escort—a tall man and slim, with an ironical mouth. Garbo was speaking to him in German but I decided that he wasn't German. Suddenly I recognized him—Jacques Feyder, the Belgian-French director, who made *The Kiss*, Garbo's last silent picture.

They began to eat. Greta had enchilada de la tapiata, a kind of Mexican pancake, dry and served with salad. She finished it and ordered a second dish—this time enchilada with a highly flavored chili sauce. Afterward she drank black coffee and smoked a denicotinized cigarette. A flower woman came by the table with her little tray of blossoms. Feyder purchased a gardenia and with a gallant gesture handed it to Garbo. She smiled at him and pinned it to the lapel of her coat.

At nine sharp she and Feyder left as quietly as they had come and walked next door to the Teatro Torrito. They sat down in the third row from the back of the tiny house and I slipped into the row just behind them. I pinched myself to be sure I am awake and sitting so close to my idol.

During the first sketch Garbo is quietly amused. I study her face and am amazed by two things—first, that she is even more beautiful off the screen than on, and younger—and, second, that she wears a light make-up, mascara and liprouge. Where is the colorless, drab, homely girl the fan writers have talked so much about? This off-screen Garbo is a lovely woman, wearing just enough make-up to accentuate her beauty.

The Hollywood sketch comes on. A puppet of George Arliss and one of Aimee Semple McPherson make their appearance. Then the Garbo puppet, dressed as Anna Christie. A hush falls on the small audience—by now everyone in the house knows that Garbo is present. They glance at her surreptitiously to see how she will react to the puppet of herself. But Garbo has seen it many times before. She chuckles throatily at the verse spoken by the little figure—particularly at the last lines:

> Dat old devil sea is a devil maybe
> but he was an angel to me.
> With photography misty I did Anna Christie
> and see what O'Neill did for me!
> If I should decide to go back home
> I could buy a half interest in Stockholm;
> I live life as I please with the world at my knees
> Singing "Skoal!" to dat old devil sea!

At the line about Stockholm Garbo laughs out loud—a good, hearty laugh—and looks up at Feyder, smiling. They are plainly very good, understanding friends.

At ten o'clock the curtain goes down on the final sketch. Garbo and Feyder slip through a side door into Adrian's Shop, next door. Adrian is the costume designer at M-G-M and I begin to feel scared—scared that my prey will slip away from me through some underground passage sacred to ladies of mystery.

But I go around in front of the shop and paste my nose against the glass of the door. Inside I see Garbo going from one object to another in the small shop, animatedly. She is gay and interested. Suddenly she spies a huge, fantastic monkey with a body of white fur and a comic red corduroy face. She stands delightedly while Adrian shows her how the arms and legs move. She is as pleased as a child.

Meantime, a crowd has collected outside the patio. With that genius peculiar to crowds, they have sensed a celebrity near-by—their greatest celebrity. But Garbo lingers in the shop until they have all gone except me. It is eleven when suddenly, much to my relief, Adrian, Garbo and Feyder come out and stroll up and down the street. Adrian is showing her the sights of the miniature village.

At eleven-twenty-five Garbo and Feyder enter Garbo's Lincoln limousine and the colored chauffeur starts off. Garbo in a Lincoln and me in a Ford! I pray my poor Lizzie will be equal to the task and set out in hot pursuit. I follow the big car so closely that I almost bump into it at several intersections. West, toward Hollywood, through Hollywood and Beverly Hills on out to the sea. As we approach Santa Monica, the chase grows exciting. Garbo lives somewhere in Santa Monica—but *where?* And after I discover where, what am I going to do about it?

Suddenly the big car slows down and turns sharply into a driveway thickly surrounded by trees. I make a note of the address and hastily survey the place. It is entirely surrounded by tall spruce trees, standing black in the blue of a California night. Not a glimpse of the house can be seen from the street. It is just the sort of place Garbo would choose. A fortress as impenetrable and hidden as she is herself. She disappears—Feyder departs alone—midnight arrives.

I settle down for a nocturnal vigil.

Only a little after daybreak, I begin to investigate my surroundings. I am in the vicinity of Brentwood, an exclusive community halfway between Santa Monica and Sawtelle. I wander about a bit and learn things. About five blocks from the Garbo ménage is the small, open market where Garbo herself comes after the fresh fruit and vegetables she loves, and the black Concord grapes for which she has a weakness. Here, too, is the drugstore to which she walks often, in the late afternoon. On such occasions she is always alone, clad in top-coat, beret and dark glasses. The proprietor tells me that she always goes straight to the magazine rack and buys all the new fan magazines—but that the clerks never speak to her unless she addresses them first. Her purchases in the drugstore seldom come to more than a dollar or two and she always pays cash, refusing to open an account.

By this time, the morning is advanced enough for me to return to my post outside the Garbo residence. The place is just as mysterious in the daytime as at night. There is no name on the mailbox. The thick wall of trees veils the house completely. On the east side a vacant lot, on the west another house, completely shut off by the same closely-planted trees. West of that, another vacant lot. I cross the lot on the east side of the house, hoping to get a view from the back—but a sheer cliff faces me. Garbo's garden ends at the cliff's edge and an iron railing runs along the brink. But, just between the last tree in the impenetrable wall of foliage, and the beginning of the railing is a tiny clear space, not more than two feet square. With a sudden burst of courage, I gain a precarious footage somewhere between earth and heaven, and, standing on this spot at peril to life and limb, I can see over a waist-high hedge—at last, a clear view of Garbo's house.

A two-story white Spanish house, with red-tiled roof. Rambling and larger than I had expected, but not pretentious. Typical of Garbo, who not only has a simple home, but runs it economically, keeping only three servants, a cook, a gardener and a chauffeur. Her bills for food average only sixty dollars a month, although both the cook and gardener live in. Besides buying in Brentwood, Garbo also goes into Los Angeles to get meat at Wreden's, a wholesale market.

On closer inspection, the atmosphere of her surroundings takes on a different aspect—one of dignity and reserve—but not necessarily of mystery.

A wide lawn surrounds the house, but at this early morning hour, it is deserted and silent. A heavy medicine ball lies on the grass. And an empty parrot cage. There is a rustle. I jump. A black and white cat strolls leisurely into view, followed by a small coal-black kitten. Hastily I snap some pictures and clamber down from my dangerous perch.

Garbo is nowhere to be seen so I decide to go and see the neighbors. Their house is only a few feet from Garbo's, but completely screened by foliage. My visit reveals only one thing—Garbo's neighbors have never met her nor exchanged a single word with her. I seem to know more about her after one evening of research than the people who had lived beside her for months.

I returned to my vantage point. This time through a small gap in the tree-wall I can see a figure lying on the grass in a patch of sunshine. It is Garbo. She is curled up under an old robe with only her bare legs visible. She talks to the cats. She sings in a deep pleasant voice a German song—Schubert's Serenade. At twelve the cook comes out, bringing luncheon on a tray. Garbo speaks to her in English, asking for some Swedish bread! They talk for a moment—gesturing toward the empty cage. They are bewailing the fact that the parrot has flown away. Both are despondent, but Garbo especially feels the loss. For she loves all sorts of birds and animals, and is apt to take her whole crew of pets with her when she goes away for a week or two. When her kittens were at a veterinary hospital she went to see them every day.

Leaving Garbo to eat her luncheon in solitude, I take up my post across the street. Hours of waiting. Being Sunday, she prolongs her solitary sunbath. At last she goes in the house and before long a lone figure emerges from the heavily shadowed driveway. She wears a polo coat and the inevitable beret, a white skirt and blue navy jacket and heavy flat-heeled shoes. She walks vigorously and so fast that I have difficulty in keeping up with her, even at a discreet distance. Through back streets, down into the canyon behind her home, then into the hills on the other side she plunges, with me fast on her heels. At last she doubles back and toward the ocean, winding up finally at a house in a side street very near the sea. The mailbox tells me that it is the home of Viertel, the director. Mrs. Viertel, a German, played Marie Dressler's part in the German version of *Anna Christie* and coached Garbo in the language. They are close friends, and when she is not working, Garbo goes almost every day to the Viertels, and almost as often to the Feyders. Those two families are her closest friends, and she is gay and sociable when she is with them.

About four-thirty the entire Viertel family, including a crew of youngsters, emerges from the house with Garbo. They all pile into a Buick sedan. Garbo drives. She's an erratic chauffeur and the cab which I hastily summon (having left my own Lizzie parked before her house) has difficulty following her devious route. But finally we end up at the Feyder home in Brentwood, some four miles away.

By this time I was quite proficient at looking over fences, so with a paean of praise for Spanish patios, where all is open for the world to see, I manage to find a place from which I can view the Feyder festivities.

The entire French colony seems to have gathered there—among others I recognized Mirande, the writer, Gregore, the actor, and André Luguet and his wife. The place is alive with children. There are three small Feyders and several small Luguets.

Garbo comes into the patio, beret in hand. Her hair hangs almost straight to her shoulders, parted on one side as she wore it in *Anna Christie*, and without any attempt at coiffure. But she still wears a light make-up like that of the night before.

She talks to the children and plays with them. Obviously she loves them and they adore her. Then she talks to Feyder about the picture she is soon to begin and seems anxious about her work. Contrary to the accepted opinion, she adores her work and has no desire to give it up. And before each new picture, she is as nervous as an amateur. After each picture is completed, she is certain that she has given a bad performance and talks of leaving the screen. When the picture is a success—as it always is!—she decides to try once more. And because she is so engrossed in her work, she loves to talk about it even during her hours of relaxation.

Finally, she turns from Feyder, and leaning on the back of a chair, engages in conversation with Mirande. She is gay, laughing, full of life—not at all the sombre melancholy figure I had expected her to be. The patio is alive with laughter and conversation.

Garbo stays just an hour. Then takes her departure alone. No one tries to stop her or to insist upon going with her. All seem to take it as a matter of course that she should leave suddenly and by herself. They understand her desire to be alone.

Again she strides along the quiet roads and back streets. She seems to know every stone—she walks alone from two to three hours every day either early in the morning or late in the afternoon—whether she is working or not.

There is no sign of life anywhere, except for the tall solitary figure of Garbo. She turns up the driveway, dark and gloomy now that the sun has set.

It is my last sight of her for the day. There is no sound from the house and there are lights only in the bedroom and kitchen. Apparently she is having her dinner in bed, just as she frequently does when she is working.

It is eight-thirty. The golden moon hangs low in the cloudless California sky. The air is sweet with the scent of blossoms drifting down from distant hills. I watch the big house and see the lights being extinguished one by one. Then everywhere there is silence and peace. The garden lies quiet.

Garbo is asleep.

JAMES HARVEY ON *CAMILLE*

This anatomy of Garbo's greatest performance appeared in James Harvey's final book, Watching Them Be: Star Presence on the Screen from Garbo to Balthazar *(2014). Harvey, who died six years later at the age of ninety, wrote only three books—this one and* Romantic Comedy in Hollywood: From Lubitsch to Sturges *and* Movie Love in the Fifties. *Every one of them is essential reading.*

Bᴜᴛ ᴛʜᴇɴ ᴄᴀᴍᴇ *ᴄᴀᴍɪʟʟᴇ* ɪɴ 1937, and it was, by common agreement, beyond any Garbo experience so far. "Seeing her here," wrote Otis Ferguson in *The New Republic*, "one realizes that this is more than there are words for, that it is simply the most absolutely beautiful thing of a generation." And there was a lot more like this in most of the notices. (Not enough to get her an Academy Award, however.)

Irving Thalberg, the film's producer, and the main architect of her M-G-M career, saw it right away. She's never been quite like this before, he said, she's never been so good—as he watched the first rushes with the movie's director, George Cukor. But how could he tell? asked Cukor (as he would later recount)—"she's just sitting there." Thalberg's answer to this was that she was "unguarded," more than she had ever been. (Thalberg died just weeks later, at thirty-seven—it was the only big public funeral Garbo was ever known to attend.)* And it's true: it's almost a new Garbo, relaxed into her role from the beginning with a freedom we have never quite felt in her before (compare her first appearance in *Grand Hotel*). Besieged as that freedom quickly is in the film, first by Prudence in the carriage (Laura Hope Crews—the "Aunt Pittypat" of *Gone with the Wind*), then at the theater by their fellow courtesan Olympe (Lenore Ulric), the one fussing at her about money, the other about men. Where Prudence is avaricious, Olympe is jealous and spiteful—and they are both noisy and quarrelsome, with Garbo's Marguerite caught between them, laughing resignedly, but saying finally, "You really are a fool, Olympe," in simple sad acknowledgment.

The theater is an ornate Belle Époque music hall. It has gypsy dancers on the stage and formally dressed gentlemen on the prowl in the lobby. Garbo's Marguerite passes through it all at first, obliquely but surely, a lovely leaning diagonal among the upright top-hatted men and the pillow-shaped overdressed women—and then regards it gravely from the top of a staircase (a private moment). Next you see her on display in her box, seeming very gay—she is a pro, after all. And beyond that she has this deeply *humorous* presence, sitting there, biding her time. Even her relation to her own finery—fingering the fur on her wrap, tapping her necklace with a fingernail, playing idly with her jeweled opera glasses—feels amused. This is the scene that Thalberg saw—and it's wonderful.

Prudence, now seated beside her, is pointing out to her the very rich

---

* Although even her attendance has been disputed.

Baron de Varville (Henry Daniell) in the seats below them just at the moment when Marguerite is focusing her opera glass on the improbably handsome Armand Duval (Robert Taylor). "I didn't know that rich men ever looked like that," she says gutturally, lowering the binoculars and her voice at the same time. A lascivious sound.

Out in the lobby at the entr'acte, having turned to make sure that the young man has seen and followed her, she looks at him invitingly, head back, eyes widening, eyebrows arching: a *well-why-not?* look and smile, the most enchanting invitation you could imagine, reckless and gay. But as often with her at such moments, the enchantment has a surprising depth: a powerful benignity, a largesse of spirit that seems Garbo's alone. (It makes your own heart pound.)

They seem almost fated to meet, she says to him—sliding her arm into his and returning with him to her box. Inside, she steps away and leans back to look at him up and down—savoring her catch—then sits. He sits next to her. He tells her that he has been hoping for this meeting for a long time, adding: "You don't believe me?" "No," she says, looking straight ahead and laughing softly: she doesn't believe it, but she doesn't mind hearing it. Since he first laid eyes on her four months ago he's been following her around Paris, he tells her, and proceeds to give details of his sightings. But if all that is true, she says—beginning to be impressed—why hasn't he spoken to her before this? Because before this we hadn't met, he says—as she turns now to look at him. "And you hadn't smiled at me until now," he adds. "And now? Since you've met me?" she says, turning away again, with a smile that looks more like a wince (the kid's an innocent—what must he *really* think of her?). "Now I *know* that I love you," he answers gravely, "and have loved you since that first day." She turns to look at him again, with wonder—into his eyes, then above them, her gaze traveling over and around the face. That observing ironic distance of hers—something she somehow maintains through each encounter with others—seems to have been breached.

But then Prudence returns to the box and the confusion of identities is cleared up: he is not the Baron. But stay, says Marguerite tenderly, to the mortified (and far from rich) Armand, "even if you're not the rich Baron."

She is not sorry for the mistake, she says. But when he goes out before the curtain to buy her "some marrons glacés," the rich Baron enters and she goes off with him. When Armand returns, the box is empty. She has to live, after all (we've already heard about her bills).

"I'm not always sincere," she tells Armand in this same sequence—regretfully. "One can't be in this world, you know." But what she calls "insincerity" is really another name for her triumphant (as we register it here) worldliness, her social brilliance. She has fun with this skill in action, and so do we. But even "just sitting there" she seems remarkable enough. Her Marguerite is a virtuoso turn but not a diva one. Rather than overwhelming or overbearing you, she keeps her usual and essential distance. And her character becomes like those people in Shakespeare that Harold Bloom especially celebrates, the "heroic vitalists," as he calls them, the ones like Falstaff and Cleopatra, who are not larger than life but "life's largeness" itself. Like them, Garbo's Marguerite finally transcends even her own story. And within it, she comprehends everyone else: she simply *knows* more than anyone else, and knows *them* better than any of them (Armand included) could ever know her. And she is alive with this comprehension, making you feel that much more alive as you watch her.

When she encounters Armand again, it is after one of her long illnesses in bed. She is at an estate auction of another once high-living Paris courtesan (she wants to bid to keep Olympe from hiring—and inevitably abusing— the late woman's elderly coachman). Armand is there, too—and she finds out that he is the unnamed man who kept calling and leaving flowers for her while she was sick. And she offers him one of her little arias of feminine inconsequence, inviting him to the party the following night at her place. "It's my birthday," she says, covering her mouth with her kerchief, looking stricken-eyed at him. But his seriousness keeps intruding. As when he now makes her a pointed present of a leather-bound volume, *Manon Lescaut*, warning her that the story ("about a woman who lives only for pleasure") is a sad one: the heroine dies. "Then I'll keep it," she says, taking the book, "but I won't read it," adding, "I hate sad thoughts"—kittenish now. But then another thought comes: "However" (a beat) "we all die," she says, looking up at him brightly—he'd better know that any subject can provide her with a stage to be dazzling on. Though this one gets slightly out of her control with her next words: "But perhaps someday this book" (holding it and looking at it) "will be sold again at an auction after *my* death . . ." Armand is disturbed by this. "I thought you didn't like sad thoughts," he says. "I don't," she replies, brightening again, squeezing his forearm, and twinkling up at him, "but they come sometimes." And off she goes. She can handle *him*, all right—it's quite clear.

But at the birthday party, that's not so clear. Here—instead of the airhead Manon imitation we've just been watching—she seems truly like a girl, young and a little silly. Can those locks of Shirley Temple curls be meant to encourage that idea? In any case they suit her, however surprisingly. As does her alarmingly low-cut huge-skirted white party gown, exposing her beautiful eloquent shoulders more nakedly than ever. "I want to hear the joke!" she cries pettishly, at the head of her birthday table, when a dirty story starts to circulate around it behind cupped hands, greeted with whoops and howls of laughter, especially from the women, and disapproved of by Armand, who is seated next to her. Not, he says, that he doesn't know all the stories himself (Marguerite rolls her eyes at the others)—"In fact I told Gaston most of them," he adds, with an embarrassing lack of conviction. Then, lowering his voice: "But I'd rather they weren't told at your table." Now she seems embarrassed. "Oh come, come," she says softly. "You must remember"—lifting her glass to him—"I'm not a colonel's daughter just out of the convent." No indeed. But this concession to his decorum, with that curious toasting gesture, is touching.

But she is overexerting. And Armand seems the only one at her party who notices that she is, when she leaves the room where she has been dancing boisterously with Gaston (Rex O'Malley), coughing into the handkerchief she seems always to have clutched in her hand, and goes through the jolly crowd out of the light and into her darkened bedroom alone, where there is an Empire couch with two candles burning at its head, like a bier. She sinks onto the couch, into the darkness, the candlelight gleaming off her shoulders and hair, as she falls backward with open mouth to breathe, then sitting up again, bending forward, over and into that billowing white skirt, to reach for one of the candles, rising with it and going off right to her dressing table mirror. It's one slowly flowing movement—her long legato line, what Cukor called her plastique—both beautiful and disturbing.

But never mind: she's in front of her mirror now, darkness behind her, popping another pill from her little tin, sucking on it and pinning what looks (and sounds) like a paper flower to the top of her hair, and appearing, for the first time in the film, sort of tarty, even tough (coughing is hard). When Armand comes silently in behind her, she looks at him in her mirror. "You look ill too," she says. He tells her she is killing herself. "If I am," she replies, "you're the only one who objects." And when she gives him her hand to return to the party, he stands still in the shadows, lifts it to his mouth, and kisses it. "What a child you are," she says—seeming quite detached from what he is doing with the hand, sucking on her lozenge and observing him speculatively. "Your hand is so hot," he says, holding on to it. She comes closer, her tone is kinder: "Is that why you put tears on it? To cool it?" she asks playfully. But he doesn't want to be talked to this way, he wants her to take him seriously. Besides, somebody should be looking after her: "And I could if you'd let me," he says. This tears it. She draws away from him. "Too much wine," she says coldly, "has made you sentimental."

She, on the other hand, is *not* sentimental—she is not even romantic. Her "insincerity" is her lifeline: her need to stay on the surface when there is only meaninglessness below—or self-deception. She offers him "some good advice": he should be married, not hanging out with people like her friends and her—and she is no better than they are. He turns away. "What on earth am I going to do with you?" she says softly, kneading her kerchief in one hand and leaning toward him across the couch between them. The question is real, and he is encouraged, seizing her by the shoulders and declaring: "No one has ever loved you as I love you!" It's too much: his urgency seems to break against and over her like a wave, leaving her beached in his hands, her head lolling to one side, looking up at him. "That may be true," she says in a dead voice, "but what can I do about it?"

Still, she doesn't want to let him go, especially if he goes in anger. "Why don't you laugh at yourself as I laugh at myself? And come and see me once in a while in a friendly way?" But he can't be appeased in that way, and he is beginning to wear her down—until she makes a crucial concession: "I believe you're sincere at least," she says. Return tomorrow, she says at last. No, to-night, he says—and she agrees. She will get rid of the party guests first, and then he can come back. This is not like the marrons glacés errand, is it? he says. She gives him her key. He kneels at her feet like a knight errant. Bending from the waist, she kisses him lightly all over his upturned face, roaming over it with her mouth the way she'd done with her eyes that first time in the opera box.

The problem, as both she and we are aware, is likely to be her current lover and supporter, the Baron. We've already seen her, in an earlier sequence with him, behaving like a mistress, saying goodbye to him as he leaves for Russia. They are affectionate with each other, but he would like her to be sorrier about his approaching absence than she is. The Baron is the one with whom she most clearly demonstrates her honest sort of insincerity, giving little moues of concern when he speaks of his going, half reclining on a lounge (she has been ill—this is before she encounters Armand at the auction) as the Baron sits beside and leans over her while she plays with the monocle that hangs from a chain on his neck, like a petted daughter with Daddy. She is not meaning to deceive him—nor does she—but only to play out with credit the necessary scene between them. We know that he is bad news—not only because the genre requires it but because he is played by Henry Daniell, who has a cruel mouth and who was already typed in movies as a suave villain.

And instead of Armand it's the Baron who turns up later that night. He hasn't gone to Russia after all. He has a key, too, and he lets himself in with it—just when she is expecting Armand. Who is the midnight supper laid out for? inquires the Baron. "You," she replies, without skipping a beat. "I have learned never to believe a man when he says he's leaving town." But she is panicked. She had been playing the piano when he came in—a waltz full of arpeggio excitement; now she asks him to play, he does it so beautifully. And knowing that Armand (with *his* key) may arrive at any moment, she whispers to her maid and surrogate mother, Nanine (the wonderful Jessie Ralph, who played Peggotty in Cukor's *David Copperfield*), to bolt the door. Marguerite leans on the piano as the Baron at the keyboard plays—with his nasty smile.

And as the tension between them grows, the scene gets uglier. She is committed to playing out her deception (a real one this time), even past the point, soon reached, where she can suppose she has any hope of fooling him. And he is reduced to taking whatever satisfaction he can from her growing discomfort. Each of them is angry at the other for the situation they are in, and at themselves. And the exacerbated feelings rise to an almost operatic pitch when Armand rings and knocks futilely outside, and the Baron plays with equivalent force and vehemence, and Marguerite keeps him playing, bantering with him rather than going to the door, where the noise is getting louder. "I'll tell you who it is," she says—then, with a hearty roguishness: "I could say" (a beat) "that there is someone at the wrong door . . ." And they both laugh unpleasantly—Varville's self-dislike finding an echo in her own, a hysterical one, mounting to something like a shared rapture between them. "*Or*—if not the wrong door—the great romance of my life!" The Baron likes this joke even more, his piano crescendos, the camera bears down on them (the only bravura camera move in the film) as she leans, almost falling, toward the keyboard and the Baron, laughing helplessly—laughing together as the scene fades out. "It might have been," she says (the guttural voice) and laughs some more.

Can she really come back from that? you wonder. It's a nightmare culmination of what we've seen (and admired) as her social brilliance, a kind of final "insincerity." But in the next sequence she seeks Armand out in his chambers and there they become lovers. But not before (a Garbo necessity) she has looked at his family pictures. Especially of his long-married parents: "And they loved each other all that time?" she asks. And now it's her turn to drop a tear. Why? he asks. "It's impossible to believe in such happiness," she says.

But she is tempted by belief. And it helps that he is almost as nice as he is handsome. You have only to look at her looking at him to feel her feeling for him (and Taylor, one of her less objectionable leading men, hardly distracts you from it)—the sheer fondness, as strong as a passion, both doting and distanced at once. He is, after all, *very* unworldly. As she registers once again when he tells her they can live together in the countryside on what he calls his fortune, seven thousand francs. She replies that she spends more than that in a month—"and I was never too particular about where it came from, as you probably know."

But this is just the sort of knowingness that he wants her to leave behind. And so she does. "It's heaven!" she tells him, waking in his arms when he first carries her into their country home. And later, together on their hillside, she presses her face against the earth. But the Baron's château is visible from that same hillside. And Armand, prone to jealousy, is growingly despondent. "I always know he's there," he tells her. "But I am always here," she says, pulling him toward her, her voice almost mewing with concern and tenderness. Before telling him that he has come to "mean everything" to her—"more than the world, more than myself." But when he asks her to marry him, she is frightened. She is almost *too* happy.

But the "brilliant" Marguerite reappears—after Duval père (Lionel Barrymore in his most unctuous mode) visits and prevails on her to give up his son for the sake of his future in society. She agrees, of course (does she ever *not?*), and resolves to make Armand believe she no longer loves him by returning to the rich Baron—proving her love (to *us* at least) by abandoning it. But the urgency of Garbo's suffering in these scenes makes you almost forget the formulaic contrivances. In her curls again, in another (or the same) naked-shoulder white dress, she joins Armand in their sitting room—where she performs an ugly caricature of her social self, repelling his concern with cynical rejoinder, even making him afraid, as he says, that she no longer loves him. "Well, perhaps I don't really," she replies, looking wan and drawn, pushing herself with hands on his shoulders up and out of his arms, leaning into her own heaviness to move away. "Only last night you were ready to give up everything for me," he says. "Well, that was last night," she says, biting off the words; "people sometimes say things they don't mean at night." And you feel all her revulsion at what she's having (as she sees it) to do— she's drawing on her bitterness just to get through it—until she tells him that she is leaving him tonight ("Baron de Varville is expecting me") and, throwing on her cape, scuttles from the room, a sudden crablike darting motion out the door, and over the hill in the moonlight to the Baron's château.

And from then on she really *is* killing herself—with the full compliance of the Baron, who is getting his own back for what she's done to him before this, as we see when the unhappy couple appear at a Paris gambling club where Armand, equally embittered now, publicly reviles Marguerite and challenges the Baron to a duel. They both survive, we soon learn, but as a consequence, Armand is exiled from Paris. He gets back, in the final sequence, to reunite with the ailing Marguerite, but only just before she dies.

Before that, however, there's the struggle—in Nanine's strong but loving arms, with Marguerite begging, imploring her to let her get out of bed (he's here!). Being helped to a chair and then somehow managing to stand for him, she seems emptied of everything except that uncanny radiance—greeting Armand—who catches her in his arms just in time. And holds her: forgive me, he begs her—as she gazes up at him raptly—of *course* she forgives him (she makes a faint little "oh" sound). He knows now, he says, that no good can come to either of them apart. "I know that, too," she says—as if she has always known it, in spite of the suffering she's put herself through. Now, with her riveted moist-eyed gaze, her mouth-half-open smile, her total absorption in the face and voice above her, she's on a level of ecstatic "knowing" beyond even his—and it's almost enough. We'll go back to the country again, he says, and we'll go today. And she responds with delight to this—but then collapses. She dies in his arms while he's still trying to talk her around—opening her eyes and frowning slightly, as if a worried thought had come to her and passed. Then lapsing into serenity, her head thrown back—Armand relaxes his hold—just as it so often had been at the eagerest points of her life.

"You actually see her do it," said Cecelia Ager's *PM* review about Garbo's dying in this scene, "sense the precise moment when her lovely spirit leaves her fascinating clay." And so you can (that passing frown, I think). The "clay" goes without saying, of course. But it's as if the "spirit" had never been so lovely as here—it's as if all those other movies, all those finally redeemed whores, had been a rehearsal for this one, for this pinnacle. As if *now* you can see what she's been getting at—right? As Alistair Cooke saw it even before this in *Anna Karenina*—in the "protective tenderness" she wrapped around the other characters (even Fredric March, according to him). And the moral beauty of her Marguerite has its final, purest, and most piercing expression in these final scenes, in which this "tolerant goddess" (Cooke again)—who has always somehow seemed, even when at her most desperate, to have retained a goddesslike final control—is reduced here to a hapless humanity, even a piteous one. With Garbo trapped in confining close-up, tossing her head on the pillow as she struggles against Jessie Ralph's Nanine to get out of bed, and then being too weak to make it, then crying, even whimpering, until her friend and maid helps her, weeping herself as she does.

And she remains "Garbo" at such moments, never losing her essential dignity—or her distance from us. She still inspires awe, but in *Camille* that is more than it ever has been before about the tragic magnanimity she imbues the character with. Her Marguerite is above everything a kind of great soul—with a way of being in the world that feels rich and generous even when it's most challenged. She is moving even when she *isn't* dying. "Woman is the world and man lives in it," George Balanchine once said, gnomically and characteristically. And among the great stars of the past, it seems to me, it's Garbo who comes the very closest to showing us what that means.

EDWARD G. ROBINSON IN *ALL MY YESTERDAYS*

*A major star (*Little Caesar, Double Indemnity, Key Largo*), Robinson was known for his superb private art collection.*

I NEVER PLAYED WITH GARBO. She was as mysterious and unreachable to me as she was to you—except that one day in the remodeled house the bell rang, and against all my principles I answered the door myself. There, through the peephole, I saw a lady with a floppy hat holding a package. And the lady said: "Is Mr. Robinson in? My name is Garbo."

I opened the door. She came in, shook hands with me stiffly in the European manner, asked my pardon for intruding, but there was a matter of some importance she wished to discuss with me if I could spare her a moment or two. Greta Garbo in my house! I was overwhelmed, awed, and as nervous as a cat.

I took her into the living room; she glanced at the pictures on the wall approvingly but did not look at them closely. She refused to sit down, toyed with the string on her package, having some trouble with the knots, refused to let me help her, and finally unveiled a painting.

Was it worth buying?

It was a landscape by an artist I had never heard of. It had quite a decent feeling about it, though far from masterly. It could be called a daub except that it was brooding and sylvan and rather like her—or at least the image that you and I had come to have about her.

"Is it worth—" she started to ask, and I interrupted, I hope, politely.

"Don't tell me the price yet," I said. "Tell me if you like it."

"I do at night," she said. "In the morning I am not so sure."

"Then," I said, "live with it for a few weeks before making up your mind today."

"But it is necessary," she insisted, "that I make up my mind today."

"Do not be forced into a decision you might regret."

"You are right, Mr. Robinson," she said. "I do not like to be forced until I am certain. Yet, he needs the money."

"The artist?"

"No, the man who bought it from the artist and now needs to sell it in order to eat."

"In that case," I said, "you are not buying a picture; you are giving charity. How much charity does he want?"

"Two hundred dollars."

"For two hundred dollars," I told her, "you are getting a very nice picture. And if you find you do not like it, you can always give it away or put it in a closet."

"That is excellent advice, Mr. Robinson," she said, "but two hundred dollars is still quite a lot of money. Can I take it off my tax?"

"I don't know, Miss Garbo," I said. "I suggest you talk to your accountant."

"He will charge me," she said. Again refusing help, she wrapped the picture again. "I will buy it. It is nice. It is about forests. And I like forests."

She started for the door. I followed her and opened it for her.

"Thank you very much for your time, Mr. Robinson," she said, and then suddenly she smiled that *Ninotchka* smile. "You also have nice pictures. Very nice. Thank you. Good bye."

I never saw her again.

GLIMPSES OF GARBO

✺

IRENE MAYER SELZNICK IN *A PRIVATE VIEW*

[Our tennis court] had lights. Only once were they turned on at night, and that was for Garbo, who had an urge to play after the preview of *Anna Karenina*. I don't know whose tennis shoes she wore, but I do know that never before or since have I seen her in such high spirits. We never knew each other well, but more than twenty years later she gave me another surprise. Our mutual friend Sam Spiegel, who occasionally had lunch with us on Christmas Day, one year proposed bringing Garbo, but on second thought he came alone and asked us to join her and him at his place later in the day. Jeff and Danny, well into their twenties, were beside themselves with delight. Assuming she might be less than delighted, I said that we'd better make it brief and not impose.

I underestimated Garbo, who put me to shame. She came forward eagerly to meet the boys, saying, "Did you know I knew your mother before you did?" She made it sound an astonishing treat as she told all about the Adlon Hotel in 1924. I was pretty fascinated myself, because she had never before given any hint that she remembered. She was charm itself as she linked them not only with me, but with my father and with their father. They were bowled over.

Christmas gets to everyone, even Garbo. As I was leaving, she took me aside and said what, at least for the moment, she clearly felt: she wished she had children. "You have everything," she said. "I have nothing. I envy you."

Doug and Mary gave a dinner party for one of the male members of the Royal Family, here from London more or less incognito . . . Afterward there was general dancing, and I became a wallflower. I sat on a couch with another young actress, who said, "I don't like to dance," in one of the loveliest voices I'd ever heard. It was strongly accented, very low and whispery as though it just took too much energy to talk. It would be years before the public would be privileged to hear that voice: "Gimme a visky, ginger ale on the side, and don't be stingy, baby." Garbo, of course. I had heard of her: She'd come from Sweden, had made one American picture and there were great possibilities for her future. Indeed there were! We talked about the party, about clothes, about movies; we discovered we were born the same year, 1906 [*sic*], that we both had trouble sleeping; I took hot milk before going to bed, she liked chocolate, "something sveet." That's all. I never saw her again, except in films.

NED ROREM IN *THE PARIS AND NEW YORK DIARIES OF NED ROREM*

1951: Lunch at Charles de Noailles's in Grasse. Cocteau is the only other guest. He speaks of Garbo. "Because she has carte blanche she only goes when she's not invited. Last week in Paris she knocked unexpectedly at my door. I was busy, *mais que voulez-vous?* There's only one Greta. I took her to eat at Véfour. In her baby French we talked of how sad, how sad that she was afraid to mime the Phèdre that Auric and I had created for her last year. After coffee she vanished into the afternoon."

January 1961: I passed twenty Christmas days in Manhattan slush where for the new year I took Joe LeSueur to Ruth Ford's and there was Garbo. (Annually the Scotts receive what are called "celebrities," all very on-stage. When Garbo, uninvited, walked in, they were all suddenly off-stage. For who can do better? Joe whispered, "Is that who I think it is? Promise that whether or not we meet her, we must say we did! Her eyes are larger than anyone's have a right to be.")

BILLY WILDER IN CAMERON CROWE'S *CONVERSATIONS WITH WILDER*

One day I saw her running, exercising, up Rodeo Drive. Rodeo then had a track in the middle where you could run. So she was running up Rodeo and she was very sweaty, and I stopped her and said, "Hi, how are you? I'm Billy Wilder." And she said [imitating her smoky accent], "Yes, I know you." "Would you like to have a martini or something to drink? I live right around the corner, Beverly Drive." She said, "Yes, I would like to." So I took her home. It was in the afternoon, and she collapsed in the chair and I said, "I will call my wife, she is upstairs, to come and fix us a drink." And I said, "Aud, come on down, guess who we have here." She says, "Who, Otto Preminger?"—somebody like that. And I said, "No, Greta Garbo." And she said, "Oh, go on, go *fuck* yourself!" And I said, "No, honestly." So she came down and I introduced her, and Aud fixes a martini, really strong, big, and [Garbo] had that thing in one gulp, and then another one and another one. They drink them like beer, the Swedish—martinis . . . And we started to talk about pictures and she said [does accent] "I would like to make a picture about a clown." I said, "Oh, that's fine." "I always am a clown, and I am wearing a mask, and I will not take the mask off. I will only be in a picture as a clown" . . . So she wanted to play the clown, and not show her face. A clown who grins all the time. I said, "That might be difficult." She said, "I play a clown. I always play a clown [in life] . . . I will always be a clown."

LON CHANEY

They liked each other, Fritiof Billquist tells us. "How are you, Garbo girl?" was Chaney's greeting when they shared a table for lunch. His advice to her was, "Don't let anyone influence you; just be yourself." In one picture he was playing a blind man and Garbo watched him spraying his eyeballs with a thick gray fluid to look blind. "But Lon," she exclaimed, "is that necessary? Suppose it damaged your eyesight?" "I don't think it will," he replied, smiling. "One must do something for the dough." When later she asked her interpreter, Borg, what dough was, "Money," he told her. She nodded thoughtfully. "Lon's right. There's a lot one has to do for one's money."

INGMAR BERGMAN IN *THE MAGIC LANTERN*

Garbo, in Stockholm, visits him in what was her old studio and what had been Mauritz Stiller's room.

Suddenly she took off her concealing sunglasses and said, "This is what I look like, Mr. Bergman." Her smile was swift and dazzling, teasing.

It is hard to say whether great myths are unremittingly magical because they are myths or whether the magic is an illusion, created by us consumers; but at that particular instant there was no doubt. In the half-light in that cramped room, her beauty was imperishable. If she had been an angel from one of the gospels, I would have said her beauty floated about her. It existed like a vitality around the big pure features of her face, her forehead, the intersection of her eyes, the nobly-shaped chin, the sensitivity of her nostrils. She immediately registered my reaction, was exhilarated and started talking about her work on Selma Lagerlöf's *Gösta Berling's Saga* . . .

[Later] she leant over the desk so that the lower half of her face was lit by the desk lamp.

Then I saw what I had not seen! Her mouth was ugly, a pale slit surrounded by transverse wrinkles. It was strange and disturbing. All that beauty and in the middle of the beauty a shrill discord. No plastic surgeon or make-up man could conjure away that mouth and what it told me. She at once read my thoughts and grew silent, bored. A few minutes later we said goodbye.

I have studied her in her last film, when she was thirty-six. Her face is beautiful but tense, her mouth without softness, her gaze largely unconcentrated and sorrowful despite the comedy. Her audience perhaps had an inkling of what her make-up mirror had already told her.

IRENE GALITZINE (RUSSIAN PRINCESS AND
FASHION DESIGNER)

The first time I met her was on the Onassis' boat, in Monte Carlo in the mid-1950s. There was a great party. But the day after, my husband and I left for a trip with some friends and I saw her for a very short time, but it was amazing 'cause I had been loving her since I was a little girl. Then I saw her again in Greece, I don't remember the year. I was on the *Creole*, the boat of Stavros Niarchos who was taking us to a little island that he had recently bought and wanted us to visit. When we arrived in front of the island, we saw another boat there. It was the Onassis' *Christina*. There were some people with him, and among these people were Garbo with a companion, named George Schlee. He was Russian and he said he was a relative of mine. I did not think so and I did not like him very much. It was on that occasion that I had the possibility to know her well. She was shy, reserved, almost complexed. Then, when she drank, she melted, she changed. I remember that my husband and Prince Aldobrandini courted her and asked her, "Why could you quit the movies? Why such crime?" And she replied, "Who? Me in the movies? I don't remember being in the movies."

MARION DAVIES IN *THE TIMES WE HAD*

One night Greta Garbo came to the beach house with Jack [Gilbert]. She walked in the door saying, "Hullo. I'm tired," then the first thing she did was to take off her high heels and throw them in the hall. She said, "You got a pair of bedroom slippers?"

I said yes.

I was getting them for her when I heard sounds. I found her jumping on my four-poster bed, testing the mattress. She was jumping so hard, her head was hitting the canopy. She said, "Good mattress."

When she got the slippers she said to me, "Get me a knife." She slit the backs off my slippers and put elastic bands around them. "Thank you," she said and went downstairs.

She didn't dance at all. She just sat in one corner with Jack Gilbert. Everybody was looking at her, saying hello and all that, and it sort of annoyed her. She was terrifically shy; she didn't want to mingle with anybody. It wasn't snobbishness, just shyness. I never saw the like of it in anybody else.

KEN MURRAY

Murray's Los Angeles revue, Blackouts—*chorus girls, funny skits—opened in 1942 and ran for 3,844 performances! Young congressman Richard Nixon saw it a dozen times: "Thank God for* Blackouts," *he told Murray. "I don't know where else I could take a lot of these dull political people I have to entertain." (Fun for Pat!)*

"Garbo," said Murray, "was in several times on the QT. We'd reserve a seat for her in the balcony, and she'd slip in after the curtain went up and leave just before the curtain came down. When there were stars in the audience, I'd usually introduce them. Bob Hope would come on stage and do half an hour. W. C. Fields, Jack Benny and George Burns also came up and ad-libbed with me. Of course, I never put Garbo in that position."

Of course. But what was she doing there in the first place?

HOWARD GREER (COUTURIER)

We were talking one day between fittings. "I suppose everyone who is famous comes into this shop," said Garbo. "Don't they frighten you? People always frighten me."

DAGMAR GODOWSKY (SILENT FILM STAR), INTERVIEWED BY JOHN KOBAL IN *PEOPLE WILL TALK*

John Kobal: Didn't you also know Garbo?

Dagmar Godowsky: Ohhhhh, *very* well . . . I used to see her a great deal. She was very, very shy . . . terribly interested in astrology. Isn't it funny, you remember certain habits of people . . . I really couldn't tell you if she was intelligent. I wouldn't know. She talks *very* little about herself. Practically not at all. I think she's amazed at the success she's made . . . just as Valentino, were he still alive today, would not have believed that he is still a saga.

JK: Did they ever meet, Garbo and Valentino?

DG: I don't know if they met. She's only met a great many people recently. She didn't like to meet people. She likes the way we used to be together. She's a good listener. I never heard her talk very much. How intelligent is she? I don't know . . . but she's a good listener.

TALLULAH BANKHEAD IN JOHN KOBAL'S *PEOPLE WILL TALK*

And Garbo has dined at my home. Miss Garbo. Greta. Whatever they want to call her. I always say Garbo, the way people say Tallulah. I've only seen her here and at Salka Viertel's about six times in my life, and that's over a long period of time . . . The first time I met her, I had never seen anything so beautiful. She hadn't then started the suntan; her face was as white as snow. No lipstick, but her eyelashes, which are her own, made up very heavily. And her skin looked as if she had an electric light bulb inside, it was so transparent. And she laughed at everything I said, so I thought she had a marvelous sense of humor! And she was ingratiating and charming and poured wine for people, and the few times I've met her she never said, "I tink I go home" or whatever she's supposed to say.

VIRGILIA PETERSON ROSS IN *THE NEW YORKER*, 1931

Six lively people were gathered in someone's Hollywood drawing-room one rainy night when the doorbell rang and Miss Greta Garbo was announced. She came in wearing a beret over her straight blonde hair, a tailored suit, a man's shirt and tie, and a pair of flat-heeled oxfords. When the guests saw her face with its delicate pallor ungarnished except for the excessive, beaded eyelashes, their talk abruptly died away. She sat silent while they made sporadic comments on the weather and stole furtive looks at her. She was alone, bottled in by a childish lack of interest, inarticulate, uncomfortable, offering no access to herself. She was unwilling, perhaps unable, to share in the social responsibility of the occasion. She was indifferent to its human aspects.

She had made the effort to come and now, awkwardly, she hid behind her beauty. The party soon scattered. Miss Garbo had frozen the evening.

HEDDA HOPPER IN *FROM UNDER MY HAT*

When Garbo was upset she would stride the full length of her dressing-room gallery; back and forth, back and forth, like some female Captain Bligh. At each dressing-room window along the gallery, fascinated eyes would follow her.

Joan Crawford, who had the room next to mine, would dash in and whisper, "What do you suppose is wrong now?"

"How should I know?"

"Let's find out."

We never did . . .

The picture [*As You Desire Me*] ended with regrets—"See you soon," "Wonderful working with you"—the usual thing. Three weeks later I glimpsed Garbo on the lot, waved, called, "Hi, there!" She gave me a frightened glance and flew off in the opposite direction.

BILLY BALDWIN (INTERIOR DECORATOR) IN *BILLY BALDWIN REMEMBERS*

George Schlee had called to say that they were having some trouble finding the right color for Garbo's bedroom walls and could I help? I asked my assistant, Edward Zajac . . . to come along—and he was practically overcome with excitement. I told him just to be calm, and gave him as part of his assignment the job of memorizing the number from one of Garbo's telephones. If I was to be running back and forth supervising workmen, her number would be indispensable.

Miss G. opened the door herself, dressed in denim jeans and a man's pale-pink shirt. She and George Schlee took us through the apartment. The painter waited in the hall.

A large L-shaped living room was filled with sunlight from two long walls of windows facing south and east. All the colors were rosy and warm; there were beautiful curtains of eighteenth-century silk, a Louis XV Savonnerie carpet, the finest quality *Régence* furniture, and wonderful Impressionist paintings. I knew Miss G. spent a lot of time browsing through antique shops. How many times had I seen her on walking tours shopping with the Baron Eric de Rothschild, the two of them making a spectacular couple indeed. Their time had not been wasted, either. Her living room was a delight.

Except for the corner nearest the door. Here it was windowless and rather dark, furnished only with a red damask *lit de repos* that had belonged to the former Duchess of Marlborough, Mme Balsan, and a coffee table on which several bottles of vodka were all open and consumed to varying depths. Laughing, Miss G. said, "You can see that this is where I live."

I felt a little tug on my sleeve, and Miss G. beckoned me playfully with a crooked finger to follow her. She led me to a room that had been intended as a bedroom (her own bedroom was, of course, the only one in the apartment, since there were never any guests), with three walls lined with closets. With obvious pleasure she slid all the doors back and forth, revealing hundreds of dresses. "Master Billy," she giggled, "I have never worn a single one."

All four of us, with the painter in tow, trooped off to the problem bedroom. As we passed through the hall, Garbo mortified Eddie Zajac by telling him: "There's no point in looking at the telephones—all the numbers have been removed."

The bedroom, which overlooked the East River, was a nice square room, practically empty, waiting for its background. Miss G. picked up a small candle shade of shirred mulberry-colored silk and held it up for us to see. "This shade," she said, "was on a candle in a dining car in Sweden—in the first train I was ever on." Then she lit a candle and held it beneath the shade. Our job was to paint the room the color that resulted from the candlelight shining through the silk! The painter looked desperate.

We set to work. The only way to even attempt it was with many coats of glazing. We experimented for hours by sheer trial and error, covering sample board after sample board before finally coming up with a color that was satisfactory to her. I went back to my office exhausted, promising to check back later at "Harriet Brown"'s apartment as the work progressed. But when the painter had finished, it was painfully clear that the hard-won color, when it covered all four walls, was quite a bit too strong—and we had to strip and reglaze the whole thing. Finally, we produced the impossible color of flame through mulberry-pink silk, a feat for which we deserved a Nobel prize.

Miss G., totally delighted, paid her bill in person, in full, in cash. She could have saved some money by paying with a check—who would ever have cashed it?

ALICE B. TOKLAS IN A LETTER TO CARL VAN VECHTEN, 1951

A few nights ago she [Mercedes de Acosta] rang up and said she and Cecil and Greta Garbo had rung the doorbell several times the night before but no one had answered (Basket [dog] and I really need a stronger doorbell) and could they come that evening which they did—Cecil very tousled exhausted and worshipful—she a bit shy—quite Vassarish—unpretentious but very criminal. She asked me with simplicity and frankness—Did you know Monsieur Vollard [the famous art dealer] was he a fascinating person—a great *charmeur*—was he seductive. She was disappointed like a young girl who dreams of an assignation. Do explain her to me. She was not mysterious but I hadn't the answer. The French papers say they [Beaton and Garbo] are to marry—but she doesn't look as if she would do anything as crassly innocent as that. *Expliquez-moi* as Pablo used to say to Baby [Gertrude Stein].

NOËL COWARD FROM HIS *DIARIES*

1943: Elsa's [Elsa Maxwell] dinner party. Dick Rodgers played and I sang. Garbo was there looking lovely, in fact lovelier than ever.

1955: On Thursday evening I went to Valentina's, a small cocktail party, very gay. Garbo was there for a little, looking lovely but grubby.

1957: The high spot of the week [on the Riviera] has been a lovely evening with Garbo. We picked her up at her beautifully situated but hideous villa and dined at a little restaurant on the port at Villefranche. Garbo was bright as a button and, of course, fabulously beautiful; the food was delicious, the evening glorious with lights from ships glittering in the dark sea, and the mountains rising dramatically into the sky.

1964: Last night the Ahernes came, bringing Garbo who was really enchanting . . . The next afternoon I took off from Geneva. Brian, Eleanor and Garbo (quivering with neurosis) were on the plane. They travelled tourist, presumably because La Divina feared recognition in the more sophisticated atmosphere of the first class. She needn't have worried; because no one recognized her at all.

FROM ANDREW BARROW'S *GOSSIP*

1946: Meanwhile, the world reverberated with rumours of romance between Cecil Beaton and film star Greta Garbo. The couple had been seen together in Hollywood and Beaton had recently visited the film star in Stockholm where her villa was said to be protected by savage police dogs. "Miss Garbo wishes to be left alone," said Mr. Beaton at the end of July. "We should all respect her wishes."

1947: On August 13, film star Greta Garbo, whose name was still romantically linked with that of Cecil Beaton, arrived on board the *Queen Mary*. Her name was not on the passenger list and she was shielded from photographers as she disembarked. "I just felt I wanted to see England again," she said. "I don't want anyone to know what I am going to do." On board the same ship was demure fifteen-year-old film star Elizabeth Taylor.

1951: Polling took place on October 25. That night, Lord Camrose gave a great election night party at the Savoy Hotel which was attended by Cecil Beaton and Greta Garbo, Noël Coward, Somerset Maugham, Sharman Douglas and other celebrities.

1956: On October 17, Greta Garbo who had not made a film for fifteen years but was still an object of immense curiosity value, was taken to tea at 10 Downing Street by her friend Cecil Beaton. A few hours later, the couple were seen together at Covent Garden. "I will speak to no one concerning Miss Greta Garbo," said Beaton afterwards. "I have no comment to make as to whether or not she or I were at the ballet."

RICHARD BURTON

While attending a party at which one of the guests was Garbo, I curiously asked her, "Could you do me a great favor? May I kiss your knee?" She replied, "Certainly," and I leaned over and did so. It was an experience I'll never forget.

DONALD KEENE (THE DOYEN OF EXPERTS ON JAPANESE LITERATURE) IN ON FAMILIAR TERMS

My most unforgettable memory of these people whose acquaintance I briefly made is of the time I took Greta Garbo to the theater. I felt when I met her as if I had known her name ever since I had known anyone's name. I could even remember, as a junior high school student, jocularly referring to her as Greasy Garbage. I must have seen all or nearly all of her films and I could recall how she looked in each, especially *Camille*, in which her mysterious beauty was set off by the vulgarity of the other actors. I had met Gigi, as she was called by her friends, at parties but had been unable to pronounce a word before her. It can easily be imagined how I felt when I was asked on the telephone by Jane Gunther, a close friend of Garbo, if I would like to take her to the theater. My answer was instantaneous. I was then informed where to meet her, and told that if I absolutely had to refer to her by name, I should call her Miss Brown.

We met as scheduled and went to the theater where a matinee of *The Diary of Anne Frank* was playing. We entered just as the lights were being dimmed. During the intermission "Miss Brown" held her program around her face so that no one could see her. (She must, however, have drawn the attention of some people by this unusual way of spending the quarter of an hour of the intermission.) We left just as the play was ending, while the theater was still dark. We stepped outside and I signaled for a taxi. During the five minutes or so until one came along, pedestrians gathered silently around us, and many cars in the street stopped. Although Garbo had not appeared in a film for twenty years, her face could still halt traffic.

LEO LERMAN IN *THE GRAND SURPRISE*

I am lunching again in the old dining room of the Plaza. Suddenly a great quiet. All talk and clatter ceases and all eyes are looking at two women who walk swiftly, almost stealthily, between the tables. One has a great big hat clamped down over her face and a great big coat covering herself and a very determined stride. The other is Jane Gunther, who is very pretty. She does not even give me a glance, and I have known her since she was sixteen. They both go to the far end of the room. The room resumes its chatter-clatter. Suddenly, there is an enormous rush from the far end of the room, and Miss Garbo runs the full length of the room and is gone. Later in the day I ring up Jane, who says, "She didn't really like all that attention." I say, "Well, if she didn't like all that attention, she certainly managed to get it, didn't she?"

GEORGE HURRELL IN MARK A. VIEIRA'S *HURRELL'S HOLLYWOOD PORTRAITS*

He opened his new studio on North Rodeo Drive in the fall of 1941, and one day he was surprised to find Greta Garbo in his reception area. "Alloo, Mister 'Urell. Thought I would come by and see how my new tenant was doing."

"*You're* my landlady?"

"Yes," she said. "It pleases me very much to have you on my property. Show me around, please."

Hurrell gave her the grand tour, and when she commented on the light-weight new Korona camera, he saw that here was another movie star who was "very astute and completely knowledgeable."

"Before she left, I popped the question: 'How about some shots?'"

"'Oh, no, no, Mister 'Urell, I am not photographed any more.' She waved and was gone."

JOHN LODER IN *HOLLYWOOD HUSSAR*

Every Sunday morning I used to pick up Greta and Jacques [Feyder] at the Chateau Marmont Apartments, where Jacques lived, and drive them down for the day at the beach.

One Sunday I arrived to find Greta in the kitchen scrambling eggs. I crept up behind her and kissed her on the nape of the neck.

"Don't be a fool, John. Make yourself useful. It's the table that needs laying."

SALVADOR DALÍ

In the 1940s, Salvador Dalí was eager to meet Garbo, and Jack Warner set up a meeting.

After agonizing over what to wear, Dalí finally decided on a white suit, lilac silk shirt, and heavily waxed mustache. Garbo showed up in trousers and tennis shoes—and when she was introduced to Dalí, took a long look at him and said, "One of us has got it wrong." And left.

COLLEAGUES ON GARBO

⚹

BILLY WILDER (WRITER ON *NINOTCHKA*)

The supreme movie actress of all time . . . The face, that face, what was it about that face? You could have read into it all the secrets of a woman's soul. You could read Eve, Cleopatra, Mata Hari. She became all women on the screen. Not on the sound stage. The miracle happened in that film emulsion. Who knows why? Marilyn Monroe had this same gift. That strange trick of flesh impact—that is to say, their flesh registered for the camera and came across on the screen as real flesh that you could touch, an image beyond photography.

EDMUND GOULDING (DIRECTOR OF *LOVE* AND *GRAND HOTEL*)

In the studios she is nervous. Rather like a racehorse at the post—actually trembling, hating onlookers. At the first click of the camera, she starts literally pouring off Garbo into the lens.

   . . . I don't believe that Garbo's outstanding success depends on any mystery. She has movie sex appeal, if I may say so, but her success depends more on her unique ability to work and her will to achieve the absolute concentration before the camera. When Garbo says that she is tired and wants to go home—which incidentally happens very seldom—she really is exhausted. She feels she can't give anything more and so would prefer to stop, rather than to do what she knows won't be good . . . The switch to talkies has neither changed her way of working nor her personality. She was born to be an artist. Having once got in front of a camera, nothing could stop her climbing to the top—except unperceptive producers, of course—but they weren't as unperceptive as all that!

WILLIAM DANIELS (CINEMATOGRAPHER OF NINETEEN GARBO FILMS)

Miss Garbo's understanding of camera technique is remarkable. She makes every effort to cooperate with the cameraman and she really appreciates the difficulties and different requirements of photographing scenes from various angles. She is the most patient and sympathetic player with whom I have ever been associated in pictures.

MICHAEL POWELL (DIRECTOR) ON WOODY VAN DYKE (DIRECTOR)

He was told by the studio heads of M-G-M to direct some retakes of a Greta Garbo film. She came on the set. Van Dyke was seated in his chair looking at the script of the film. She said, "Good morning." He said, "Mornin', honey," without looking up. "The script says you come through that door"—he pointed to the top of the stairs—"and you go out of that door"—pointing to the door across the splendid baroque hall at the bottom of the staircase. Garbo was used to working with Clarence Brown, a first-rate director and diplomat who handled her with kid gloves: "Miss Garbo, this," "Madame Garbo, that," but she said, "Shall we try it?" Van Dyke said, "Sure!" She went up the stairs and went through the action: "How was that?" "Swell. Now the script says you have a change of costume and you come in that door and go out the other." She was puzzled. "Aren't you going to shoot the other section first?" "Oh, we got it." A pause. Garbo looked at him. "Mister Van Dyke, don't you ever rehearse?" He was already back in the script and answered without raising his eyes: "Listen, honey, how many ways are there of coming down a staircase?"

MELVYN DOUGLAS (ACTOR IN *AS YOU DESIRE ME*, *NINOTCHKA*, AND *TWO-FACED WOMAN*)

Garbo had an extraordinary face, plastic and luminous, the kind of subject sculptors adore. When she began to play, it acquired an astonishing animation. While rehearsing or even shooting with her I could not help thinking, "My God, how astoundingly beautiful! This is really happening, somehow, right here in my arms." And, "I have never played with a woman with such an ability to arouse the erotic impulse."

CLARENCE BROWN (DIRECTOR OF *FLESH AND THE DEVIL*, *A WOMAN OF AFFAIRS*, *ANNA CHRISTIE*, *ROMANCE*, *INSPIRATION*, *ANNA KARENINA*, AND *CONQUEST*)

Greta Garbo had something that nobody ever had on the screen. Nobody. I don't know whether she even knew she had it, but she did. And I can explain it in a few words. I would take a scene with Garbo—pretty good. I would take it three or four times. It was pretty good, but I was never quite satisfied. When I saw that same scene on the screen, however, it had something that it just didn't have on the set.

Garbo had something behind the eyes that you couldn't see until you photographed it in close-up. You could see thought. If she had to look at one person with jealousy, and another with love, she didn't have to change her expression. You could see it in her eyes as she looked from one to the other. And nobody else has been able to do that on the screen. Garbo did it without command of the English language. For me, Garbo starts where they all leave off. She was a shy person; her lack of English gave her a slight inferiority complex. I used to direct her very quietly. I never gave her a direction above a whisper. Nobody on the set ever knew what I said to her; she liked that. She hated to rehearse. She would have preferred to stay away until everyone else was rehearsed, then come in and do the scene. But you can't do that—particularly in talking pictures.

We could never get her to look at the rushes, and I don't think she ever looked at any of her pictures until many years later. When sound arrived, we had a projector on the set. This projector ran backward and forward so that we could watch scenes and check continuity.

When you run a talking picture in reverse, the sound is like nothing on earth. That's what Garbo enjoyed. She would sit there shaking with laughter, watching the film running backward and the sound going *yakablom-yakablom*. But as soon as we ran it forward, she wouldn't watch it.

ROUBEN MAMOULIAN (DIRECTOR OF *QUEEN CHRISTINA*)

You did not have to tell Garbo to look like this or that, for this reason or that. No, you just had to tell her which emotion you wanted her to have produced for the scene in question. "I understand," said Garbo. And she did understand. She produced the emotion on her face. She produced it in her bodily movements . . . What was absolutely extraordinary about Garbo was that she was both photogenic *and* intuitive.

LÁSZLÓ WILLINGER (STUDIO PHOTOGRAPHER)

I never even tried to do Garbo at M-G-M. I was told not to even attempt. I talked to her. You know, it was very difficult to talk to her, 'cause she's not very bright. She wasn't then and she still isn't.

LIONEL BARRYMORE (ACTOR IN *THE TEMPTRESS*, *MATA HARI*, *GRAND HOTEL*, *CAMILLE*)

Next to Miss Garbo, the most awesome actress I have encountered in Hollywood is Margaret O'Brien.

CHARLES BOYER (ACTOR IN *CONQUEST*)

Today, there are no actresses like her. Some have more acting ability, but Garbo had a guarded mystery about her and was enchanting to be with, to work with. The most beautiful nose and face, and you could read on it all the thoughts that came to her. Her ability to project what was within was unique.

ADRIAN (COSTUME DESIGNER) ON HOW TO BECOME
A GARBO GIRL

An absolute requisite is a tall slender figure without accentuated hips—those without don't bother. The Garbo girl should begin her day in pajamas of bright colors and over them a wrapper of black silk with heavy Chinese embroidery; that is, she should be rather exotic in the morning. The Garbo girl must shun lace and frills and negligées like the plague. Little fluttering pink ribbons and sweet bits of swan's down are quite simply criminal. Such things are for sweet girls and Garbo isn't a sweet girl.

In the forenoon the Garbo girl will go for a walk in a simple, chic tweed coat and skirt with a correct blouse or jumper—the whole with a hint of the "sportiness" that Michael Arlen speaks of in *The Green Hat*. Apropos hats, this too must be simple and sporty and the hair drawn back. In no circumstances is an unruly fuzz at the ears permitted. Large pearl earrings are recommended, however.

The Garbo girl spends her afternoon in a long-sleeved, discreet dress of crêpe-de-chine or flowered satin, but in the evening she lets her elegance blossom forth in full. Gala dress should be of velvet, soft silk, moiré or even lace; taffeta and tulle are strictly forbidden, as are puffs and flounces. Instead she will have drapes and scarves to wind round her neck. The dress should be cut generously deep, especially at the back. On top of all this elegance a cape of ermine or gold lamé, and thus equipped the Garbo girl will set out for fresh conquests!

ROBERT TAYLOR (ACTOR IN *CAMILLE*)

There's something about Garbo's silences and her concentration that gets you, way down inside. The woman is one of the most powerful personalities in the world. She wears a sort of flat colorless make-up that gives her a suggestion of something out of this world . . . There's a radiation from her when you're playing an intense scene that makes you play up to it, whether you have the stuff in you or not. She simply makes you find it and give.

Also: She thought with her eyes, photographically. The muscles in her face would not move, and yet her eyes would express exactly what was needed. Working with her was perhaps my greatest acting lesson, though I probably didn't learn enough from it.

GEORGE HURRELL (STUDIO PHOTOGRAPHER)

Her features were so photogenic. You could light her face in any manner possible; any angle; up, down. Her bone structure and her proportions—her forehead, her nose was just right; the distance between here and here was just right. And her eyes were wet in such a way that you couldn't go wrong. Now, Harlow's eyes were deep-set, and you had to get the light under them or her head up, or her eyes would just get too dark. Crawford had the closest face to Garbo's, to perfect proportions. Crawford had strong jawbones, that's about all I'd say, because her cheekbones were good, and her forehead, and her eyes were good—maybe a little on the large size. Garbo was probably the sexiest gal of the whole darned bunch of them, but she didn't project it, because that wasn't her job. Sex to her probably didn't take place until it got dark. When she was working during the day, she was doing a job. She worked in a very logical way. There was no maybe about her for me. It always had a connection with the part. She never played sexy roles when I was there, so maybe that's why she didn't think she had to push the sex in the gallery.

GEORGE CUKOR (DIRECTOR OF *CAMILLE* AND *TWO-FACED WOMAN*)

It is hard to talk about Garbo, really, for she says everything when she appears on the screen. That is GARBO . . . and all you can say is just so much chit-chat. There she is on the screen. How she achieves these effects may or may not be interesting. She is what she is, and that is a very creative actress who thinks about things a great deal and has a very personal way of acting. You have to give her her head—let her do what she feels. If you remember in *Camille* when the father comes in to tell her to leave his son, she falls to the ground and puts her hand on the table. That is a very original thing to do. One must let her do these things and they happen marvelously.

COMMENTS ON GARBO

✂

DAVID THOMSON IN *THE NEW BIOGRAPHICAL DICTIONARY OF FILM*

When she died, there was plentiful evidence of how ordinary and how dull the real woman had been. And she had never managed to escape that legendary figure—or see the joke. Books appeared and her Sutton Place apartment was photographed—like a liberated shrine. For a few years arguments may persist over whether she was wise or dumb, androgynous or uninterested. But sooner or later such trivia will evaporate and a mysterious truth will be left—she was photographed. She was all in the silver.

Postscript (2021): That was written in 1975 when the generation of the grandchildren she never had was catching up with her movies and trying to place her aloneness—or was it aloofness? When she withdrew from pictures was it because she realized that the cult of movie stars might be unreliable? Attitude—her presence and her obscure, gloomy sexiness—might be on its way to attitudinizing. Had she been a bereft or uninteresting person? Had our interest in her depended on the awesome thrill of movie theaters?

Decades later, her instinct looks smart. We do not believe in movie stars anymore; we do not keep in touch with them; it seems fatuous to desire them, or believe in ourselves as romantic pilgrims. That is not her fault.

The pictures remain, in black and white, and they are poignant with the details of an odd lost tenderness. But the church of cinema is no more. And no movie stars flourish in that loss of faith. It's hard to imagine my grandchildren looking at her today and not smiling at her need to be intense. The face that could be sublime when the size of a house is now a postage stamp we have lost in our filing system.

MERCEDES DE ACOSTA IN *HERE LIES THE HEART*

She has what I consider a very striking quality, a deep purity of intention in all that she does. I believe her own greatest problem and one that causes her untold unhappiness is an underlying suspicion toward people and life itself. This trait, I am told, is a Scandinavian characteristic and is perhaps more emphasized in Greta than in many Scandinavians. Latins are just the opposite. We flow more readily with life than the Nordic race and are more out-going. We are willing to take a chance and throw our caps over the mill. Greta takes few chances. She continually draws back, and when she moves she moves cautiously and then is tortured with regret, convinced she has made a mistake.

JOHN ENGSTEAD (PHOTOGRAPHER)

I remember that first movie. I went down to Sunset Boulevard to track it down. *Torrent* or *The Tempest*, whatever it was . . . she was absolutely marvelous. The reviews were just great. She was a completely new thing on the screen. She changed everything. She just changed everything.

FRANCES MARION (LEADING SCREENWRITER)

It was always fascinating to watch Garbo; her economy of gesture, constant changing of moods revealed by her luminous eyes that never played the little tricks used by so many actresses—flashing sidelong glances or opening wide to show the entire iris. Her lashes were so long and thick they veiled her eyes, giving them an expression of "smouldering passion," according to the fan magazines. But when she was bored by anyone they burned dully like candles in daylight.

TENNESSEE WILLIAMS

The saddest of creatures, an artist who abandons her art.
  and
People who are very beautiful make their own rules.

ALEXANDER WALKER IN *STARDOM: THE HOLLYWOOD PHENOMENON*

Garbo was the greatest star the screen has produced. Among the many rare gifts that combined to make her, there was a unique one: it is the ability to suggest in one person the whole complexity of life. No wonder the source of her art finally evades us, for it is part of a much wider scheme of things. "There is a mystery in you," says John Gilbert to her in *Queen Christina*. And her answer must finally be our consolation—"Is there not in every human being?"

TALLULAH BANKHEAD IN *TALLULAH*

Forget all the bilge about Garbo. She's excessively shy. When at ease with people who do not look upon her as something begat by the Sphinx and Frigga, Norse goddess of the sky, she can be as much fun as the next gal.

JEANINE BASINGER IN *A WOMAN'S VIEW*

Her ultimate appeal lay in her exotic quality, as in a movie like *The Mysterious Lady*, where she personified love, sex, intrigue, and fantasy, a kind of fur-draped and orchidaceous escapism. This is how people want to remember her, rather than as a ski instructor who danced the chica-choca. When a woman like Garbo wraps her head in a jeweled turban and goes out into the pulsing dark of night draped in gems and sporting one luscious orchid, who is going to remember her sitting beside her son's bed and nursing him through an illness? She was simply too extraordinary to be remembered with a cold compress in her hand; we liked her better when she was willing to die for all our sins, and we were willing to let her.

MOLLY HASKELL (CRITIC)

Garbo, her own inimitable *auteur* . . . was able, of course, to survive not only good and bad directors and bad and awful leading men, but changing fashions of women, for she was timeless. More than Negri, Garbo was the woman who lived for love and, hence, was less free; enchained to the idea of absolute love, she was incapable of enjoying its intermittent savories and provisional pleasures. But her commitment carried a sense of fatalism present in many of the great twenties' films and in the tragic vision of life: a belief that certain choices are irrevocable . . . The appeal of Garbo, however provocatively she might array herself, was romantic rather than sexual, and that is the reason women liked her. Her spirit leaped first and her body, in total exquisite accord, leaped after. She yearned not for pleasure in bed but for love in eternity.

DILYS POWELL (BRITISH FILM CRITIC)

Whether or not Greta Garbo is a good actress I have no idea, but I am sure she is a great actress . . . The good actor has the chameleon's ability of matching his surroundings; his colour changes to suit his part. I am inclined to suspect that the great actor has the reverse of the chameleon's art; he changes the colour of everything around him.

ROBERT SKLAR IN *MOVIE-MADE AMERICA*

On the screen Garbo shone with an inner intensity few other performers in motion pictures came even close to. Director Fred Niblo demonstrated Garbo's power with a clever opening sequence in *The Mysterious Lady*. The film begins at a party. The camera moves among the guests. Then a woman appears at the top of a staircase. You see parts of her, her legs, her arms, you see her from the back, she moves downstairs among the others, and still you have not seen her face. It does not matter. She has created an excitement in the audience, an emotional quickening, that makes the other players appear mere mannequins. This was Garbo: if her career had any major flaw, it was that she made Hollywood's most romantic male stars look callow and inadequate beside her.

ADELA ROGERS ST. JOHNS IN *THE HONEYCOMB*

Garbo was never at any time disturbed by or conscious of the Helen of Troy screen star. The mysterious, unattainable she. Never. She wouldn't have recognized her if they'd met on the street. Garbo *acted*. By the time Stiller brought her to America, acting had become her job. In personality, her one-hundred-per-cent Swedish reactions were difficult for us to follow, her slow mind, her fear-dislike of people, the immovable stubbornness. Away from the Camera, she did not wish to be the Garbo created by the Camera, could not be, never was.

CECIL BEATON IN *THE GLASS OF FASHION*

Though Garbo has been credited with having little clothes sense and obviously pays no attention whatsoever to the rules of current fashion, she has an innate flair for what is fitting for her and is possessed of a great natural taste, being capable of appraising good clothes as well as of appreciating them. If she is unwilling to devote her time to becoming a well-dressed woman, she has succeeded, nevertheless, by the very simplicity of the clothes she wears, in creating a fashion for herself and, though nonconformist, has been an important factor in contributing to the tone of a whole period, innovating low-heeled shoes, hats that hide the face, stevedore jerkins, and cowboy belts.

Her sartorial tastes combine those of the highwayman and Robin Hood with ancient Greece. She wears large pirate hats and romantic cavalier blouses and belts, which are always unadorned and often in off colours: dull greys and browns.

At the time of her Hollywood advent, the filmmakers attempted to make Garbo conform to their pattern, frizzing her hair and dressing her in impossible houri trappings. But by degrees, as she gained more authority, Garbo was able to assert her instinct and bring her real beauty to the fore, which had previously been lost behind the unreal human façade that Hollywood had devised for her as another of its temptresses.

In her great heyday in the films her clothes were made with the utmost ease. She was never one to fuss or to insist upon film tests, believing that if anything looked well to the eye it would appear all right to the camera. Far from finicky about her hair styles, Garbo would proceed with the rough, sure taste of the artist: like Mrs. Vernon Castle before her, she intuitively knew how she wanted to look and had no need of a mirror for approval. Her personality imposed itself on her clothes to such an extent that she could turn a tea gown into a nun's habit or an evening dress into a monk's robe. This personality aura explains why Garbo can be so readily spotted in a crowd: few people have so distinctive and recognizable an appearance.

ARLETTY (FRENCH MOVIE STAR)

John Kobal: Can you explain the secret of her popularity on the screen?

Arletty: Her face, her figure, her shoulders. Not her intelligence, for sure. I couldn't take my eyes off her. The secret is that she was dumb.

JOHN FREEMAN IN THE *NEW STATESMAN*

In 1955, when M-G-M showed Camille *in London, at a revival festival.*

In a series of trivial films . . . we fell in love with her, until suddenly . . . she disappeared . . . Was it possible that the light could shine as we remembered it through a twenty-five-year-old melodrama? But we needn't have worried. From the corny melodramatics of the re-issued *Camille* she distils more femininity, more passion, more humanity, more sheer beauty than the post-war generation has ever seen. Emerging again from eclipse, she is a more refulgent star by comparison with the evanescent galaxy of hellcats and cuties who succeeded her. She died, the other afternoon, in a fierce and tearful silence, broken only by the sobbing of two very young women . . . My generation was vindicated. At least we knew how to jerk a tear.

ANDREW SARRIS (CRITIC)

Here then is the ultimate myth of Garbo in the silent era: an overflowing fountain of beauty capable of eroticizing everything and everyone around her . . . That the characters she played seemed to transcend their almost invariably unhappy fate is a tribute to her own cinematic self-sufficiency. It is not so much that the camera made love to her as that she made love to the audience through the camera. Furthermore, it was a love richly colored with irony, curiosity, and uncontrollably high spirits. In short, she seemed so much more sophisticated than the movies that enclosed her that she became their most perceptive critic.

MARIANNE MOORE IN *THE COMPLETE PROSE OF MARIANNE MOORE*

Greta Garbo's uncompromise and intensity seem to me to impart style to whatever she does; her flexible footwear whatever else others prescribe, is my most distinctive impression of her.

LOUISE BROOKS

Garbo is all movement. First she gets the emotion, and out of the emotion comes the movement and out of the movement comes the dialogue. She's so perfect people say she can't act—she is *so* great.

   . . . Louis B. Mayer found her! Looking at Greta Garbo in the Swedish picture *Gösta Berling*, in Berlin, he knew as sure as he was alive that he had found a sexual symbol beyond his or anyone else's imagining. Here was a face as beautiful as Michelangelo's Mary of the *Pietà*, yet glowing with passion. The suffering of her soul was such that the American public would forgive her many affairs in *Torrent*, Garbo's first American picture. At last,

marriage—the obstacle standing in the way between sex and pleasure—
could be done away with. At last, here was an answer to young actresses
who wanted to play good girls!

Also: You know, most directors, or at least all directors whom I've
worked for, give the choreography, the action and the words, and leave
your inner thoughts alone because on the screen, like in life, a person is
doing one thing and thinking another. Just as I'm talking to you now. You
can see that in Garbo, who I think is the greatest actress in the world,
you can see that along with her actions is this wonderful mysterious thought
line moving below, but it's harmonious, she is at one with her thoughts.

JIM TULLY (VANITY FAIR FILM REPORTER)

Garbo is the only woman in the world who has made capital out of her anemia. Her indolent movements and half-shut eyes give us an impression of
exotic sensuality. The real reason for them is fatigue. She is just no longer
able to keep her mouth shut or her eyes open. She is continually interrupting
filming with "I am tired, I must lie down" . . . At first they thought this tiredness was a pose—"I must lie down a bit" became a catchword—but medical
examination has shown that unfortunately it is genuine. And so they are
nicer now to Garbo in the studios. She is tended like a valuable animal.

ALFRED LUNT (ACTOR)

Garbo couldn't sustain a long scene. But she has probably sustained the longest scene in theatrical history, ever since 1925—her private life.

ROBERT PAYNE (BIOGRAPHER)

She is not a mystery to be solved. Inarticulate and instinctive, she is a limpid
child. Even under the scrutiny of the world, even in the jaws of Hollywood,
she does not grow up.

and

In this outrageous and corrupt age, with dictators and armies continually on the rampage, Garbo came as a benediction, reminding us that there existed in this world the perfect beauty we had all been seeking, and we saw in her beauty the promise of an unhoped-for peace. We live in a dark age, but she was all brightness. Her beauty was not simply a very appealing arrangement of planes and surfaces: It was charged with energy. It was a beauty that sprang at us and took us by the throat, and did not let us rest; and if it seemed peaceful, this too was an illusion, for a saving energy poured out of her to revive us and heal our wounds. So Athena must have appeared to the ancient Greeks and Nefertiti to the ancient Egyptians.

VIRGILIA PETERSON ROSS

She is a child, at the beck of a child's moods and caprices.

NORMAN ZIEROLD (BIOGRAPHER)

Garbo's position on such matters as closed sets and autographs must be viewed in the context of her unprecedented status as a superstar. In the thirties, touching—or even glimpsing—Greta Garbo became a national neurosis. "Forget Yellowstone and Coney Island," wrote Leonard Hall in 1932. "The sands of Hollywood are white with the bleaching bones of ferocious flappers who perished of starvation while waiting for Garbo to emerge from her Santa Monica deadfall and go down to the store for a pint of milk. Thousands have drowned while lurking behind shrubbery in the hope of seeing her come out for a walk in the rain."

CHARLES AFFRON IN *STAR ACTING: GISH, GARBO, DAVIS*

Garbo as ballerina seems as appropriate as Garbo as opera singer (*Romance*), carnival kootch girl (*Susan Lenox*), Balinese dancer (*Mata Hari*), and night club chanteuse (*As You Desire Me*). Five (including *Grand Hotel*) of la Garbo's first seven talkies display her as a performer.

In *Grand Hotel* Garbo is exposed as never before. Her other lady-of-the-stage portrayals do not call for a stance, and a sense of body so wholly discordant to her esoteric self. Their theatrical activities are quickly established, and the main business is then pursued without digression. The embarrassing passes at Siva's statue during the first sequences of *Mata Hari* are not alluded to in the rest of the film.

Her deep knee bends are particularly unforgettable (choreographed by Louis B. Mayer himself, no doubt), but they do not impede her more characteristic march through bedrooms toward the firing squad at a pace suited to her body. As the opera singer [in *Romance*] she is at first heard (dubbed) but not seen, and then during a staging of *Martha* near the film's end, she is replaced by a stand-in. The substitution is supremely obvious, and it is a shameful loss if we remember Garbo's Carmen and Melisande in *Torrent* and her repeated silent singing of *Tosca* in *The Mysterious Lady*. During the single café sequence in *As You Desire Me*, the audience within the film observes an act that we cannot see. The spatial limits in *Grand Hotel* spare us Grusinskaya's on-stage Odette-Odile, but even Garbo, usually so disdainful of the banalities of verisimilitude, accepts a degree of ballerina impersonation—we see the tension of her arms, wrists, and back; she rises on pointe to reveal her utter lassitude.

A dancer's body is always with her, and Garbo's efforts toward consistently altering her posture are justified. But they are not correct. She cannot impersonate away her physical bigness that verges on gawkiness, and the curve of her back and shoulders, the caved-in look. For that intimate relationship to the ground she treads, so dominant in her style, she would have been banished from the barre. Garbo as a dancer is something of a joke, one of the few that was appreciated by the creators of *Two-Faced Woman*. She can manage the "Chica-Choca." Her grace in the ballroom sequence of *Anna Karenina* is, however, less of a surprise than the remarkable verve of the sequence itself in a film characterized by somnambulism.

H.D. (THE POET HILDA DOOLITTLE) IN 1927

Deflowered, deracinated, devitalized, more than that, actively and acutely distorted by an odd unbelievable parody of life, of beauty ... with sewed-in black lashes, with waist-lined, svelte, obvious contours, with gowns and gowns, all of them almost (by some anachronism) trailing on the floor, with black-dyed wig, obscuring her own Nordic nimbus . . . The Censor, this magnificent ogre, had seen fit to devitalize this Nordic flower, to graft upon the stem of a living, wild camellia (if we may be fanciful for a moment) the most blatant of obvious, crepe, tissue-paper orchids.

HENRI AGEL (LEADER OF THE CATHOLIC SCHOOL OF FRENCH FILM CRITICISM)

Greta Garbo endures untainted by her incarnations; she pulverizes some, transcends others which wallow in the romantic . . . She turns toward us the tenderest and most loving face of love, she moves us by the shudder of a sensuality whose secret has been lost, the mystery of a soul impregnating a body.

And for another French point of view . . .

ROLAND BARTHES

Garbo still belongs to that moment in cinema when capturing the human face still plunged audiences into the deepest ecstasy, when one literally lost oneself in a human image as one would in a philter, when the face represented a kind of absolute state of the flesh, which could be neither reached nor renounced. A few years earlier the face of Valentino was causing suicides; that of Garbo still partakes of the same rule of Courtly Love, where the flesh gives rise to mystical feelings of perdition . . . Garbo's face represents this fragile moment when cinema is about to draw an existential from an essential beauty, when the archetype leans towards the fascination of mortal faces, when clarity of flesh as essence yields its place to a lyricism of Woman.

Viewed as a transition, the face of Garbo reconciles two iconographic ages, it assures the passage from awe to charm. As is well known, we are today at the other pole of this evolution: the face of Audrey Hepburn, for instance, is individualized, not only because of its peculiar thematics (woman as child, woman as kitten), but also because of her person, of an almost unique specification of the face, which has nothing of the essence left in it, but is constituted by an infinite complexity of morphological functions. As a language, Garbo's singularity was of the order of the concept, that of Audrey Hepburn is of the order of the substance. The face of Garbo is an idea, that of Hepburn an event.

And yet another . . .

SIMONE DE BEAUVOIR

Garbo's face had a vague expression onto which you could project anything at all; you can't project anything onto Bardot's face. It is what it is.

RAYMOND DURGNAT (CRITIC)

To see, in these early films, Garbo breathe life into an impossible part is like watching a swan skim the surface of a pond of *schmalz*, and finally, with long, slow, persistent strokes, mysteriously as natural breathing, streak to some unknown horizon.

FRITIOF BILLQUIST (BIOGRAPHER)

No film star, with the possible exception of Valentino, has achieved such popularity as Garbo after only four films. She gave women a "new look." The shop and office girls stopped being skittish à la Clara Bow and instead became white-faced, tired of life and stamped with destiny. After this, in shops, customers might well be answered with a tragic shake of the head and a sigh; it was finished. The businessman who told his secretary to type an urgent message might be sent a languishing look through half-closed lids that said more distinctly than any words: "I'm tired. I want to lie down a bit." While the only answer that the poor husband who found his wife's behavior peculiar and asked her if she wasn't happy would get would be raised eyebrows and an enigmatic smile. In France the type was called *Garboesque . . .*

Garbo asked for neither appreciation nor admiration, merely the same consideration she showed to others. Being absolutely unaffected herself, she could only stand people who were themselves without conceit, and when she suspected people of having preconceived ideas about herself, she felt uncomfortable and disappeared. She could not afford to lose any of the dear-bought solitude and composure that she needed so badly for her next part. Hers was the artistic nature's jealousy of real life.

HEDDA HOPPER

Adrian accentuated Garbo's assets and concealed her liabilities. For her he devised the high-necked, long-sleeved evening gown that swept the world of fashion in the thirties. For *As You Desire Me*, in which I played her sister, he invented the pillbox hat with string tied under her chin, which became part of every smart woman's wardrobe. He had her dripping in lace and melting costume lines for *Anna Karenina*, sent the dress industry off on an oriental kick with exotic outfits for *The Painted Veil*. Her costumes in *Grand Hotel* could be worn today and still be high fashion.

DAGMAR GODOWSKY

All she really wanted from life was a plate of okra.

JOHN LODER (ACTOR)

Garbo is a peasant at heart. We often call her the "Peasant of Chevy Chase." At a beach or out in the garden, I have seen her sitting on the ground and digging her toes and hands into the sand and soil as if she would like to burrow right into the earth. Greta Garbo is a law unto herself. She will not endure restraint or routine. In the year and a half that I have known her I cannot remember that she ever made one definite appointment, even a dinner engagement, a day in advance. "Perhaps I will drop in to see you to-morrow night" is the nearest intimation of her intentions that my wife and I ever got.

400

FEDERICO FELLINI IN *I, FELLINI*

My mother liked Garbo. Garbo films weren't my choice, but I saw a lot of
Greta Garbo. My mother said she was the greatest actress of our time, and
sometimes my mother would sit in the dark and cry. Garbo looked so white
in the black-and-white pictures that I thought she might be a ghost. I didn't
understand her films at all. She didn't compare with Tom Mix. I would sit
and watch her eyelashes.

JOHN GIELGUD

[She] is the most extraordinary individual—little girl face and now quite
short hair tied with an Alice ribbon; hideously cut dress of beautiful printed
cotton to her calves and then huge feet in heel-less black pumps. Lovely
childlike expression and great sweetness—she never stopped talking but
absolutely to no purpose—said her life was empty, aimless, but the time
passed so quickly there was never time to do anything one wanted to do!
All this with twinkling eyes and great animation, not at all the mournful
tones of her imitators . . . But I couldn't make out whether her whole attitude was perhaps a terrific pose.

HAMLIN GARLAND (AUTHOR OF *A SON OF THE MIDDLE BORDER*), FROM HIS DAUGHTER'S MEMOIR OF HIM, *A SUMMER TO BE*

They went several times a week to the motion pictures, and Jimmie and I
were with them the night Father saw Greta Garbo for the first time. Up to
then, he had become virulent at the very name, seeing "that woman" as a
female fiend, dedicated to corrupting men's souls, but this time with malice
aforethought, Jimmie and I took Mother and Father to a film called *Conquest*, the story of Maria Walewska, Napoleon's Polish love. Within ten
minutes, to Mother's and our delighted amusement, Daddy capitulated. In
short, he fell in love. "That is the most magnificent actress I have ever
seen!" he announced on the way home, recalling the countless actresses he
had seen: Duse, Bernhardt, Ellen Terry, the best of the American and Brit-

ish stage. "This girl has it all over them. She is—I hate the over-worked word but there is no other adequate—she is glorious!" Thereafter Father saw every picture Garbo ever made, some of them over and over. It's fun seeing a man in his seventies so stirred, so enraptured.

Garland would note in his diary that he and his wife had just seen Conquest *for the fifth time.*

F. SCOTT FITZGERALD

In 1934 when asked by a newspaper to list his ten favorite plays—or outstanding impressions in the theater—Fitzgerald selected three from film: Charlie Chaplin in *The Pilgrim*, Greta Garbo in her first big role, and David W. Griffith's face "as he imagined it directing the filming of *Birth of a Nation*."

ROBERT SHERWOOD (WRITER)

She is one of the most amazing, puzzling, most provocative characters of this extraordinary age. She definitely doesn't belong in the twentieth century. She doesn't even belong in this world.

JEAN NEGULESCO (DIRECTOR)

I met Greta Garbo at the Feyders'—Jacques Feyder, the French director, and his wife, Françoise Rosay . . . I had heard so much about Garbo's lonely way, about her self-imposed privacy, her strange, unexpected behavior. When I first met her I was ready to be confronted with some sort of bizarre performance. Instead, Garbo was simple, direct, and in a good mood, comfortable, with a lovely sense of humor. The Feyders' home and its ambiance gave her the comfort and security she needed . . .

When I made her portrait, I realized that her beauty was a combination of marvelous but definite asymmetrics: a big forehead, one eyebrow higher up than the other, a generous mouth with a much too liberal lower lip, a perfect nose slightly on the side in full face. Yet these asymmetrics—combined with that special sound of her voice, the body of a young warrior, the rhythm of her walk, the silent time she takes in answering—create the Garbo world she produces with her presence. This is unique, passionate, and profound.

ETHEL BARRYMORE

Hedda Hopper reports: Ethel Barrymore uses Garbo's dressing room. "Heavens above!" she cried. "It's the black hole of Calcutta." The walls were midnight blue; the chairs were uncomfortable, fragile French gilt. "I can't breathe in a place like this," Ethel complained. They brought in chintz-covered easy chairs and made it livable according to Ethel's standards.

STARK YOUNG (CRITIC)

Esthetically, the case of Miss Greta Garbo is a kind of joke on the whole theater public. The realism-democracy theory that the great public hold concerning the theater tells us that acting is just being natural, being the character, things as they are, none of the spouting and artificiality of the old fellows . . . What they think they want would be best found in a zoo, since nothing so acts like an elephant as an elephant . . . Miss Garbo solves this problem without seeming to . . . That remote entity of her spirit, a certain noble poignancy in her presence, a certain solitary fairness, a sense of mood that is giving and resisting at the same time: these defeat and break down the poor little common theory of naturalness and prose method. The player is not hoity-toity or highbrow or any of that, the public feels; she is not unnatural; she is like somebody, they don't know just who, but still . . . People's souls sense in her some concentration of magnetism that they value. There is a muteness, inaccessibility, and beauty that attracts both men and women. She presents an instance of the natural and right progress of the poetic: from the concrete toward ideality. There is in her work no cheapness of attack, it is clear that her services could not be obtained for such effects. Her mind is not patently technical, her spirit not easily flexible, so that it is mainly a larger something that comes off to the audience, and in the future there will be a fuller development and radiance of her natural resources according to her own study, training, and the influences to which she is subjected.

DENNIS GRUNES (CRITIC) IN *A SHORT CHRONOLOGY*
OF WORLD CINEMA

Grace, irony, gravity, timeless loveliness: Greta Garbo is cinema's most enchanting tragedienne—all in all, its greatest actress. From Selma Lagerlöf's 1891 novel, Mauritz Stiller's *The Saga of Gösta Berling*, sparkling with feminism and romantic passion, is the Swedish silent that made Stiller's teenaged discovery a star. Pabst's *The Joyless Street* made her an *international* star as Greta, the soul of innocence vulnerable to corruption in economically depressed Germany. For the next dozen years the Swedish actress dominated the medium that grew in renown largely for presenting her. Hollywood beckoned. Sound arrived; "Garbo Talks!" the studio advertised, and Garbo became a star again with her magnificent enactment of O'Neill's Anna Christie, a child already hauling a heavy past. She is brilliant as the stormy ballerina Grusinskaya in *Grand Hotel*, whose near co(s)mic exhaustion—"I want to be alone!"—fresh romance reverses even as a bullet, unbeknownst to her, has canceled her happiness: stillness in heartbreaking constant motion. She is intricate, thrilling, deeply moving as "Maria," who insists on truth and others' believing in her in the midst of what may be an impersonation, in *As You Desire Me*, from Pirandello. Emphatic, over-directed, her Queen Christina intrigues nevertheless; and her solemn Anna Karenina is superb. Rising to the peak of her gracious, captivating beauty, she is transcendent as Marguerite Gautier, the Lady of the Camellias, in *Camille*, possibly cinema's greatest performance. *Ninotchka* proved her peerless at satirical romance. ("Garbo Laughs!") Soon after, the world's most famous working woman retired. Europe, on whose box office returns her career profitability largely depended, was at war, and Garbo receded deeper into myth.

FRANKLIN DELANO ROOSEVELT (AS REPORTED BY JOHN
GUNTHER IN *ROOSEVELT IN RETROSPECT*)

After seeing himself in a newsreel once, he grinned. "That was the Garbo in me."

GARBO IN BOOKS

><del><</del>

ERNEST HEMINGWAY IN *FOR WHOM THE BELL TOLLS*

Maybe it is like the dreams you have when some one you have seen in the cinema comes to your bed at night and is so kind and lovely. He'd slept with them all that way when he was asleep in bed. He could remember Garbo still, and Harlow. Yes, Harlow many times. Maybe it was like those dreams.

But he could still remember the time Garbo came to his bed the night before the attack at Pozoblanco and she was wearing a soft silky wool sweater when he put his arm around her and when she leaned forward her hair swept forward and over his face and she said why had he never told her that he loved her when she had loved him all this time? She was not shy, nor cold, nor distant. She was just so lovely to hold and kind and lovely and like the old days with Jack Gilbert and it was as true as though it happened and he loved her much more than Harlow though Garbo was only there once while Harlow—maybe this was like those dreams.

SIMONE DE BEAUVOIR IN A LETTER TO JEAN-PAUL SARTRE

I took Poupette to the Champs-Élysées to see *As You Desire Me* with Stroheim and Greta Garbo—it wasn't bad.

CHARLES JACKSON IN *THE LOST WEEKEND*

On the mantel over the bar, tilted against the mirror, was a yellow card advertising the double-feature at the Select next door. Greta Garbo in *Camille*, and some other movie. It was like a summons, for God's sake. He had seen the picture three times during the week it opened on Broadway, a month or so ago. All of a sudden (but no, it was too early, it would have to wait) he had to see again that strange fabled face, hear the voice that sent shivers down his spine when it uttered even the inconsequential little sentence (the finger-tips suddenly raised to the mouth as if to cover the rueful smile): "It's my birthday." Or the rapid impatient way, half-defiant, half-regretful, it ran off the words about money: "And I've never been very particular where it came from, as you very well know." And oh the scene where the Baron was leaving for Russia—how she said "Goodbye . . . goodbye" like a little song. ("Come with me!" The shake of the head and the smile, then; and the answer: "But Russia is so co-o-old—you wouldn't want me to get ill again, would you," not meaning this was the reason she couldn't go, not even pretending to mean it.) He knew the performance by heart, as one knows a loved piece of music: every inflexion, every stress and emphasis, every faultless phrase, every small revelation of satisfying but provocative beauty. There was a way to spend the afternoon!—The bartender slid the bottle across the counter and this time he poured the drink himself.

JOHN UPDIKE IN *IN THE BEAUTY OF THE LILIES*

Teddy and Emily go to the movies. The film they see is The Temptress. *At the end of the film, Teddy asks Emily what she thought of Garbo.*

"She *is* very beautiful, though if you notice she moves rather awkwardly, with her big feet and hands, so they never show her full-length, just in close-up or from far away."

"I mean the character, I guess, not the actress."

"Oh, I *liked* her. I liked the way she went after what she wanted. Women can't really do that yet, but it's nice to think they can some day."

EVELYN WAUGH IN *VILE BODIES*

An elderly woman servant came in to announce luncheon. "What is at the Electra Palace, do you know, Mrs. Florin?"

"Greta Garbo in *Venetian Kisses*, I think, sir."

"I don't really like Greta Garbo. I've tried to," said Colonel Blount, "but I just don't."

PHILIP KERR IN *FIELD GREY*

There's been a political shoot-out inside a movie theater.

The movie was *Mata Hari*, with Garbo in the title role and Ramon Novarro as the young Russian officer who falls in love with her. I hadn't seen it myself but the movie was doing well in Berlin. Garbo gets shot by the treacherous French, and with a plot like that, it could hardly fail with Germans. The theatre manager was waiting in the lobby. He was swarthy and worried-looking with a moustache like a midget's eyebrow and, to that extent at least, rather resembled Ramon Novarro. But it was probably just as well the blonde from the box office didn't look like Garbo, at least not like the Garbo on the lobby card; her hair was frightful-looking, like Struwwelpeter.

GRAHAM GREENE IN *ENGLAND MADE ME*

Three separate references:

. . . a girl with hair like Greta Garbo's walking alone . . .

The film star's return home: He had earned about sixty crowns a few days ago translating into Swedish all the dope he could discover in the movie magazines. "The screen's greatest lover." "The mystery woman of Holly-wood." A number of people (were they hired by the hours? Minty wondered) began to cheer, and several business men, with portfolios under their arms, stopped on the pavement and scowled at the station . . . The actress was not very popular in Sweden; something disgraceful might happen; something which someone would want hushed up. If, for example, she was hissed . . . But nothing happened. A woman came out of the station in a camel-hair coat with a big collar; it was just possible to see that she was wearing grey flannel trousers; Minty had one glimpse of a pale haggard humourless face, a long upper lip, the unreal loveliness and the unreal tragedy of a mask like Dante's known too well. The movie cameras whirred and the woman put up her hands in front of her face and stepped into a car. Somebody threw an expensive bouquet of flowers (who paid for that? Minty wondered) which missed the car. A little woman in heavy black tweeds and a black veil scuttled into the car and it drove away . . .

"I love the sea," the blonde said, with Garbo in her voice.

ELLERY QUEEN IN *THE CHINESE ORANGE MYSTERY*

This woman was as unreal as a Garbo seen upon the silver screen. One might look but not touch.

TENNESSEE WILLIAMS IN *THE GLASS MENAGERIE*

Laura: Where have you been all this time?
Tom: I have been to the movies.
Laura: All this time at the movies?
Tom: There was a very long program. There was a Garbo picture and a Mickey Mouse and a travelogue and a newsreel . . .

LORRAINE HANSBERRY IN *A RAISIN IN THE SUN*

George: You're a nice-looking girl, honey, forget the atmosphere. Guys aren't going to go for the atmosphere—they're going to go for what they see. Be glad for that. Drop the Garbo routine. It doesn't go with you.

FROM W. H. AUDEN'S "SONG OF THE BEGGARS"

"And Garbo's and Cleopatra's wits to go astraying,
In a feather ocean with me to go fishing and playing . . ."

GEORGE ORWELL IN *KEEP THE ASPIDISTRA FLYING*

Gordon halted outside a great garish picture-palace, under the weary eye of
the commissionaire, to examine the photographs. Greta Garbo in *The
Painted Veil*.

FRANÇOIS MAURIAC (FRENCH NOBELIST WRITER)

Nonetheless, I saw her: or rather, at that vague hour of the gloaming, I
glimpsed a marvelous form—similar, it is true, to so many others. Everything that her veil, which stopped just above her mouth, failed to conceal
disappeared beneath the layer of powder and paint which, nowadays, covers the entire population of women. I thought how strange it is that the
cinema requires this excess of makeup of its stars, in order to be able to give
us a face's pure essence. The screen, that mysterious barrier, allows only the
imperishable elements of that nose, that mouth, to filter through. Could it
be that the paste and unguents are there to absorb and dissolve all that is
ephemeral? The thought that God had in creating a face like this makes itself visible in this design, which is of such a celestial simplicity, cleansed of
every blemish, readied for Eternity.

Beautiful in town, beautiful in the country, beneath lamps and in the
sunlight, she has, moreover, a quality of beauty that the camera prefers,
and this sensibility, this transparency, that makes her "feel" the characters that she is responsible for interpreting, that she's not playing them,
that she has neither "gimmicks" nor apparent artfulness, that she always
seems to be shooting a documentary about herself, taken by a chance surprise by a clever cameraman, and finally, that nothing that happens within
her remains closed and enchained, that everything runs through her and
the audience too, that she constitutes with her body, her voice, her face,

her walk, the atmosphere that she moves with her, an ensemble of intelligible signs, a living language that never has need of either commentary or translator. Beautiful and human, Greta Garbo is like the child, the dog, and the leaf on the tree; she even surpasses them by a lightning bolt, an accent.

EDWARD ST. AUBYN IN *NEVER MIND*

Just as a novelist may sometimes wonder why he invents characters who do not exist and makes them do things which do not matter, so a philosopher may wonder why he invents cases that cannot occur in order to determine what must be the case. After a long neglect of his subject, Victor was not as thoroughly convinced that impossibility was the best route to necessity as he might have been had he recently reconsidered Stolkin's extreme case in which "scientists destroy my brain and body, and then make out of new matter, a replica of Greta Garbo."

And, most famously, in the movies . . .

SUNSET BOULEVARD

Norma Desmond: "Still wonderful, isn't it? And no dialogue. We didn't need dialogue—We had faces. There just aren't any faces like that anymore. Only one: Garbo. Those idiot producers, those imbeciles! Haven't they got any eyes? Have they forgotten what a star looks like?"

And then there's George Baxt's The Greta Garbo Murder Case, *a spy story set in Santa Monica during the war. On hand: Marion Davies, Salka Viertel, Samuel Goldwyn, Erich von Stroheim, et al. Garbo finally gets to play Joan of Arc in a movie called* Joan the Magnificent, *but as she reports,* "Goldwyn says it was too terrible to release, so now it sits somewhere in storage, unwanted, unloved, like me."

GARBO IN SONGS

✳

"YOU'RE THE TOP" —COLE PORTER, 1934

You're the National Gallery,
You're Garbo's salary . . .

"THESE FOOLISH THINGS" —ERIC MASCHWITZ, 1936

The smile of Garbo and the scent of roses,
The waiters whistling as the last bar closes.

"I CAN'T GET STARTED" —IRA GERSHWIN, 1936

I've been consulted by Franklin D.;
And Greta Garbo's asked me to tea . . . [variant: gave me her key]

"MY NAME IS JACK" —MANFRED MANN, 1968

My name is Jack, and I live in the back
Of the Greta Garbo's Home for wayward boys and girls.

"AH! SI VOUS CONNAISSIEZ MA POULE"
—MAURICE CHEVALIER HIT, 1938

Marlène et Darrieux
N'arrivent qu'en deux
La Greta Garbo
Peut mêm' retirer son chapeau.

"CELLULOID HEROES" —RAY DAVIES (THE KINKS), 1972

Don't step on Greta Garbo as you walk down the boulevard,
She looks so weak and fragile that's why she tried to be so hard.

"BETTE DAVIS EYES" —DONNA WEISS AND
JACKIE DeSHANNON, 1974

She's got Greta Garbo standoff sighs
She's got Bette Davis eyes.

"KING OF THE SILVER SCREEN" —ALICE COOPER, 1977

I could've been Greta Garbo
If I was born in another time.

"VOGUE" —MADONNA, 1990

Greta Garbo, and Monroe,
Dietrich and DiMaggio . . .

"GRETA" —MYLÈNE FARMER, 1986

Greta rit, et moi je rougis
Greta tremble, la mort lui ressemble
Greta meurt, j'entends dieu qui pleure

Greta aime, divine infidèle
Baisers froids comme elle
Je l'aime

"JUST LIKE GRETA" —VAN MORRISON, 2005

Just like Greta Garbo
I want to be alone.

"DU BIST MEINE GRETA GARBO" —ROBERT STOLZ AND
WALTER REISCH, 1930

Du bist meine Greta Garbo
Bist die schönste Frau der Welt,
Blond bist du wie Greta Garbo
Nur hast du nicht soviel Geld.

(You are my Greta Garbo—
You're the most beautiful woman in the world.
You're as blond as Greta Garbo,
But you don't have her kind of money.)

And a variety of other songs, in a variety of languages . . .

FILMOGRAPHY

⤛⤜

This filmography, which originally appeared in Barry Paris's *Garbo*, includes, in addition to the standard cast and credits, the producers, the number of production days, the production costs, the domestic and foreign earnings, and the profit or loss on all M-G-M Garbo films. The apparent discrepancy between cost and profit figures is due to the omission of distribution and advertising expenses in M-G-M's method of accounting for its production costs.

How Not to Dress (1921), advertising film for Paul U. Bergstrom department store (PUB) in Stockholm. Produced by Hasse W. Tullbergs. Directed by Captain Ragnar Ring. Running time: c. 5 min.

Our Daily Bread (1922), advertising film for bakery products of the Consumer's Cooperative Association of Stockholm. Produced by Fribergs Filmbrya. Directed by Captain Ragnar Ring. Running time: c. 8 min.

Peter the Tramp (Luffar-Petter) (1922). Produced, directed, and written by Erik A. Petschler. Photography by Oscar Norberg. Released in Stockholm, December 26, 1922. Slapstick comedy of a soldier and his romantic highjinks. Cast: Erik A. Petschler (Fire Lieutenant Erik Silverjalm and Max August Peterson), Greta Gustafsson (Greta), Helmer Larsson (artillery captain), Fredrik Olsson (police officer), Tyra Ryman (Tyra), Gucken Cederborg (mayor's wife). Running time: c. 75 min.

The Saga of Gösta Berling (1924). Produced by Svensk Filmindustri. Directed by Mauritz Stiller. Screenplay by Mauritz Stiller and Ragnar Hyltén-Cavallius from the novel by Selma Lagerlöf. Photography by Julius Jaenzon. Costumes by Ingrid Günther. Released in Stockholm, March 10 (Part I) and March 17 (Part II), 1924. A defrocked minister sins long and hard before falling in love with, and being redeemed by, a pure young countess. Cast: Lars Hanson (Gösta Berling), Gerda Lundeqvist (Majorskan Samzelius), Otto Elg-Lundberg (Major Samzelius), Sixten Malmerfeldt (Melchior Sinclair), Karin Swanström (Gustafva Sinclair), Jenny Hasselqvist (Marianne Sinclair), Ellen Cederström (Countess Martha Dohna), Mona Mårtenson (Countess Ebba Dohna), Torsten Hammarén (Count Henrik Dohna), Greta Garbo (Countess Elisabeth Dohna). Running time: 91 min. (U.S. condensed version); other prints exist ranging in length from 105 to 165 min.

Die Freudlose Gasse (Joyless Street) (1925). Produced by Sofar Film. Directed by G. W. Pabst. Screenplay by Pabst and Willy Haas from the novel by Hugo Bettauer. Photography by Guido Seeber. Released in Berlin, May 18, 1925. In corrupt, chaotic post-war Vienna, a young woman on the verge of prostitution is saved by a Yankee lieutenant. Cast: Jaro Fürth (Councillor Franz Rumfort), Werner Krauss (butcher of Melchior Street), Asta Nielsen (Maria Lechner), Greta Garbo (Greta Rumfort), Valeska Gert (Frau Greifer), Einar Hanson (Lieutenant Davy), Agnes Esterhazy (Regina Rosenow), Loni Nest (Rosa Rumfort), Egon Stirner (Henry Stuart). Running time: 96 min.

All of Garbo's subsequent films were produced for Metro-Goldwyn-Mayer.

Torrent—originally *Ibanez' Torrent* (1926). Produced by Irving Thalberg. Directed by Monta Bell. Screenplay by Dorothy Farnum from the novel *Entre Naranjos* by Vicente Blasco Ibáñez. Titles by Katherine Hiliker and H. H. Caldwell. Wardrobe by Kathleen Kay & Maude Marsh and Max Rée. Edited by Frank Sullivan. Photography by William Daniels. Released February 21, 1926. In a Spanish village, a mother-dominated young politician and a budding diva, of different classes, are continually separated and bitterly reunited. Cast: Greta Garbo (Leonora), Ricardo Cortez (Don Rafael Brull), Gertrude Olmstead (Remedios), Edward Connelly (Pedro Moreno), Lucien Littlefield (Cupido), Martha Mattox (Doña Bernarda Brull), Lucy Beaumont (Doña Pepa), Tully Marshall (Don Andreas). Running time: 68 min. (6,679 feet). Production days: 23. Cost: $250,000. Earnings: domestic $460,000; foreign $208,000; total $668,000. Profit: $126,000.

The Temptress (1926). Produced by Irving Thalberg. Directed initially by Mauritz Stiller, who was replaced by Fred Niblo. Screenplay by Dorothy Farnum from the novel *La Tierra de Todos* by Vincente Blasco Ibáñez. Titles by Marion Ainslee. Photography by Tony Gaudio. Edited by Lloyd Nosler. Wardrobe by André-ani. Released October 10, 1926. A married woman follows her lover, an engineer, to the wilds of Argentina with resultant tragedy and ruin. Cast: Greta Garbo (Elena), Antonio Moreno (Robledo), Roy D'Arcy (Manos Duros), Marc McDermott (M. Fontenoy), Lionel Barrymore (Canterac), Virginia Browne Faire (Celinda), Armand Kaliz (Torre Blanca), Alys Murrell (Josephine). Running time: 95 min. (8,862 feet). Production days: 83. Cost: $669,000. Earnings: domestic $587,000; foreign $378,000; total $965,000. Loss: $43,000.

Flesh and the Devil (1927). Produced by Irving Thalberg. Directed by Clarence Brown. Screenplay by Benjamin Glazer from the novel *The Undying Past* by Hermann Sudermann. Titles by Marion Ainslee. Photography by William Daniels. Edited by Lloyd Nosler. Wardrobe by André-ani. Released January 9, 1927. An unfaithful wife vamps two soldier buddies and meets a violent end after luring one of them into resuming their affair. Cast: Greta Garbo (Felicitas), John Gilbert (Leo Von Sellinthin), Lars Hanson (Ulrich von Kletzingk), Barbara Kent (Hertha Prochvitz), William Orlamond (Uncle Kutowski), George Fawcett (Pastor Breckenburg), Eugenie Besserer (Leo's mother), Marc McDermott (Count Von Rhaden). Running time: 95 min. (8,759 feet). Production days: 43. Cost: $373,000. Earnings: domestic $603,000; foreign $658,000; total $1,261,000. Profit: $466,000.

Love (1927). Produced by Irving Thalberg. Directed by Edmund Goulding. Screenplay by Francis Marion from the novel *Anna Karenina* by Leo Tolstoy. Titles by Marion Ainslee and Ruth Cummings. Photography by William Daniels. Edited by Hugh Wynn. Wardrobe by André-ani. Released November 29, 1927. A woman leaves her husband and child for her lover, then realizes she is losing him as well. Cast: Greta Garbo (Anna Karenina), John Gilbert (Vronsky), George Fawcett (Grand Duke), Emily Fitzroy (Grand Duchess), Brandon Hurst (Karenin), Philippe de Lacy (Seryosha). Running time: 84 min. (7,351 feet). Production days: 48. Cost $488,000. Earnings: domestic $946,000; foreign $731,000; total $1,677,000. Profit: $571,000.

The Divine Woman (1928). Produced by Irving Thalberg. Directed by Victor Seastrom. Screenplay by Dorothy Farnum from the play *Starlight* by Gladys Unger. Titles by John Colton. Photography by Oliver Marsh. Edited by Conrad A. Nervig. Wardrobe by Gilbert Clark. Released January 14, 1928. A great stage star—vaguely based on Sarah Bernhardt—finds true love with a soldier. Cast: Greta Garbo (Marianne), Lars Hanson (Lucien), Lowell Sherman (M. Legrande), Polly Moran (Mme. Pigonier), Dorothy Cumming (Mme. Zizi Rouck), John Mack Brown (Jean Lery), Cesare Gravina (Gigi), Paulette Duval (Paulette). Running time: 80 min. (7,135 feet). Production days: 35. Cost: $267,000. Earnings: domestic $541,000; foreign $390,000; total $931,000. Profit: $354,000. This is the only Garbo film that has not survived.

The Mysterious Lady (1928). Produced by Harry Rapf. Directed by Fred Niblo. Screenplay by Bess Meredyth from the novel *War in the Dark* by Ludwig Wolff. Titles by Marion Ainslee and Ruth Cummings. Photography by William Daniels. Edited by Margaret Booth. Wardrobe by Gilbert Clark. Released August 4, 1928. A Russian spy double-crosses her chief in favor of her Austrian lover. Cast: Greta Garbo (Tania), Conrad Nagel (Karl), Gustav von Seyffertitz (General Alexandroff), Edward Connelly (Colonel Von Raden), Albert Pollett (Max), Richard Alexander (General's Aide). Running time: 96 min. (7,757 feet). Production days: 31. Cost: $337,000. Earnings: domestic $543,000; foreign $551,000; total $1,084,000. Profit: $369,000.

A Woman of Affairs (1928). Produced by Irving Thalberg. Directed by Clarence Brown. Screenplay by Bess Meredyth from the novel *The Green Hat* by Michael Arlen. Photography by William Daniels. Edited by Hugh Wynn. Gowns by Adrian. Released January 19, 1929. Star-crossed English lovers, thwarted by their families and by scandal, go separate ways to self-sacrifice. Cast: Greta Garbo (Diana), John Gilbert (Neville), Lewis Stone (Hugh), John Mack Brown (David), Douglas Fairbanks, Jr. (Geoffrey), Hobart Bosworth (Sir Montague), Dorothy Sebastian (Constance). Running time: 108 min. (8,716 feet). Production days: 39. Cost: $383,000. Earnings: domestic $850,000; foreign $520,000; total $1,370,000. Profit: $417,000.

Wild Orchids (1929). Produced by Irving Thalberg. Directed by Sidney Franklin. Screenplay by Hans Kraly, Richard Schayer, and Willis Goldbeck from an original story, "Heat," by John Colton. Photography by William Daniels. Titles by Marion Ainslee. Edited by Conrad Nervig. Gowns by Adrian. Released March 30, 1929. A bored but faithful wife has a near-affair with a Javanese prince before finally reconciling with her much older husband. Cast: Greta Garbo (Lillie Sterling), Lewis Stone (John Sterling), Nils Asther (Prince De Gace). Running time: 102 min. (9,558 feet). Production days: 36. Cost: $322,000. Earnings: domestic $622,000; foreign $543,000; total $1,165,000. Profit: $380,000.

The Single Standard (1929). Produced by Hunt Stromberg. Directed by John S. Robertson. Screenplay by Josephine Lovett from the novel by Adela Rogers St. John. Photography by Oliver Marsh. Titles by Marion Ainslee. Edited by Blanche Sewell. Gowns by Adrian. Released July 27, 1929. A San Francisco debutante and "free soul" has a seagoing love affair but finally decides her husband and child are more important. Cast: Greta Garbo (Arden Stuart), Nils Asther (Packy Cannon), John Mack Brown (Tommy Hewlett), Dorothy Sebastian (Mercedes), Lane Chandler (Ding Stuart), Robert Castle (Anthony Kendall), Mahlon Hamilton (Mr. Glendenning), Kathlyn Williams (Mrs. Glendenning). Running time: 73 min. (6,559 feet). Production days: 45. Cost: $336,000. Earnings: domestic $659,000; foreign $389,000; total $1,048,000. Profit: $333,000.

A Man's Man (1929). Directed by James Cruz. Screenplay by Forrest Halsey from the 1925 play by Patrick Kearney. Romance between a soda-fountain boy and a Hollywood actress. Cast: William Haines, Josephine Dunn, May Busch, Sam Hardy. In brief documentary footage, Garbo, John Gilbert, and director Fred Niblo make cameo appearances as themselves at a movie premiere.

The Kiss (1929). Produced by Albert Lewin. Directed by Jacques Feyder. Screenplay by Hans Kraly from a story by George M. Saville. Photography by William Daniels. Edited by Ben Lewis. Gowns by Adrian. Released November 15, 1929. A jealous husband, discovering his wife in a clinch with a young man, is murdered and the wife is defended in court by her former lover. Cast: Greta Garbo (Mme. Irene Guarry), Conrad Nagel (André), Anders Randolf (M. Guarry), Holmes Herbert (Lassalle), Lew Ayres (Pierre), George Davis (Durant). Running time: 89 min. (5,749 feet). Production days: 40. Cost: $257,000. Earnings: domestic $518,000; foreign $387,000; total $905,000. Profit: $448,000.

Anna Christie (1930). Produced by Irving Thalberg. Directed by Clarence Brown. Screenplay by Frances Marion from the play by Eugene O'Neill. Photography by William Daniels. Edited by Hugh Wynn. Gowns by Adrian. A fallen woman saves a sailor from drowning and they fall in problematic love. Released March 14, 1930. Cast: Greta Garbo (Anna), Charles Bickford (Matt Burke), Marie Dressler (Marthy), George F. Marion (Chris), James T. Mack (Johnny the Priest), Lee Phelps (Larry). Running time: 74 min. (8,263 feet). Production days: 30. Cost: $376,000. Earnings: domestic $1,013,000; foreign $486,000; total $1,499,000. Profit: $576,000.

Anna Christie (1930), German version. Produced by M-G-M. Directed by Jacques Feyder. (Other production credits same as above.) Cast: Greta Garbo (Anna), Theo Shall (Matt), Salka Steuermann [Viertel] (Marthy), Hans Junkermann (Chris), Hermann Bing (Johnny). Running time: 82 min. Production days: 20. Cost and earnings figures combined with the English version above.

Romance (1930). Produced by Paul Bern. Directed by Clarence Brown. Screenplay by Bess Meredyth and Edwin Justus Mayer from the play *Signora Cavallini* by Edward Sheldon. Photography by William Daniels. Edited by Hugh Wynn and Leslie F. Wilder. Gowns by Adrian. Released August 22, 1930. A bishop tells his grandson the story of his heartbreaking affair with an opera star. Cast: Greta Garbo (Rita Cavallini), Lewis Stone (Cornelius Van Tuyl), Gavin Gordon (Tom Armstrong), Elliott Nugent (Harry), Florence Lake (Susan Van Tuyl), Clara Blandick (Miss Armstrong), Henry Armetta (Beppo). Running time: 76 min. (7,081 feet). Production days: 30. Cost: $496,000. Earnings: domestic $733,000; foreign $523,000; total $1,256,000. Profit: $287,000.

Inspiration (1931). Produced by Irving Thalberg. Directed by Clarence Brown. Story and screenplay by Gene Markey, loosely derived from Alphonse Daudet's *Sappho*. Photography by William Daniels. Edited by Conrad A. Nervig. Gowns by Adrian. Released February 6, 1931. An artist's model loves a stuffy young diplomat but leaves him for the sake of his career. Cast: Greta Garbo (Yvonne), Robert Montgomery (André), Lewis Stone (Delval), Marjorie Rambeau (Lulu), Judith Vosselli (Odette), Beryl Mercer (Marthe), John Miljan (Coutant), Edwin Maxwell (Julian Montell). Running time: 74 min. (7,159 feet). Production days: 32. Cost: $438,000. Earnings: domestic $725,000; foreign $402,000; total $1,127,000. Profit: $286,000.

Susan Lenox: Her Fall and Rise (1931). Produced by Paul Bern. Directed by Robert Z. Leonard. Screenplay by Wanda Tuchock from the novel by David Graham Phillips. Dialogue by Zelda Sears, Edith Fitzgerald, and Leon Gordon. Photography by William Daniels. Edited by Margaret Booth. Gowns by Adrian. Released October 16, 1931. To escape her rape-minded "fiancé," a farm girl runs away, joins a carnival, and eventually finds love with a feisty engineer. Cast: Greta Garbo (Susan Lenox), Clark Gable (Rodney), Jean Hersholt (Ohlin), John Miljan (Burlingham), Ian Keith (Robert Lane), Alan Hale (Mondstrum), Hale Hamilton (Mike Kelly), Hilda Vaughn (Astrid), Russell Simpson (Doctor). Running time: 76 min. (7,143 feet). Production days: 49. Cost: $580,000. Earnings: domestic $806,000; foreign $700,000; total $1,506,000. Profit: $364,000.

Mata Hari (1931). Produced by M-G-M. Directed by George Fitzmaurice. Original story and screenplay by Benjamin Glazer and Leo Birinski. Dialogue by Doris Anderson and Gilbert Emery. Photography by William Daniels. Edited by Frank Sullivan. Gowns by Adrian. Released December 31, 1931. The legendary Dutch spy poses as a dancer in Paris, makes good headway with two Russian officers, but keeps her date with the firing squad. Cast: Greta Garbo (Mata Hari), Ramon Navarro (Lt. Alexis Rosanoff), Lionel Barrymore (General Shubin), Lewis Stone (Adriani), C. Henry Gordon (Dubois), Karen Morley (Carlotta), Alec B. Francis (Caron), Blanche Frederici (Sister Angelica). Running time: 90 min. (8,740 feet). Production days: 43. Cost: $558,000. Earnings: domestic $931,000; foreign $1,296,000; total: $2,227,000. Profit: $879,000. Domestic reissue of 1940 and 1941: $81,000 earnings, $27,000 profit.

Grand Hotel (1932). Produced by Paul Bern. Directed by Edmund Goulding. Screenplay by William Drake from the novel and play by Vicki Baum. Photography by William Daniels. Edited by Blanche Sewell. Gowns by Adrian. Released April 12, 1932. The intertwining stories of troubled, all-star guests at Berlin's Grand Hotel. Cast: Greta Garbo (Grusinskaya), John Barrymore (Baron von Gaigern), Joan Crawford (Flaemmchen), Wallace Beery (Preysing), Lionel Barrymore (Otto Kringelein), Jean Hersholt (Senf), Robert McWade (Meierheim), Purnell B. Pratt (Zinnowitz), Lewis Stone (Dr. Otternschlag), Tully Marshall (Gerstenkorn). Running time: 113 min. (10,545 feet). Production days: 49. Cost: $700,000. Earnings: domestic $1,235,000; foreign $1,359,000; total $2,594,000. Profit: $947,000.

As You Desire Me (1932). Produced by Paul Bern. Directed by George Fitzmaurice. Screenplay and dialogue by Gene Markey from the play by Luigi Pirandello. Photography by William Daniels. Edited by George Hively. Gowns by Adrian. Released June 2, 1932. A cabaret artist from Budapest has amnesia and is torn between her sadistic "protector" and the man who claims to be her true husband. Cast: Greta Garbo (Maria/Zara), Melvyn Douglas (Count Bruno Varelli), Erich von Stroheim (Carol Salter), Owen Moore (Tony Boffie), Hedda Hopper (Mme. Mantari), Rafaela Ottiano (Lena), Warburton Gamble (Baron), Albert Conti (Captain). Running time: 71 min. (6,533 feet). Production days: 42. Cost: $469,000. Earnings: domestic $705,000; foreign $658,000; total $1,362,000. Profit: $449,000.

Queen Christina (1933). Produced by Walter Wanger. Directed by Rouben Mamoulian. Screenplay by H. M. Harwood and Salka Viertel from a story by Salka Viertel and Margaret Levino. Dialogue by S. N. Behrman. Photography by William Daniels. Music by Herbert Stothart. Edited by Blanche Sewell. Gowns by Adrian. Released December 26, 1933. The Swedish queen falls in love with a Spanish ambassador and abdicates her throne. Cast: Greta Garbo (Queen Christina), John Gilbert (Don Antonio de la Prada), Ian Keith (Magnus), Lewis Stone (Chancellor Oxenstierna), Elizabeth Young (Ebba), C. Aubrey Smith (Aage), Reginald Owen (Prince Charles Gustavus), George Renevent (French ambassador). Running time: 97 min. (9,298 feet). Production days: 68. Cost: $1,144,000. Earnings: domestic $767,000; foreign $1,843,000; total $2,610,000. Profit: $632,000.

The Painted Veil (1934). Produced by Hunt Stromberg. Directed by Richard Boleslawski. Screenplay by John Meehan, Salka Viertel, and Edith Fitzgerland from the novel by W. Somerset Maugham. Photography by William Daniels. Edited by Hugh Wynn. Music by Herbert Stothart. Gowns by Adrian. Released December 7, 1934. In China, a doctor's wife has an affair with a diplomat but finds salvation by helping her husband and his cholera victims. Cast: Greta Garbo (Katrin), Herbert Marshall (Walter Fane), George Brent (Jack Townsend), Warner Oland (General Yu), Jean Hersholt (Herr Koerber), Bodil Rosing (Frau Koerber), Katherine Alexander (Mrs. Townsend), Cecilia Parker (Olga), Soo Yong (Amah). Running time: 83 min. (7,785 feet). Production days: 59. Cost: $947,000. Earnings: domestic $538,000; foreign $1,120,000; total $1,658,000. Profit: $138,000.

Anna Karenina (1935). Produced by David O. Selznick. Directed by Clarence Brown. Screenplay by Clemence Dane, Salka Viertel, and S. N. Behrman from the novel by Leo Tolstoy. Photography by William Daniels. Edited by Robert J. Kern. Music by Herbert Stothart. Gowns by Adrian. Released August 30, 1935. A woman leaves her husband and child for her lover, then loses him, too. Cast: Greta Garbo (Anna Karenina), Frederic March (Vronsky), Freddie Bartholomew (Sergei), Maureen O'Sullivan (Kitty), May Robson (Countess Vronsky), Basil Rathbone (Karenin), Reginald Owen (Stiva), Reginald Denny (Yashvin). Running time: 95 min. (8,545 feet). Production days: 46. Cost: $1,152,000. Earnings: domestic $865,000; foreign $1,439,000; total $2,304,000. Profit: $320,000.

Camille (1936). Produced by Irving Thalberg. Directed by George Cukor. Screenplay by Zoe Akins, Frances Marion, and James Hilton from the novel and play *La Dame aux camélias* by Alexander Dumas *fils*. Photography William Daniels. Edited by Margaret Booth. Music by Herbert Stothart. Gowns by Adrian. Released January 22, 1937. A beautiful courtesan forsakes her beloved so as not to ruin his life and career. Cast: Greta Garbo (Marguerite), Robert Taylor (Armand), Henry Daniell (Baron de Varville), Lenore Ulric (Olympe), Laura Hope Crews (Prudence), Lionel Barrymore (Monsieur Duval), Rex O'Malley (Gaston), Elizabeth Allan (Nichette), Jessie Ralph (Nanine). Running time: 108 min. (9,929 feet). Production days: 75. Cost: $1,486,000. Earnings: domestic $1,154,000; foreign $1,688,000; total $2,842,000. Profit: $388,000. Domestic reissue of 1954 and 1955: $300,000 earnings, $134,000 profit.

Conquest (European title: *Marie Walewska*) (1937). Produced by Bernard H. Hyman. Directed by Clarence Brown. Screenplay by Samuel Hoffenstein, Salka Viertel, and S. N. Behrman from the novel *Pani Walewska* by Waclaw Gasiorowski and a play by Helen Jerome. Photography by Karl Freund. Edited by Tom Held. Music by Herbert Stothart. Gowns by Adrian. Released November 4, 1937. The love affair between Napoleon and the Polish countess-patriot Marie Walewska. Cast: Greta Garbo (Marie Walewska), Charles Boyer (Napoleon), Reginald Owen (Talleyrand), Alan Marshal (Captain d'Ornano), Henry Stephenson (Count Walewski), Leif Erickson (Paul Lachinski), Dame May Whitty (Laetitia Bonaparte), C. Henry Gordon (Prince Poniatowski), Maria Ouspenskaya (Countess Pelagia). Running time: 112 min. (10,183 feet). Production days: 127. Cost: $2,732,000. Earnings: domestic $730,000; foreign $1,411,000; total $2,141,000. Loss: $1,397,000.

Ninotchka (1939). Produced and directed by Ernst Lubitsch. Screenplay by Charles Brackett, Billy Wilder, and Walter Reisch from a story by Melchior Lengyel. Photography by William Daniels. Edited by Gene Ruggiero. Music by Werner R. Heymann. Gowns by Adrian. Released November 9, 1939. A Soviet woman commissar comes to Paris, strictly on business, but falls in love with a decadent French playboy in spite of herself. Cast: Greta Garbo (Ninotchka), Melvyn Douglas (Count Leon d'Algout), Ina Claire (Duchess Swana), Sig Rumann (Iranoff), Felix Bressart (Buljanoff), Alexander Granach (Kopalski), Bela Lugosi (Commissar Razinin), Gregory Gaye (Count Rakonin). Running time: 110 min. (10,068 feet). Production days: 57. Cost: $1,365,000. Earnings: domestic $1,187,000; foreign $1,092,000; total $2,279,000. Profit: $138,000. Reissue of 1952 and 1953: Earnings $63,000 domestic; $506,000 foreign; $569,000 total. Profit: $416,000.

Two-Faced Woman (1941). Produced by Gottfried Reinhardt. Directed by George Cukor. Screenplay by S. N. Behrman, Salka Viertel, and George Oppenheimer from the play by Ludwig Fulda. Photography by Joseph Ruttenberg. Edited by George Boemler. Music by Bronislau Kaper. Gowns by Adrian. Dance direction by Bob Alton. Released December 31, 1941. A ski instructress impersonates an invented twin in order to compete with a glamorous rival and win back her own husband. Cast: Greta Garbo (Karin), Melvyn Douglas (Larry Blake), Constance Bennett (Griselda Vaughn), Roland Young (O. O. Miller), Robert Sterling (Dick Williams), Ruth Gordon (Miss Ellis), Frances Carson (Miss Dunbar), Bob Alton (dancer). Running time: 94 min. (8,236 feet). Production days: 60. Cost: $1,247,000. Earnings: domestic $875,000; foreign $925,000; total $1,800,000. Loss: $62,000.

BIBLIOGRAPHY

Acosta, Mercedes de. *Here Lies the Heart*. Reynal, 1960.

Affron, Charles. *Star Acting*. E. P. Dutton, 1977.

Agate, James. *Around Cinemas (Second Series)*. Home & Van Thal, 1948.

Agee, James. *On Film*. McDowell Obolensky, 1958.

Aherne, Brian. *A Proper Job*. Houghton Mifflin, 1969.

Alliluyeva, Svetlana. *Twenty Letters to a Friend*. Harper & Row, 1967.

Astor, Mary. *A Life on Film*. Delacorte, 1971.

Baldwin, Billy. *Billy Baldwin Remembers*. Harcourt Brace Jovanovich, 1974.

Bankhead, Tallulah. *Tallulah*. Harper & Brothers, 1952.

Barrow, Andrew. *Gossip*. Hamish Hamilton, 1978.

Baxt, George. *The Greta Garbo Murder Case*. St. Martin's, 1992.

Bazin, André. *What Is Cinema?*. Vol. 1. University of California Press, 1967.

Beaton, Cecil. *The Glass of Fashion*. Doubleday, 1954.

Behrman, S. N. *People in a Diary*. Little, Brown, 1972.

Bergman, Ingmar. *The Magic Lantern*. Viking, 1988.

Bickford, Charles. *Bulls Balls Bicycles & Actors*. Paul S. Eriksson, 1965.

Billquist, Fritiof. *Garbo*. G. P. Putnam's Sons, 1960.

Bret, David. *Greta Garbo: Divine Star*. The Robson Press, 2012.

Broman, Sven. *Conversations with Garbo* (aka *Garbo on Garbo*). Viking, 1992.

Brown, Shane, ed. *Silent Voices*. 2017.

Brownlow, Kevin. *The Parade's Gone By*. Alfred A. Knopf, 1969.

Bruno, Michael. *Venus in Hollywood*. Lyle Stuart, 1970.

Cary, Gary. *Anita Loos*. Alfred A. Knopf, 1988.

Chandler, Charlotte. *I, Fellini*. Random House, 1995.

Conway, Michael, Dion McGregor, and Mark Ricci. *The Films of Greta Garbo*. Citadel, 1963.

Cooke, Alistair, ed. *Garbo and the Nightwatchman*. McGraw-Hill, 1971.

Corliss, Richard. *Greta Garbo*. Pyramid, 1974.

Coward, Noël. *The Noël Coward Diaries*. Little, Brown, 1982.

Cuthbertson, Ken. *Inside*. Bonus Books, 1992.

Daum, Raymond. *Walking with Garbo*. HarperCollins, 1991.

Davies, Marion. *The Times We Had*. Bobbs-Merrill, 1975.

de Mille, William C. *Hollywood Saga*. E. P. Dutton, 1939.

Durgnat, Raymond, and John Kobal. *Greta Garbo*. Studio Vista, 1965.

Ebert, Roger. *Book of Film*. Norton, 1997.

Eyman, Scott. *Ernst Lubitsch: Laughter in Paradise*. Simon & Schuster, 1993.

———. *Lion of Hollywood*. Simon & Schuster, 2005.

Fairbanks, Douglas, Jr. *The Salad Days*. Doubleday, 1988.

Feyder, Jacques, and Françoise Rosay. *Le Cinéma: Notre métier*. Skira, 1944.

Fountain, Leatrice Gilbert. *Dark Star*. St. Martin's, 1985.

Genthe, Arnold. *As I Remember*. Reynal & Hitchcock, 1936.

Gilbert, Julie. *Opposite Attraction*. Pantheon, 1995.

Goodman, Ezra. *The Fifty-Year Decline and Fall of Hollywood*. Simon and Schuster, 1961.

Greene, Graham. *England Made Me*. William Heinemann, 1935.

———. *Graham Greene on Film*. Simon & Schuster, 1972.

Grunes, Dennis. *A Short Chronology of World Cinema*. Sands Films Cinema Club, 2010.

Gunther, John. *Roosevelt in Retrospect*. Harper & Brothers, 1950.

Gutner, Howard. *MGM Style*. Lyons Press, 2019.

Haskell, Molly. *From Reverence to Rape*. Holt, Rinehart and Winston, 1974.

Hemingway, Ernest. *For Whom the Bell Tolls*. Scribner, 1940.

Higham, Charles. *Merchant of Dreams*. Donald J. Fine, 1993.

Hopper, Hedda. *From Under My Hat*. Doubleday, 1952.

Infante, G. Cabrera. *A Twentieth Century Job*. Faber and Faber, 1991.

Isherwood, Christopher. *Lost Years*. HarperCollins, 2000.

———. *Prater Violet*. Random House, 1945.

Kael, Pauline. *Kiss Kiss Bang Bang*. Calder & Boyars, 1970.

Kerr, Philip. *Field Grey*. Marian Wood Books / Putnam, 2011.

Kobal, John. *People Will Talk*. Alfred A. Knopf, 1985.

Lacouture, Jean. *Greta Garbo: La Dame aux camélias*. Editions Liana Levi, 1999.

Lennig, Arthur. *Stroheim*. University of Kentucky Press, 2000.

Lerman, Leo. *The Grand Surprise*. Alfred A. Knopf, 2007.

Loder, John. *Hollywood Hussar*. Howard Baker, 1977.

Lord, Isabel Garland. *A Summer to Be*. University of Nebraska Press, 2008.

Marion, Frances. *Off with Their Heads!* Macmillan, 1972.

McClennan, Diana. *The Girls*. St. Martin's, 2000.

Moore, Marianne. *The Complete Prose of Marianne Moore*. Viking/Penguin, 1986.

Mordden, Ethan. *Movie Star*. St. Martin's, 1983.

Negulesco, Jean. *Things I Did and Things I Think I Did*. Simon & Schuster, 1984.

Palmborg, Rilla Page. *The Private Life of Greta Garbo*. Doubleday, Doran, 1931.

Palmer, Lilli. *Change Lobsters and Dance*. Warner, 1976.

Paris, Barry. *Garbo*. Alfred A. Knopf, 1995.

Payne, Robert. *The Great Garbo*. Praeger, 1976.

Pensel, Hans. *Seastrom and Stiller in Hollywood*. Vantage Press, 1969.

Powell, Michael. *A Life in Movies*. Alfred A. Knopf, 1987.

Queen, Ellery. *The Chinese Orange Mystery*. Blakiston, 1934.

Rifkind, Donna. *The Sun and Her Stars*. Other Press, 2020.

Rorem, Ned. *The Paris and New York Diaries of Ned Rorem*. North Point Press, 1983.

Russo, Vito. *The Celluloid Closet*. Harper & Row, 1981.

Sarris, Andrew. *You Ain't Heard Nothin' Yet*. Oxford, 1998.

Schanke, Donald A. *"That Furious Lesbian."* Southern Illinois University Press, 2003.

Schickel, Richard. *The Men Who Made the Movies*. Atheneum, 1975.

Selznick, Irene Mayer. *A Private View*. Alfred A. Knopf, 1983.

Sjöwall, Maj, and Tomas Ross. *The Woman Who Looked Like Greta Garbo*. Norstedts Förlag, 1990.

Sklar, Robert. *Movie-Made America*. Random House, 1975.

Stanley, Leonard, and Mark A. Vieira. *Adrian: A Lifetime of Movie Glamour, Art and High Fashion*. Rizzoli, 2019.

St. Johns, Adela Rogers. *The Honeycomb*. Doubleday, 1969.

———. *Love, Laughter and Tears*. Doubleday, 1978.

Swenson, Karen. *Greta Garbo: A Life Apart*. Scribner, 1997.

Swindell, Larry. *The Reluctant Lover: Charles Boyer*. Doubleday, 1983.

Toklas, Alice B. *Staying on Alone*. Liveright, 1973.

Tyler, Parker. *The Hollywood Hallucination*. Simon and Schuster, 1944.

———. *The Three Faces of Film*. A. S. Barnes, 1960.

Tynan, Kenneth. *Letters*. Random House, 1994.

Updike, John. *In the Beauty of the Lilies*. Alfred A. Knopf, 1996.

Vickers, Hugo. *Loving Garbo*. Random House, 1994.

Vidal, Gore. *Palimpsest*. André Deutsch, 1995.

Vieira, Mark A. *George Hurrell's Hollywood*. Running Press, 2013.

———. *Greta Garbo: A Cinematic Legacy*. Harry N. Abrams, 2005.

———. *Hurrell's Hollywood Portraits*. Harry N. Abrams, 1997.

———. *Irving Thalberg*. University of California Press, 2010.

Viertel, Salka. *The Kindness of Strangers*. Holt, Rinehart and Winston, 1969.

Wagner, Walter. *You Must Remember This*. G. P. Putnam's Sons, 1975.

Walker, Alexander. *The Celluloid Sacrifice*. Hawthorn Books, 1967.

———. *Stardom*. Michael Joseph, 1970.

Wilson, Victoria. *Stanwyck*. Simon & Schuster, 2013.

Young, Stark. *Stark Young: A Life in the Arts*. Vol. 2, *Letters, 1900–1962*. Louisiana State University Press, 1975.

Zierold, Norman. *Garbo*. Stein and Day, 1969.

Zolotow, Maurice. *Billy Wilder in Hollywood*. G. P. Putnam's Sons, 1977.

ACKNOWLEDGMENTS

※

My warmest thanks to Kerstin Lind Bonnier for her help with everything Swedish, including vetting text (and accents), and dealing for me with the repositories of Garbo photographs in Stockholm. We met at a dinner at Diane Johnson's in Paris many years ago, and it was friendship at first sight.

Of course, thanks to Vicky Wilson, friend, colleague, and unofficial niece (also biographer of Barbara Stanwyck), for important images, including the *Modern Screen* cover picture of Garbo and Stokowski, plus endless encouraging and productive talk.

And to Mindy Aloff, for much indispensable talk about Garbo, for connecting me to the appropriate people at Disney, and for introducing me to the obscure 1931 publication *Television*, with its image of Garbo on the cover of its first issue.

And to film teacher, archivist, and writer Jeanine Basinger, for her deep knowledge and unwavering support—and humor. We've worked together on six of her own books, and so I know very well the value of her appreciation, and the acuity of her gentle suggestions.

And to the unfailingly helpful and super-efficient Ivan Shaw, corporate photography director for Condé Nast.

One of the finest of Garbo biographies is that by Barry Paris (1995), which I have ruthlessly filleted. I am deeply grateful to Barry for his generosity in allowing me to reproduce the Garbo filmography from his book, and also for sharing with me letters and documents concerning Claire Koger, Garbo's maid and companion of forty years. We have been friends ever since our first meeting, in Pittsburgh, as he was working on his essential biography of Louise Brooks.

And it was Barry who led me to the admirable Richard Schmidt, who became Claire's friend and, eventually, her legal guardian, and who has been wholeheartedly supportive of this project.

Anyone writing about Garbo or just interested in her owes an immense debt to the website "Garbo Forever," which as I understand it was founded some years ago by a group of young Garbo-lovers in Europe, and which is filled with wonderful material unavailable anywhere else.

Another writer about Garbo (and about Cecil Beaton, whose literary executor he is) is the remarkable Hugo Vickers, perhaps the leading chronicler of Britain's royal family. Not only has he been unremittingly generous with photographs and documents and advice, but he is as prompt and efficient as he is generous. Vickers's own *Loving Garbo: Greta Garbo, Cecil Beaton and Mercedes de Acosta* is a brilliant anatomy of that tangled tragi-comedy.

I want to thank Anka Muhlstein for speaking to me so candidly about Cécile de Rothschild, her aunt. And to thank the people who spoke to me about the Garbo they knew or had encountered—Cora Sue Collins, Michael J. Arlen, Leon Dalva, and Leonard Stanley, who is also the person we are indebted to for the salvaging and publication of Adrian's unfinished memoir.

In a category of his own is Mark Vieira. His own book—*Greta Garbo: A Cinematic Legacy*—is the most knowledgeable take we have on Garbo's relationship to Hollywood. His contributions to *this* book are almost impossible to exaggerate, beginning with his genius for bringing out the finest qualities in photographs, from studio stills to ancient snaps. His lifelong passion for Garbo, his general knowledge, his network of collectors and experts solved endless problems. His relentless work ethic combined with his unfailing good humor and modesty have made our professional collaboration a joy—and given me a new friend.

AT FSG, THE PUBLISHER of *Garbo*, I've been fortunate enough to enjoy yet again my ongoing relationships within what I like to call "the working press." Jonathan Galassi, the head honcho, is always ready to step in when needed. Ileene Smith—now "editor at large," and always a friend—has presided benignly from the heights of her at-largeness. Alex Merto is the jacket's wonderful designer, and a universal favorite. Nina Frieman, the production manager, has kindly and knowledgeably dealt with my anxieties over paper, ink, the duotone process, et cetera. Nina, like me, venerates Andy Hughes, the legendary head of production and design at Penguin Random House.

For years now I've had the pleasure of working with Scott Auerbach as my production editor. We understand each other on such matters as commas and semicolons and paragraphing, and the need to break for lunch. Luckily, we rarely disagree. What luck!

As for "my" designer, Abby Kagan, what can I say? We see with the same eye. We can happily spend a quarter of an hour solving a single thorny layout problem. Neither of us can believe we're being financially rewarded for having the kind of fun we have together—made possible during the pandemic by shared screens. We're not only colleagues, we're pals and partners, and would even be co-conspirators if there was anybody to conspire against. And imagine the joy of spending so much time working with images of Garbo! As for Leo, a certain black lab . . .

Finally, fervent thanks to young Ian Van Wye, officially Ileene's assistant but already everybody's go-to person (and himself an editor). He does whatever needs to be done, easily, promptly, and perfectly. He's the future.

INDEX

✢

Page numbers in *italics* refer to images.

434

PERMISSIONS ACKNOWLEDGMENTS

Kenneth Tynan's profile of Garbo courtesy of the literary estate of Kenneth Tynan, copyright © 1954 Tynan Literary, LLC.

Excerpt from Lilli Palmer's *Change Lobsters and Dance* courtesy of the Harrison family.

Excerpt from *Watching Them Be: Star Presence on the Screen from Garbo to Balthazar*, copyright © 2014 by James Harvey. Reprinted by permission of Farrar, Straus and Giroux.

Excerpt from *Billy Baldwin Remembers*, copyright © 1974 by William W. Baldwin. Reprinted by permission of Mariner Books, an imprint of HarperCollins Publishers. All rights reserved.

ILLUSTRATION CREDITS

Howard Mandelbaum's Photofest has been as fruitful—and efficient—as it has always been through my decades of working with it. Not even the pandemic has gotten in the way of its impeccable and always good-natured service.

Nancy Kauffman of the George Eastman Museum has been exceptionally organized, helpful, and patient. It's been a pleasure working with her.

Emma Nichols of Sotheby's in London was unfailingly calm, pleasant, and effective in dealing with the Cecil Beaton images in the book.

Margaret Adamic of the Disney Corporation was a pure pleasure to deal with. Thank you, Margaret.

Two earlier biographers of Garbo—Barry Paris, an old friend, and Hugo Vickers, a new one—provided me with crucial images.

The Estate of Edward Steichen was appropriately cautious and formal, and then charmingly humanized by Steichen's granddaughter, Francesca Calderone-Steichen, a new friend.

The Svensk Filmmuseum, the Svenska Filminstitutet, and the Rosenbach Museum (Jobi Zinc) were flawless in their dealings with me, as were the New York *Daily News* and *The New York Times*/Redux. Garrett Mahoney, John McElwee/Greenbriar Picture Shows, and Marc Wanamaker/Bison Archives were all especially generous.

And a heartfelt thank-you to David W. Packard for his assistance and for providing images from the Packard Humanities Institute Collection for this publication. The debt that those of us who care for the preservation of film owe to him is incalculable.

Pages 2–19: The Swedish Film Institute

Page 22: Greta Garbo in *The Saga of Gösta Berling*: © AB Svensk Filmindustri (1924). Photograph by Julius Jaenzon / The Swedish Film Institute

Page 24: Mauritz Stiller: The Swedish Film Institute

Pages 26–29: © AB Svensk Filmindustri (1924). Photograph by Julius Jaenzon / The Swedish Film Institute

Page 41: Greta Garbo in *Vanity Fair*: Arnold Genthe / Genthe photograph collection, Library of Congress, Prints and Photographs Division

Page 64: Greta Garbo and Mauritz Stiller: Ruth Harriet Louise / John Kobal Foundation / Getty Images

Page 67: Greta Garbo and John Gilbert: © 2021 The Estate of Edward Steichen / Artists Rights Society (ARS), New York. Image courtesy of Condé Nast.

Page 102: Greta Garbo and her mother: The Swedish Film Institute

Page 147: Mercedes de Acosta: George Hoyningen-Huene, Mercedes de Acosta, 1934. Collection of The Rosenbach, Philadelphia, Acosta 22:2.

Pages 212–213: *Ninotchka* trade ad: Courtesy of the Media History Digital Library at the Internet Archive

Page 251: Photograph of Greta Garbo's art collection: PL Gould / Getty Images

Page 257: Photographs by Cecil Beaton: © The Cecil Beaton Studio Archive. Images courtesy of Condé Nast.

Page 260: Photograph of Greta Garbo, Anthony Head, and Cecil Beaton: Fox Photos / Getty Images

Page 268: Photograph of Greta Garbo in front of a fruit stand: Tom Wargacki / WireImage / Getty Images

Page 280: "Garbo's will leaves best pal in poverty": © Daily News, L.P. (New York). Used with permission.

Pages 304–305: Salon on East 52nd Street: Tony Cenicola / *The New York Times* / Redux

Page 308: Greta Garbo in *A Woman of Affairs*: © 2021 The Estate of Edward Steichen / Artists Rights Society (ARS), New York. Image courtesy of Condé Nast.

Page 330: Greta Garbo and Mickey Mouse: © Disney